W9-CCT-127

WAVES AND BEACHES

About the Author

Willard Bascom has been curious about the effects of waves and beaches on each other for over thirty years. He was born in New York in 1916 and studied engineering at the Colorado School of Mines. After working in various mines and tunnels, he began investigating waves and beaches in 1945 for the Waves Project of the University of California at Berkeley.

Bascom is best known for his work in directing the first deep ocean drilling (the Mohole Project) for the National Academy of Sciences, and for his invention in 1959 of dynamic positioning, a technique for holding a ship above a hole in deep water without anchors, which made scientific deep ocean drilling possible and which is now widely used by the offshore oil industry.

He has participated in many exciting explorations, including successful undersea searches for diamonds off Southwest Africa, tin throughout Southeast Asia, and a Spanish galleon in the Bahamas. His most recent book is *Deep Water, Ancient Ships*, about marine archaeology. Bascom is now director of the Southern California Coastal Water Research Project.

WAVES
and BEACHES

THE DYNAMICS
OF THE OCEAN SURFACE

Revised and Updated

WILLARD BASCOM

Illustrations by the Author

ANCHOR PRESS/DOUBLEDAY
GARDEN CITY, NEW YORK   1980

Grateful acknowledgment is made to the following sources:

Excerpts from *Rendezvous with Rama,* copyright © 1973 by Arthur C. Clarke. Reprinted by permission of Harcourt Brace Jovanovich, Inc.

Excerpts from *Typhoon* by Joseph Conrad. Reprinted by permission of Doubleday & Company, Inc.

Excerpts from *The Odyssey,* by Homer, translated by E. V. Rieu, copyright © 1946 by the Estate of E. V. Rieu. Reprinted by permission of Penguin Books Ltd.

Excerpts from *Deep Water, Ancient Ships* by Willard Bascom. Copyright © 1976 by Willard Bascom. Reprinted by permission of Doubleday & Company, Inc.

Anchor Press Edition: 1980
ISBN: 0-385-14845-3
Library of Congress Catalog Card Number 79-7038

Copyright © 1980 by Willard Bascom
Copyright © 1964 by Educational Services Incorporated

ALL RIGHTS RESERVED
PRINTED IN THE UNITED STATES OF AMERICA
FIRST REVISED EDITION

For Anitra and Roddie

Contents

Preface

THIS NEW VERSION OF WAVES AND BEACHES REQUIRED only minor modification of the text and diagrams of the previous edition. After all, the nature of waves and beaches—and the principles that govern them—have not changed in the last fifteen years. However, new information has been added to this book. Since its first publication, there has been substantial technological creep. Ideas have been revised, new wave laboratories and test devices have been built, and ships have had new confrontations with waves.

Several kinds of waves are described here that were not mentioned in the earlier version. These include capillary waves, internal waves, and rogue waves. Huge new supertankers and bulk cargo ships cannot pass through the canals and so must go around Africa and South America, where they encounter very large waves and make fair-sized waves themselves. Drilling rigs now operate in much rougher waters, such as those of the North Sea and off Alaska. New instruments are now available for research, including synthetic aperture radar, laser altimeters, and high-frequency sonars.

All these subjects are dealt with briefly in the new sections. So are some new subjects that will be of interest to persons who wish to enlarge their outlook on ocean affairs.

For example, there is a section on ship stability, followed by another on why ships sink and a discussion of the astonishing number of modern ships that are simply "overwhelmed by the sea." Another new chapter discusses six ways we can obtain power from the sea and the problems of so doing.

Finally, there are five accounts of waves and storms taken from great works of literature. These stories give a subjective account of what the sea is like in its moments of utter violence. Statistics and scientific measurements, however accurate and impressive, simply cannot describe the fury of the sea as well as an experienced seaman who can also write.

In the last fifteen years, I believe, the probable audience for this book has become more knowledgeable as a result of the public discussion of oceanography matters and a rising interest in marine affairs. However, the book's original objective—to attract interest to the science of oceanography by giving an understandable account of a few aspects of that very broad field—remains unchanged. I have been told by dozens of persons who are now professional oceanographers or are somehow involved in the field that WAVES AND BEACHES was one of their first texts and that it did indeed influence their choice of careers.

For that I am thankful.

Willard Bascom
1979

APPRECIATIONS AND ACKNOWLEDGMENTS

As MUCH AS POSSIBLE, I HAVE TRIED TO GIVE CREDIT throughout this book to the various scientists, engineers, and writers whose work I have described and from whose writings I have quoted. Hundreds of letters and telephone calls went out asking for help with photographs, descriptions, and concepts. Virtually everyone responded helpfully and promptly—and in some cases their photographs or their work could not be used, even after a lot of effort. I thank them all and would like to acknowledge a few by name.

Much of my first thinking on the subject of shorelines was influenced by *Shorelines and Shoreline Development* by Professor D. W. Johnson of Columbia University—now long out of print and superseded by newer views on the subject. My earliest teachers were John Isaacs and Morrough P. O'Brien, from whom I am still learning. Once I was properly stimulated by these three, the rest was all fun.

For new textual material in this edition I am most grateful to my colleagues at the Scripps Institution of Oceanography, especially including John Isaacs, Walter Munk, Francis Shepard, Steve Costa, Gerald Wick, Gerald Kuhn, David Sheres, and Nancy Mancino. Marshall Orr of the Woods Hole Oceanographic Institution contributed much on internal waves, with some help from Vicky Cullen. Lawrence Draper of the Institute of Oceanographic Services in England contributed information on exceptional waves, and Alan Carr of the same organization went to great lengths to find photographs of English beaches. Professor E. P. Clancy of Mount Holyoke College generously allowed me to use his material on tides, Robert Haring sent papers and photographs of Exxon's huge wave tower, and Arnold Bouma of the U. S. Geological Survey sent data and sonograms of subsea sand forms. John Marriner and Ed Horton quickly responded with helpful material on naval architecture. Lieutenant John Nelson of the National Ocean and Atmospheric Administration, Lucile Lehmann of the University of Florida Coastal Engineering Center, William McNeice of the Corps of Engineers in California, and Andre Szuwalski of the Coastal Engineering Research Center each deluged me with information on the Tsunami Warning Service, beach changes, and shoreline engineering.

Terry Hendricks and Rick Grigg taught me surfing terms, and Larry Moore of *Surfing* magazine arranged for me to use some of their photographs. The Waterways Experiment Station, the David Taylor Ship Research and Development Center, and the National Research Council's Marine Board also dug deep into their files and came up with photographs. Sid and Hazel Bahrt of Pembroke, Maine, were kind enough to make a special trip to New Brunswick, Canada, to photograph the tidal bore as well as the high and low tide conditions especially for this book.

Thanks also to Doreen Leland of Honolulu, Harry Oppenheimer of Johannesburg, R.S.A., Jim Dawson of Lloyd's of London, and Commander William Swansburg of the U. S. Coast Guard, all of whom furnished photographs. Also to the tourist organizations of Bermuda, Australia, Thailand, Miami, and Daytona Beach, who responded with information and pictures.

Finally to Rhoda, my bride of thirty-three years, who once rode the Dukws in the surf and has since traveled to many a remote part of the world with me while I explored waves and beaches, thanks for the typing and the encouragement.

Prologue

Is THERE ANYONE WHO CAN WATCH WITHOUT FASCINATION the struggle for supremacy between sea and land?

The sea attacks relentlessly, marshaling the force of its powerful waves against the land's strongest points. It collects the energy of distant winds and transports it across thousands of miles of open ocean as quietly rolling swell. On nearing shore this calm disguise is suddenly cast off, and the waves rise up in angry breakers, hurling themselves against the land in final furious assault. Turbulent water, green and white, is flung against the sea cliffs and forced into the cracks between the rocks to dislodge them. When the pieces fall, the churning water grinds them against each other to form sand; the sand already on the beach melts away before the onslaught.

But the land defends itself with such subtle skill that often it will gain ground in the face of the attack. Sometimes it will trade a narrow zone of high cliff for a wide low beach. Or it may use some of its beach material in a flanking maneuver to seal off arms of the sea that have recklessly reached between headlands. The land con-

stantly straightens its front to present the least possible
shoreline to the sea's onslaught.

When the great storm waves come, the beach will temporarily retreat, slyly deploying part of its material in a
sandy underwater bar that forces the waves to break prematurely and spend their energies in futile foam and turbulence before they reach the main coast. When the
storm subsides, the small waves that follow contritely return the sand to widen the beach again. Rarely can either
of the antagonists claim a permanent victory.

This shifting battleground is the surf zone. The two
combatants—waves and beaches—are the heroes of this
book.

The Metric System

A LARGE PART OF THE WORLD AND MOST U.S. SCIENTISTS use the metric system. The U.S. public and most engineers are more familiar with English units. Both systems will be with us for a long time, and it is well to be conversant with both.

This book uses the units of the original authors or the charts from which data were taken. In some cases both metric and English equivalents are given for the reader's convenience. Often the numbers used are approximations, and for that purpose it is easy to multiply meters by 3 to convert the measurement to feet or to think of two kilometers as one nautical mile (actually it's 2.08).

A few conversions are given below:

10 feet	=	3.05 meters
1 meter	=	3.28 feet
1 nautical mile	=	1.85 kilometers
1 kilometer	=	0.54 nautical miles
10 liters	=	2.65 gallons
1 gallon	=	3.78 liters
1 pound	=	.453 kilograms
1 kilogram	=	2.21 pounds
1 fathom (6 feet)	=	1.83 meters

Waves come in many kinds and sizes; it is best to think of them as a continuous spectrum extending from waves so small they can hardly be seen to waves so long they are not noticed. Somewhere in the midst of the spectrum are the waves with which we are all familiar.

THE WAVE SPECTRUM

Waves range in size from the ripples in a pond to the great storm waves of the ocean and the tides whose wave length is half the distance around the earth. In order to

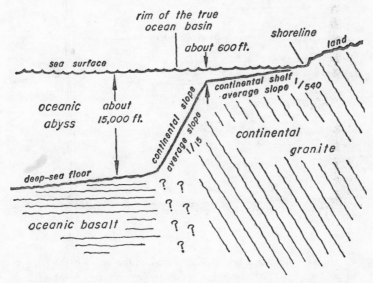

FIG. 2. The contact between ocean and continent. (Slopes are greatly exaggerated.)

be able to discuss such widely varying kinds and sizes of waves it is necessary to agree on a standard set of names for the parts of a wave.

The principal ones are defined as follows:

Crest: The high point of a wave
Trough: The low point of a wave
Wave height: Vertical distance from trough to crest
Wave length: Horizontal distance between adjacent crests
Wave period: The time in seconds for a wave crest to trav-
                  erse a distance equal to one wave length

(There is a direct relationship between wave period and wave length, but wave height is independent of either.)

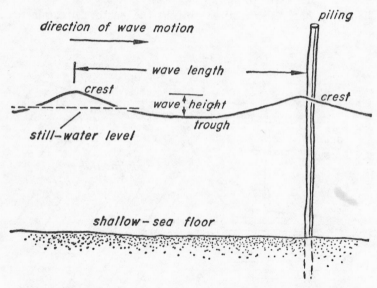

FIG. 3. The parts of a wave. The period of the wave is the time in seconds for two successive crests to pass a fixed point such as the piling.

Waves are classified according to their period, which ranges from less than one second to more than ten thousand seconds. The energy spectrum diagram prepared by Professor Walter Munk of the Scripps Institution of

Oceanography shows that the energy in the ocean is distributed among several major groups of waves, each with a characteristic range of periods.

Beginning at the lower end of the spectrum with the very-short-period waves, we have in order: ripples, with periods of fractional seconds; wind chop, of one to four seconds; fully developed seas, five to twelve seconds; swell, six to twenty-two seconds; surf beat, of about one to three minutes; tsunamis, of ten to twenty minutes; and tides, with periods of twelve or twenty-four hours. Thus there are many kinds of waves, each generated and developed in a special way.

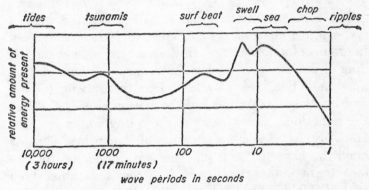

FIG. 4. The ocean wave spectrum. (After Walter Munk)

All the waves just mentioned are called *gravity waves* because, once they are created, gravity is the force that drives them by attempting to restore the original flat water surface. Each wave is made up of two parts: the crest that rises above the average sea level and the trough that extends below it. As a group of waves moves over the surface each crest seems to be forever attempting to overtake the trough ahead, fill it in, and restore equilibrium.

The wave source, whatever it was, worked against gravity. One can whimsically imagine that gravity must be eternally frustrated by its inability to fill in the hollow trough that keeps escaping just ahead of the surface-restoring water in the crest.

One special form of wave *not* driven by gravity is possibly the most abundant kind of wave on the sea. The first tiny ripples that a light breeze raises on a glassy sea surface, or on the slopes of larger waves, are called *capillary waves*—capillary because they are controlled by surface tension and respond to the same forces that cause water to rise in capillary (very-small-bore) glass tubing. The capillary force at the discontinuity between water and glass is stronger than gravity, so the water moves upward.

These waves are often one or two millimeters high, a few centimeters from crest to crest, and are usually seen in groups of a dozen or so. In the sea they arise when the drag of moving air stretches the surface and wrinkles the uppermost thin layer of water where there seems to be a more systematic alignment of the molecules of H_2O. Thus the size, slope, and velocity of these tiny waves are governed by the elasticity or tension of the surface film. As might be expected in a phenomenon dominated by surface tension, the wave crests are rounded rather than peaked. Unlike gravity waves, the shorter wave lengths move faster. Capillary waves give way to the development of ripples, which are at the bottom of our wave spectrum and which lead to the growth of larger waves.

The simultaneous existence of so many kinds and sizes of waves on the surface of the ocean, coming from different sources, moving in many directions, and changing inexplicably from day to day, made it difficult for us to learn the ways of waves.

Toss a pebble in a puddle. The impulse generates a

series of similar waves, which move outward in all directions. The simple circular pattern is clear until the first
waves reach shore and are reflected backward. Now the
pattern is not so simple, for the wave fronts of the returning waves interfere with the outgoing waves. The two sets
of waves form curious patterns with diamond-shaped
high points where crests coincide. As the reflections from
the other sides of the puddle are added, the interference
pattern becomes very complex. For a few moments there
is a hopeless jumble of high points moving in all directions; then the whole surface flattens back to mirror-like
calm. You could perform that seemingly simple experiment a hundred times and still not clearly understand
what happened.

In the ocean the situation is far more complicated.
First, the source of the waves is rarely an impulse at a
point—usually it is gusty wind blowing over a broad area
that creates very irregular wave shapes. Second, waves
change in character as they leave the generating area and
travel long distances. Third, usually several sets of waves
with different periods and directions are present at the
same time. Fourth, waves are greatly influenced by the
undersea topography. When they approach shore and
move into shallow water, the wave fronts bend and the
waves break, expending their energy in foam and turbulence. Plainly, questions about the manner in which
waves are born, develop, travel, and die could not be answered by casual observers.

Ocean waves are so hopelessly complex that thousands
of years of observations produced only the obvious explanation that somehow waves are raised by the wind. The
higher the wind, the bigger the waves, of course.

The description of the sea surface remained in the
province of the poet, who found it ". . . troubled, un-

settled, restless. Purring with ripples under the caress of a
breeze, flying into scattered billows before the torment of
a storm and flung as raging surf against the land; heaving
with tides breathed by the sleeping giant beneath." A fan-
ciful but quite useless description of the wave spectrum.

Now, after over a hundred years of scientific work, including a concentrated effort for the last thirty years,
most of the major features of waves and their causes can
be satisfactorily explained in mathematical terms and reproduced experimentally. In fact, the theoreticians have
become so bold as a result of the success of their complicated equations that there is danger the study of waves
will fall entirely into the hands of those who have never
been to sea. In this book the descriptive wave researchers
will make a determined last stand, and the mathematical
description will be held to a minimum.

THE EDGE OF THE LAND

The crust of the earth is slowly but constantly shifting.
The continents act much like great rafts of rock, floating
on the viscous interior of the earth. Consequently, if a
load is added to the top of the raft—by a huge volcanic
outpouring of lava or the accumulation of a great mass of
ice—the raft will sink a little and sea level will appear to
rise. By the same reasoning, as erosion removes mountains
and large ice sheets melt, the load is lightened and the
land rises. To illustrate, a number of embayments on the
Alaska coast that were used as harbors a century ago are
now too shallow to be navigable because that part of the
continent has risen. Other forces deep in the earth also
cause the great blocks of continental rock to move up and
down and the ocean level to rise and fall. These major

crustal movements occur very slowly, but as they do, the shoreline, which is especially sensitive to such changes, advances and retreats.

Many geologists classify coasts according to whether they are submerging or emerging from the sea and whether erosion of rock or deposition of sediment has the upper hand. For example, much of the central California coast, from Monterey to Mendocino, is rising. This movement is evidenced by the existence of terrace-like remnants of old sea bottom now well above the sea. Along our northwest coast (Puget Sound) and northeast coast (Hudson River Valley to Maine), large segments are described as "drowned topography," meaning that the land has sunk relative to sea level. Since the original topography was largely hills and valleys, in both these areas the shoreline is very irregular. Beaches tend to be narrow, short, and rocky; they do not form an important part of the coast.

Most of the rest of the east coast from New Jersey to Florida is nearly straight because the submerged land has a long gentle slope that extends from many miles inland to the edge of the continental shelf, a hundred miles offshore. This coast is stable, not having changed its elevation with respect to the ocean for a long period of time. It is characterized by an almost continuous line of sandy barrier islands with great wide beaches. Between these elongated islands and the mainland is a series of shallow bays and lagoons. Thus the basic geology of a coast depends on its history of motion relative to the ocean. If there is an ample sand supply and if enough time elapses without a major change in elevation, the beach will become an influential part of the coast.

Most coasts have a rather complicated geologic history. Relative to sea level they have at various times emerged and submerged again, each time retaining some features left from the previous situation. Moreover, since the marine processes are usually interrupted before they are complete, there are relatively few examples of finished

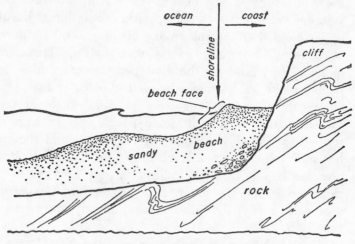

FIG. 5. Coast, shoreline, and beach.

work. The geologist is thus forced to observe changing situations and guess how the process started and what forms it will eventually produce. His principal concern is to determine the mechanism that causes the changes and the rate at which the changes are taking place. Then, perhaps, he can forecast the future.

Let us start by clearing up three terms that may cause some confusion. A *shoreline* is the line of contact between water and land. A *coast* is a large physiographic feature often extending several miles inland from the shore and several hundred miles along it. By comparison a beach is a relatively small feature whose limits are defined by the effects of waves.

A *beach* is an accumulation of rock fragments subject to movement by ordinary wave action. Beaches may be composed of any kind or color of rocky material, ranging in size from boulders to fine sand. Since most of the beach material along the most heavily populated part of the U.S. coast consists of a light-colored sand—the product of the weathering of granitic rock into its two main constituents, quartz and feldspar—most Americans tend to think of beaches as stretches of white sand. But many Pacific island beaches are made of black sand—formed by the disintegration of dark volcanic rocks. Many English beaches are composed of small flat stones called shingle, formed from the destruction of sea cliffs made of sedimentary rock. Many Alaska beaches consist of large cobbles. And for a hundred miles along the coast of Baja California, Mexico, the beach is made of two materials: a flat sandy portion that is exposed only at low tide, while immediately above and behind the sand great cobble ramparts rise to a height of thirty feet or more. So one's idea of a beach depends on one's experience. In this book, for convenience, all beach material will be called sand, although it is recognized that all of the features described may be formed in pebbles or shingle or cobbles.

There are two ways to think about beaches: (1) as small closed systems in which the sand moves either on- and offshore at the whim of the waves, or alongshore in accordance with currents; (2) as geologic units of considerable size.

BEACHES AS MAJOR COASTAL FEATURES

Later in this book the first of these beach processes will be discussed in some detail, but in considering the mechanisms by which beaches shift with the waves one tends to think on a small scale and to lose sight of the fact that beaches are often of grand enough scale to be worthy of study as major coastal features. Although the comprehensive consideration of beaches in this physiographic sense is beyond the scope of this book, let us at least briefly consider the three forms that beaches are most likely to take when they are treated as geologic units. A beach can be simply a narrow strip of sand separating the rocky cliffs of land from the sea; a spit or a bay-mouth bar; a barrier island.

The first form—beaches that are narrow, of limited extent, and on which the sand is a shallow veneer over the rock—is indicative of a youthful shoreline. That is, not much time has passed, geologically speaking, since the last change in sea level. What little sand there is has been created in place by the undermining of the cliff and the grinding of the rocks by wave action. Many beaches of the California-Oregon coast are in this category. These so-called pocket beaches extend between rocky headlands and often have sheer cliffs behind; in the winter months storms strip off most of the sand, exposing cobbles and the underlying rocks.

The second form, in which spits and bay-mouth bars are created by wave action, requires more time to develop. In it, rough coasts tend to be straightened by wave forces and ragged shorelines smoothed. Headlands extending into the sea are attacked because wave energy is focused on them by the underwater topography. Waves striking the coast at an angle create longshore currents which transport sand and seal off the mouths of relatively quiet bays.

The sequence of events in one form of coastal straightening is illustrated in Figure 6. At stage one, bold

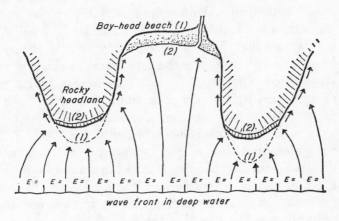

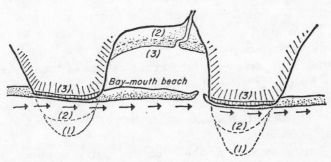

FIG. 6. Waves straighten a rocky coast. *Top:* Zones of equal wave energy in deep water are concentrated by wave refraction so that headlands are attacked. *Bottom:* Eventually headlands are cut back and furnish enough sand to build a straight continuous beach.

headlands project into ocean where they are attacked by waves whose energy is concentrated there by the process of wave refraction. As the headland retreats and the cliffs are reduced to rocky fragments, currents caused by the

waves striking the shore obliquely transport the smaller
particles into the relatively quiet water at the head of the
bay where they form a beach (stage two). Later, the
headlands cut back and the bay becomes shallow, as in
stage three. The longshore coastal currents, which were
disorganized by turbulence around the headlands in the
earlier stages, now become dominant and sweep sand
along the coast, creating bay-mouth beaches. With a
straight shoreline, sand can be transported considerable
distances, passing headlands and bays alike in its longshore migration. Eventually, at the land's end, the water
deepens and the transporting current spreads out and is
reduced in velocity so that the sand it has been carrying
drops to the bottom. These embankment-like deposits in
which the outermost end is surrounded by water are
called spits. They form wherever there is a supply of
sand, a transporting current, and a dumping ground.

There are two famous spits at the entrance to New
York Harbor. Sandy Hook, to the south, was built by materials supplied by the erosion and retreat of the Navesink
Highlands. It grew steadily until it reached an equilibrium situation in which the new sand added to the tip is
just equal to that removed by the tidal currents at the
harbor mouth.

Rockaway spit, northeast of the harbor entrance, was
built with sand from the Long Island coast and grew at
the rate of two hundred feet a year (one mile in twenty-
three years) for a long period until the present series of
groins and jetties were built. Frequently these rivers of
sand flowing along a coast are supplied by the erosion of
valuable property. This erosion creates one form of a
beach problem; later the sand is deposited where it is not
wanted—still another problem.

The beaches of the north Pacific coast are composed of

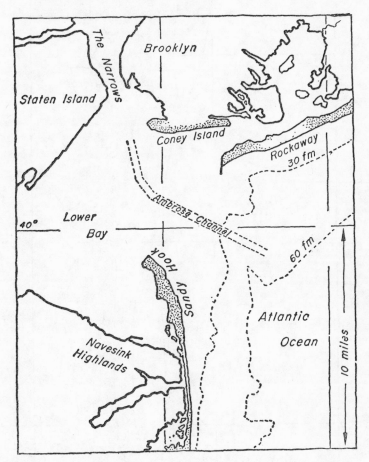

FIG. 7. Spits at New York Harbor entrance (Sandy Hook and Rockaway).

an abundance of fine dark sand made from the disintegration of an inland basaltic plateau and brought to the sea by the Columbia River. The sand is distributed by wave and current action so that both north and south of the river mouth great spits have formed, straightening the

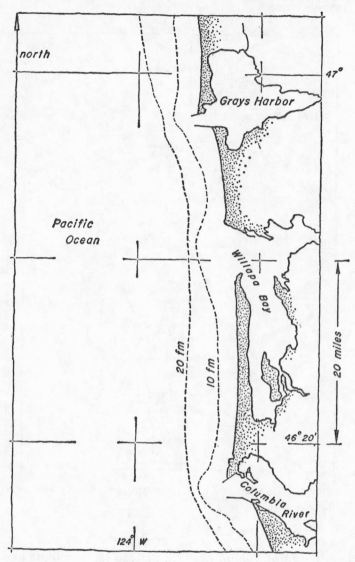

FIG. 8. Bay-mouth bars on the Washington coast near the Columbia River entrance.

coast by sealing off bays and headlands. These spits are continually widening, as evidenced by a series of sandy ridges or growth lines, and the underwater sandbars opposite bay entrances are constantly shifting. The observer, feeling the shudder of the beach and hearing the roaring of the great winter breakers, gets an impression of natural forces in violent conflict and sometimes wonders why the changes are not more rapid.

The third major beach form, the barrier island, makes up a major part of the east and Gulf coasts of the United States and much of the coasts of Holland and Poland. A half dozen major cities are built on these sandy strips, including Atlantic City, Miami Beach, and Galveston. Sometimes called barrier beaches or even offshore bars (an unfortunate term which leads to confusion), these islands vary in width from a few yards to a mile. They may be dozens of miles long and are, in places, separated from the mainland by shallow bays many miles wide.

When sand is blown by the wind into dunes, as at Kitty Hawk, North Carolina, where the Wright brothers first flew, the hills on these islands may rise to a height of nearly a hundred feet. Between them and the main coast there is a chain of bays, marshes, and tidal lagoons, which in many places has been developed into an inland waterway where small craft can move safely along the coast. These large sandy shoreline forms are accumulated beach deposits which are now so large and permanent they no longer fit our definition that limits a beach to the area in which the sand is moved by ordinary wave action.

Since beaches owe their existence to wave action, they have a dynamic quality. That is, beach materials are always in motion—as long as there are waves—although this mobility is not readily apparent to the casual observer.

The motion of the beach material may be parallel to

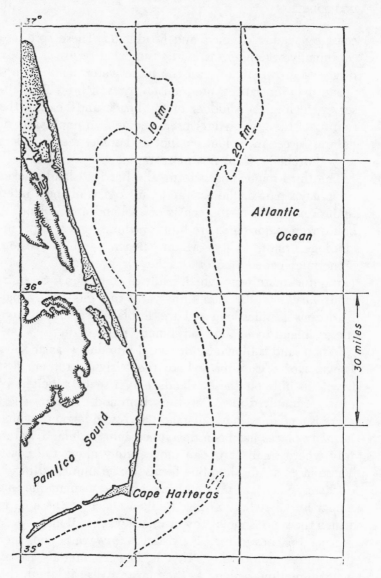

FIG. 9. Barrier beaches extend along much of the U.S. east coast. Cape Hatteras, on a long narrow ridge of sand, lies well off the main Carolina coast.

the shoreline, in which case it is transported by along-shore currents, or it may be moved toward or away from the land by wave action. There are two major beach forms created by the waves: berms and bars. Berms are flat, above-water features that make up the familiar part of the beach. Bars are underwater ridges of sand that parallel the shoreline and are seldom seen except at unusually low tides. On most beaches there is a constant exchange of sand between these two features, the direction of the transport depending on the character of the waves. When the waves are large and follow close upon each other, as they do under storm conditions, the berm is eroded and the bar builds up. When calm conditions return, the small waves rebuild the berm at the expense of the bar. For this reason the above-water part of a beach is generally much narrower in the stormy winter months than in the summer. This is convenient for the hordes of bathers who come to sun themselves on the wide summer berm and swim in the low surf.

The steeply sloping seaward side of the berm against which the waves are in constant contact is the beach face. The face might also be described as the zone within which the shoreline wanders as the waves rush up the beach and wash back down it.

It is necessary to set limits on the extent of a beach to keep the discussion of its properties within reasonable bounds. In the seaward direction, beaches extend outward as far as ordinary waves move the sand particles. By experiment and repeated measurement, this limit has been found to be about thirty feet below the low-tide level. This is an arbitrary but satisfactory limit that is generally accepted. Above water, the beach extends landward to the edge of the permanent coast. The latter may consist of a cliff, sand dunes, or man-made structures. In the geological sense these are not really permanent, but they endure far longer than the small-scale beach features that concern us here.

Most shorelines and beaches are very recent features, geologically speaking. This is because we are living in an interglacial calm between periods when great ice sheets cover the earth and sea level is much lower. The present high sea level has existed with little change for about four thousand years, but for the previous twelve thousand years or so it had been steadily rising. This means that few shorelines have reached steady-state conditions. For example, the city of Pisa, Italy, now over two miles from the sea, was a port less than a thousand years ago. Excavations in the ancient city of Ephesus on the coast of Turkey have uncovered a colonnaded marble road from the harbor where distinguished visitors in Roman times could make a triumphal entry after landing. The point of debarkation is now over a mile from the sea. Such changes will, of course, continue.

This rather broad description of the major features of waves and beaches is intended to illuminate the subject generally so that the ideas developed in the following chapters will fit into a recognizable framework.

II

Ideal Waves

THE SHAPE AND MOTION OF THE OCEAN SURFACE AS WAVES pass across it are very complicated. It is little wonder that even after thousands of years of observation, seafarers developed no very satisfactory explanation of the mechanics of wave motion. Ancient mariners knew in a general way that waves were generated by the winds, that they continued to travel outside the storm area, and that on entering shallow water they would rise up and break, expending their energy on a beach or against a rocky headland. These characteristics were easily observable.

A major difficulty in explaining their origin and motion came from the fact that waves are so irregular. Shipboard observers could see that when a breeze suddenly sprang up, a previously calm sea would first become rippled, and that in time and as the wind increased, these ripples would grow into larger and larger waves. Soon the ship would be surrounded by a full-fledged storm with large irregular masses of water moving on all sides, often breaking on the deck. There was no longer any chance to observe—the problem was to survive. Out away from the

generating area the waves were noticed to be somewhat
more regular. But even at a distance the observations
were confused by the simultaneous existence of several
trains of waves from different storms and by the curious
effect of the underwater topography.

Observers on shore would see high waves intermixed
with low ones; several would arrive in quick succession,
then the time between waves would be long; some would
break, others not. In the midst of a period of calm
weather and blue skies, suddenly, great waves would arrive at a shore. No general set of rules for wave behavior
could be worked out that seemed to cover all the conditions observed. They could only say, "That is just the nature of waves."

The obvious way to attack such a complicated problem
is to deal with each of the components, one at a time, in
their simplest form. The first problem was to define wave
properties or dimensions and to determine the relationship between them. Then it would be necessary to
discover what size and duration of storm and what velocity of wind created what kinds and sizes of waves. Finally
the relationship between wave motion and the depth of
water would have to be worked out.

It seems easy now, with the advantage of hindsight, to
organize the wave research program that could have been
carried out many years ago, but, of course, nothing so systematic happened. Casual observations of many wave
characteristics gradually led, step by step, to sufficient understanding that a beginning could be made on wave
theory.

One can imagine that several of the important properties of waves were first thoughtfully noted many thousands of years ago by someone living on the shore of the
Mediterranean Sea. Probably this early scientist was re-

garded as the village loafer; probably he made his observations in a little cove with clear shallow water, a sandy bottom, and an occasional stalk of seaweed. He would sit on one shore and watch the waves of the sea move into the cove.

One bright and sunny day when no breeze blew to ruffle the surface of the water, a series of regular waves entered the cove, moved across it, and broke on the beach at its head. Idly this scientist-by-accident tossed a stick into the water and watched it float there, noting its position in relation to a rock on the opposite shore. It would

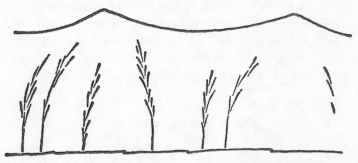

FIG. 10. Motions of seaweed indicate the movements of water particles as a wave passes.

rise and fall, move back and forth, as waves passed under it, but it did not move shoreward with the waves. There was nothing new or startling here; he, and others, had seen this countless times before. But suddenly this man saw in his mind the fact that waves are only moving forms and that the water stays in the same place. The stick, and the water around it, moved in a slow circular oscillation as each wave passed.

Now he looked more carefully at the seaweed stalks growing upright from the bottom. As a crest approached, he noticed, the upper part of the weed moved toward it; as the crest passed, the weed continued to point toward it until a new crest approached. Fragments of weed suspended in the water that were neither floating nor sinking, moved in slow vertical circles, one for each passing wave. Here was a basic principle of hydrodynamics: objects in the water tend to do what the water they displace would have done. The water particles also must be moving in circles.

With these simple observations oscillatory waves were discovered. This was an accomplishment roughly equivalent to Newton's observation that an apple falls to the ground because of the force of gravity. Everyone had seen, but no one had thought about what it meant. Unlike Newton, the early wave-observer was not capable of expressing what he had seen in mathematical terms.

THE FIRST WAVE THEORY

Much, much later, in 1802, Franz Gerstner, of Czechoslovakia, produced the first rather primitive wave theory. He described how water particles in a wave move in circles, and he pointed out that those in the crest of a wave move in the direction of wave advance and those in the trough move in the opposite direction. Gerstner noted that before returning to its original position each water particle at the surface traces a circular orbit, the diameter of which is exactly equal to the height of the passing wave. He observed that the surface trace of a wave is approximately a trochoid, the curve described by a point on a circle as the circle is rolled along the underside of a line. Presumably he knew that if the wave height is small compared to the length, as it is for most water waves, the shape of the trochoid approaches that of a sine curve.

Such was the theoretical beginning. Gerstner's work was found later to have several inconsistencies, but it attracted the attention of the Weber brothers, Ernst and Wilhelm, of Germany, who became the first experi-

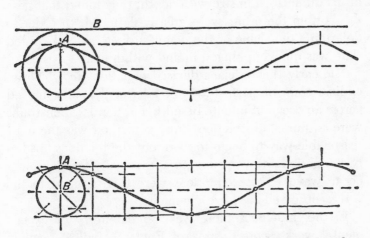

FIG. 11. Geometrical wave forms for waves of equal lengths and heights. *Top:* A trochoidal wave is generated by point A as outer circle rolls along the underside of line B. *Bottom:* A sine wave is generated by projecting the position of point A to equal increments of time as it rotates about a stationary center B.

mentalists. In 1825 they published a book about their findings with a wave channel. It was a glass-walled tank five feet long, a foot deep, and an inch wide. They filled this tank on various occasions with brandy and mercury as well as with water. To make waves they would suck up some of the fluid with a tube and let it fall back again. Thus began the study of waves under controlled conditions. The flat-sided tank, the opportunity to study one wave at a time at eye level, and the chance to repeat an experiment over and over until understanding was achieved, overcame the major difficulties of studying waves in nature.

The Webers discovered that waves are reflected from a vertical wall without loss of energy; they watched suspended particles to confirm the theory that the circular orbits diminished in size with depth; they found that near the bottom the orbits were greatly flattened. In order to determine the shape of the water surface, a chalk-dusted slate was quickly plunged in and withdrawn.

The early theoreticians devised equations in which an endless train of perfect waves, all exactly alike, moved across an ocean of infinite breadth and depth. Their trains were an unreal abstraction, but the method was the most reasonable way to begin to work out the relationships between period and wave length and velocity for sinusoidal ocean waves. These equations were then applied to the waves observed in wave channels.

In the mid-1800s there was a great flurry of experimental work. Scott Russell, of England, built a channel about one foot square and twenty feet long. Near one end was a removable sluice gate that created a small reservoir. To make waves, Russell would suddenly raise the gate and allow the water to rush down the channel as a solitary wave or wave of translation. This impulse produced normal waves, which would then reflect back and forth between the ends, sixty reflections giving him an effective channel length of twelve hundred feet. He made the first careful measurements of wave velocity. In France, Henri Bazin made similar experiments in a larger channel and obtained similar results.

The development of equations and the serious attempt to understand theoretically what the waves in tank and ocean were doing was a big step. But we must remember that with equations the experimenter has true models in his wave channel; without them he has only a plaything.

TABLE I

THE PROGRESS OF WAVE RESEARCH
AS HIGHLIGHTED BY MILESTONES IN THE LITERATURE

1802 Franz V. Gerstner, "Theory of Waves," Czechoslovakia.

1825 Ernst Weber and Wilhelm Weber, "Experimental Studies of Waves," Austria.

1837 J. Scott Russell, "Report on Waves," British Association for the Advancement of Science.

1845 Sir George Airy, "On Tides and Waves," Encyclopedia Metropolitan, England.

1863 W. J. M. Rankine, "On the Exact Form of Waves Near the Surface of Deep Water," Royal Society of London.

1864 Thomas Stevenson, "The Construction of Harbors," England.

1877 Lord Rayleigh, "On Progressive Waves," London Mathematical Society.

1880 George G. Stokes, "On the Theory of Oscillatory Waves," England.

1904 D. D. Gaillard, "Wave Action in Relation to Engineering Structures," U. S. Army Engineers.

1911 Vaughan Cornish, "Waves of the Sea and Other Water Waves," England.

1925 Sir Harold Jeffries, "On the Formation of Water Waves by the Wind," England.

1931 H. Thorade, "Probleme der Wasserwellen," Germany.

1932 Horace Lamb, "Hydrodynamics," England.

1942 Morrough P. O'Brien, "A Summary of the Theory of Oscillatory Waves," Beach Erosion Board, U.S.A.

1947 H. U. Sverdrup and W. H. Munk, "Wind, Sea and Swell," Hydrographic Office, USN.

1955 W. J. Pierson, G. Neumann, and R. W. James, "Practical Methods for Observing and Forecasting Ocean Waves by Means of Wave Spectra and Statistics," U.S.A.

1963 "Ocean Wave Spectra," USN Oceanographic Office and U. S. National Research Council Symposium.

The theoretical and experimental work done today is more complicated because it is now realized that ocean waves are not really sinusoidal, or any other pure mathematical shape. Now real ocean waves are dealt with statistically as combinations of great numbers of small waves. Model work today is done for the same reason that it was done long ago—to simplify the problems by working under controlled conditions. The Mediterranean cove has been replaced by the experimental wave channel and the irregular swell by precision generators.

Today dozens of fluid mechanics laboratories have facilities for modeling waves and determining their effects on beaches and ships. These facilities range from the tabletop ripple-makers to huge tanks that can create breakers eight feet high on full-size dam models. Let us begin this research into the nature of waves by experimenting in the simple form of wave channel shown in Figure 12.

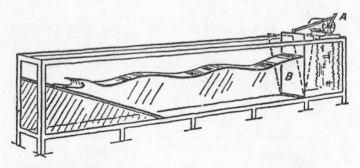

FIG. 12. Glass-sided wave channel. A variable-speed motor with an adjustable yoke drives a paddle, hinged at the bottom, to generate waves with periods of 0.7 to 1.4 seconds and heights up to one foot. The waves on the backside of the generator are absorbed by special screens.

PLATE 1. The surface of the deep ocean in a storm shows a large wave with the top being blown off. Concepts of wave period and length tend to lose their meaning in such conditions. *U. S. Coast Guard*

PLATE 2. During hurricane Carol in October 1954 the surface of the sea was photographed by the Navy's Hurricane Hunters. Violent winds of over 100 miles an hour caused the hair-like streaks and the large breaking waves. *U. S. Navy Photo*

PLATE 3. The Coast Guard cutter *Pontchartrain*, on weather patrol in the North Atlantic, battles waves that are very hilly if not mountainous. Chopping ice to maintain stability is routine for small vessels in far northern waters. *U. S. Coast Guard*

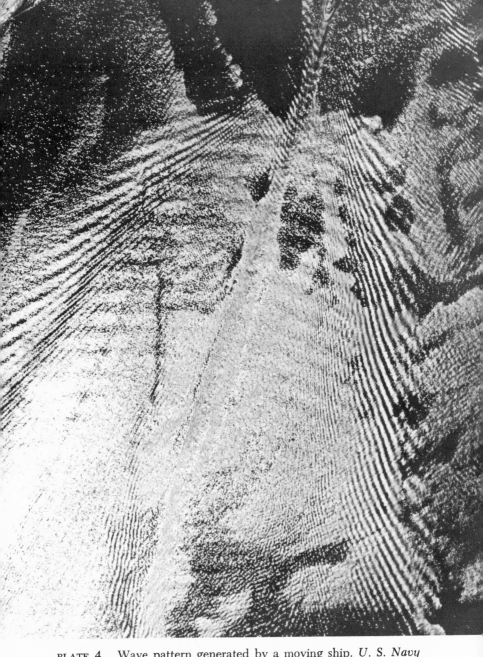

PLATE 4.   Wave pattern generated by a moving ship. *U. S. Navy Photo*

PLATE 5. Large Navy oiler refueling a much smaller destroyer amid heavy seas off the coast of Japan in a 1963 exercise. The difference in the response of the ships to the same waves is apparent. *U. S. Navy Photo*

PLATE 6. In August 1973 the *Neptune Sapphire*, a large container ship, lost its bow to a rogue wave in the Agulhas Current off South Africa. *Durban Daily News*

PLATE 7. The aircraft carrier *Bennington* returned from a typhoon off Okinawa in early 1945 with part of its flight deck folded down over the bow. The stout steel deck, fifty-four feet above the water-line, obviously encountered some very angry waves. *U. S. Navy Photo*

PLATE 8. FLIP, the Floating Laboratory Instrument Platform of the Marine Physical Laboratory, can be towed about looking a little like a large tubular barge or can flip to this position, in which it ignores most waves. When vertical it extends 55 feet above water and 300 below. It has served as a wave gauge against which the passage of 80-foot waves was observed. *Scripps Institution of Oceanography*

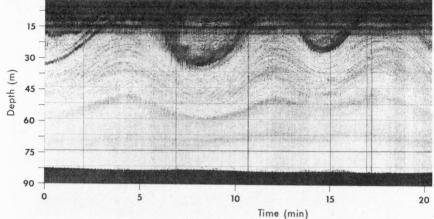

PLATE 9. Acoustic record of internal waves about thirty meters high in Massachusetts Bay. The dark reflections come from zooplankton, which seem to live along layers of equal density. *Marshall Orr, Woods Hole Oceanographic Institution*

PLATE 10. Record of breaking internal waves, an event that causes large-scale mixing of warm surface water with the cooler water beneath. The diagonal lines are sound reflections from a density-measuring instrument used to confirm the mixing. *Marshall Orr, Woods Hole Oceanographic Institution*

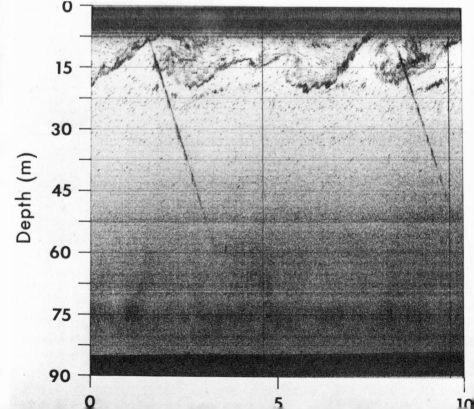

THE WAVE CHANNEL

The first problem of the researcher is to generate an endless train of ideal waves so that their properties can be studied. The simplest form to generate and the easiest to understand mathematically are sine waves.

The main features of a wave channel are evident in the illustration. It is simply a glass-sided tank that permits the researcher to look inside a wave. At one end is a movable paddle which fits closely but can slide against the walls of the tank; it is hinged at the bottom and driven at the top by a connecting rod, which, in turn, is attached to an arm on a variable-speed electric motor. The point of attachment of the rod to the motor arm is adjustable so that the height of the waves can be varied. (The farther out on the arm, the bigger the waves.) The period of the model waves is adjusted by changing the speed of the motor. At the other end of the tank the waves break on a beach, which may merely absorb the waves, and prevent confusing reflections, or be part of the experiment. The moving paddle also generates waves on its back side, and it is customary to fill this space with some material, such as synthetic honeycomb, that immediately dissipates these unwanted waves in local turbulence. Finally, a checkerboard of squares is marked on the glass walls so that wave height and length can be read directly.

THE FUNDAMENTAL PROPERTIES OF WAVES

Now we are equipped to learn the fundamental properties of waves. In the usual fashion of experimenters, our plan is to vary one thing at a time, keeping all others con-

stant and measuring the changes produced. First, the
motor is run at one revolution per second; then its speed
is increased in a series of steps while the water depth and
the arm setting stay the same. Changing motor speed is
equivalent to changing the period—the time for the flap to
complete one cycle. This control also changes the wave
length, as one would expect. However, we notice that
wave height is not affected because the amount of motion
of the flap is the same. Wave length depends upon period;
wave height does not.

In the ideal conditions of this channel, the first experimental data confirm that pure sine waves are being produced. We rediscover that the wave length L is equal to
5.12 times the square of the period.

$$L = \frac{g}{2\pi}T^2 \text{ or } 5.12T^2$$

where g is the acceleration of gravity (32 ft/sec/sec) and
T is period in seconds. Thus a one-second wave would be
5.12 feet long. Wave velocity is usually designated by C,
and $C = \sqrt{\dfrac{gL}{2\pi}}$. A one-second wave in the tank verifies
the relationship by moving at 5.1 feet per second.

But, as the period is increased, one soon finds that these
relationships for length and velocity do not hold exactly
in this wave tank for periods of over one second. Why?
Because in the shorter period range we have been dealing
with "deep-water waves." A "shallow-water wave" is one
that is traveling in water whose depth is less than half the
wave length; that is, if the depth of water is small compared to the wave length, the effect of the bottom is
sufficient to alter substantially the character of the waves.
With the still-water depth in our tank at 2.5 feet, increasing the period has produced waves which "feel the bot-

tom" and are affected by it. In the full expression for wave velocity, water depth (d) is taken into account:

$$C = \sqrt{\frac{gL}{2\pi} \tan h \frac{2\pi d}{L}}$$

The final term contains the ratio $\frac{d}{L}$ or $\frac{\text{water depth}}{\text{wave length}}$. Most wave researchers find it convenient to describe waves in terms of their d/L and use a simplified version of that equation. For a d/L of more than 0.5 (a deep-water wave) the hyperbolic tangent of $\frac{2\pi d}{L}$ is so close to one it can be neglected, as we did earlier. On the other hand, if the depth is quite small compared to the wave length ($d/L = 0.05$) the $\tan h \frac{2\pi d}{L}$ can be replaced by simply $\frac{2\pi d}{L}$. Then, after cancellation, the wave-velocity expression becomes merely:

$$C = \sqrt{gd}$$

This, too, is very convenient, especially when one is working with seismic sea waves which are so long that for them even the deepest ocean is shallow water. But for values of d/L between 0.05 and 0.5 we must use the longer form of the equation. If the length-velocity equations get too sticky one can always get a copy of "Functions of d/L," compiled by Robert Wiegel of the University of California's Fluid Mechanics Laboratory, and look up the answers.

We first observed that the wave height seemed to be independent of both the period and wave length, but further experiments show this is not quite so. If we hold the period constant at one second (with the wave length remaining 5.12 feet) and gradually increase the wave height, we discover that waves higher than 8 inches (0.75 feet) have unstable crests. That is, they tend to break as they travel down the tank. On repeating the experiment with other heights and lengths we discover that the angle at a wave crest may not be smaller than 120° or the wave will break. Stated in another way, the wave height may not be greater than one-seventh of the wave length.

This relationship of height to length (H/L) is called wave steepness.

In reviewing the notes on these last experiments we find that as the waves became steeper they also increased slightly in velocity until at 1:7, the maximum, they moved perhaps 10 percent faster than the theoretical speed. However, since ocean waves rarely achieve such steepness —only in violent storms—it is customary to neglect this increase.

FIG. 13. Maximum wave steepness is 1:7.

When the waves move onto the abruptly shoaling beach at the end of the tank they change character in another way. As the depth decreases the waves are said to peak up; that is, their height increases rapidly. At the same time the shallow water causes the wave length to decrease, and the result is a suddenly steepened wave. In a very short distance the crest angle decreases below the critical 120° and the wave becomes unstable. The crest, moving more rapidly than the water below, falls forward and the wave form collapses into turbulent confusion, which uses up most of the wave's energy.

ORBITAL MOTION

Until now we have considered only the movement of the wave form along the surface. Now it is time to look inside the wave at the motion of the individual water particles. What do they do as a wave passes?

Since the water particles themselves cannot be seen, it is necessary to add a number of small markers to the water—they will do whatever the water does. The markers should be liquid, the same density as the water, and easily visible. One material commonly used by wave researchers is a light oil (xylol and butyl phthalate) whitened and weighted with zinc oxide. The mixture is commonly known as "gunk." By trial and error it can be mixed to almost exactly the same density as the water,

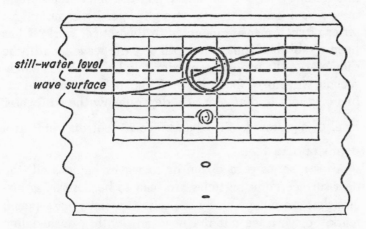

still-water level
wave surface

FIG. 14. Section of a wave channel with tracings on glass opposite orbiting water particles showing the change in orbit size and shape with depth.

and when the experiment is otherwise ready, droplets of gunk are inserted in the channel at several depths by means of a long glass tube topped by a bulb. The white globules rise or sink so slowly that they act the same as water and the results are not affected.

Now when waves are generated it is possible to see the orbital motion of these water-like particles and actually to trace it out in grease pencil on the glass side of the channel. The Webers used approximately this method one hundred and fifty years ago. The solid lines in Figure 14 show the appearance of the side of the channel after the orbits of four particles of gunk at different depths have been traced out. All the orbits of particles in a vertical line describe circles in the same direction at the same time; they are in phase.

The surface particle described a circular orbit exactly equal to the height of the wave. The next one down made a somewhat smaller circle. The third orbit is not only smaller but is slightly flattened, and the one at the bottom moves back and forth in a straight line. By combining a series of such measurements with theoretical work, it has been established that at a depth of $\frac{1}{9}$ the wave length, the diameter of the orbit is approximately halved. Thus a one-second wave 0.75 foot high is found to have particle orbits 0.37 foot in diameter at a depth below the still-water level of 0.57 foot $\left(\dfrac{5.12}{9} \right)$ and of 0.18 foot diameter at a depth of 1.14 feet.

After a series of a dozen or so waves has passed, the near-surface gunk particles are seen to be describing circles that are not precisely opposite the first grease pencil mark. So we trace out the new path with a dashed line and find that the new orbit is a little farther from the wave generator.

MASS TRANSPORT

This difference is the result of a phenomenon called mass transport. Until now we had supposed that the water returned to its original position after each wave passed, but now we find that when waves are steep the orbital circles of the water particles do not exactly close. The water itself is transported by the passing wave form, although its progress is very slow compared to the wave velocity. The volume of water so moved is negligible for waves of small steepness (the usual circumstances) and can be disregarded for all practical purposes.

However, the existence of this mass transport is a serious matter to the theoreticians. The early workers, including Gerstner and W. J. H. Rankine, concerned themselves only with "rotational flow," in which each particle completed a perfect circle as the wave form passed. Later, Sir George Airy and G. G. Stokes developed the "irrotational theory," which requires that the water move forward slightly as the wave form passes. This actual motion of the water is proportional to the square of the height of the waves and is much more pronounced at the surface than a short distance down. In a wave channel there is an imperceptibly small return flow of water along the bottom in the opposite direction to compensate for the surface transport by the waves.

One final experiment remains to be performed. We must now examine what happens to the water particles as the wave is transformed into a breaker by the sloping beach at the end of the tank. The breaking motion is too rapid to permit a particle's path to be traced in crayon on the side of the tank. Moreover, each breaker tends to disintegrate the droplets of gunk and throw them up on the beach. A more sophisticated method of recording the motion is now required. This technique uses a fast movie camera, with proper lighting, and demands a good sense of timing on the part of those who will add the gunk and start the cameras.

With the equipment set up and a series of one-second waves rolling down the channel, one person must dip the gunk-dropper into a just-broken wave and make a trail of visible droplets while the other starts the camera. These droplets trace out the water motions inside the next breaking wave. After about a dozen tries with variations of camera speed (64 to 500 frames a second) it is reasonable to assume that the desired motion may have been captured on film at least once. Later, after processing, the pictures must be projected one frame at a time on a sheet of paper so that the successive positions of the marker drops can be plotted. When the change in positions of a series of drops is marked on the grid, along with the trace of the water surface, the result is a chart of the water motion in a breaking wave. For the same number of pictures the length of each line is directly proportional to the velocity of the water particle.

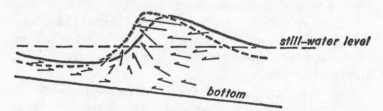

FIG. 15. Movement of water particles as a wave breaks in wave channel (from motion picture analysis).

There are many other experiments that can be made in wave tanks and we shall consider some of them in a later chapter. But now, full of confidence that we understand waves both in theory and by actual test, we fling open the laboratory door, stride to the edge of the cliff, and look to sea.

Good grief! The real waves look and act nothing like the neat ones that endlessly roll down the wave channel or march across the blackboard in orderly equations. These waves are disheveled, irregular, and moving in many directions. No alignment can be seen between a series of crests; some of the crests actually turn into troughs while we are watching them.

Should we slink back inside to our reliable equations and brood over the inconsistencies of nature? Never! Instead we must become outdoor wave researchers. It means being wet, salty, cold—and confused.

III

Wind Waves

THERE ARE MANY KINDS OF WAVES IN THE OCEAN. THEY DIF-
fer greatly in form, velocity, and origin. There are waves
too long and low to see and waves that travel on density
interfaces below the sea surface. Waves may be raised by
ships, or landslides, or the passage of the moon, or earthquakes, or changes in atmospheric pressure. Probably
there are kinds of waves that have not yet been discovered. But most waves, and the waves which are most important to mankind, are those raised by the wind.

Let us begin the life story of a wave with a perfectly
smooth water surface such as a mirror-like pond. Suddenly a breeze begins to blow. Waves are born as the air
pressure on the surface changes and the frictional drag of
the moving air against the water creates ripples. Once a
ripple has formed, there is a steep side against which the
wind can press directly. Now the energy can be transferred from air to water more effectively and the small
waves grow rapidly. In the ocean the same thing happens,
but with no nearby shore to limit wave development the
waves soon develop into a sea.

Of course, it would be rare indeed for a constant wind to blow on an entirely undisturbed ocean surface. Usually there are "old seas"—waves generated earlier by winds elsewhere. If the new wind and these existing waves are moving in about the same direction, the old waves are rapidly enlarged. If the two are opposed, the wind will flatten the sea surface as the new waves cancel the old. For the moment let us ignore this complexity.

Because winds are by nature turbulent and gusty, there are local variations in the air velocity and the pressure on the surface. As a result, wavelets of all sizes are created simultaneously.

As the waves continue to grow, the surface confronting the wind becomes higher and steeper and the process of wave building becomes more efficient—up to a point, that is, for there is a limit on how steep a wave can be. Steepness is the ratio of the height of a wave to its length, and the limit is about 1:7. A wave seven feet long can be no more than one foot high. When small steep waves exceed this limit they break, forming whitecaps. A sea surface covered with such waves is said to be choppy. When the wind blows the top off a wave, causing a breaking wave at sea, some of the energy goes into turbulence but most is contributed to longer, more stable waves. The result is that a long wave can accept more energy and rise higher than a shorter wave passing under the same wind. Therefore, as the sea surface takes energy from the wind, the small waves give way to larger ones, which can store the energy better. But new ripples and small waves are continually being formed on the slopes of the existing larger waves. Thus in the zone where the wind is moving faster than the waves, there is a wide spectrum of wave lengths. At the same time, however, the longest waves continue to accumulate energy from the smaller waves.

Although the wind produces waves of many lengths, the shortest ones reach maximum height quickly and are destroyed while the longer ones continue to grow.

Three factors influence the size of wind waves. These are (1) the wind velocity, (2) the duration of the time the wind blows, (3) the extent of the open water across which it blows (the fetch). A simplified idea of the development of waves in the generating area is given in Figure 16. In this generating area (often a storm) wind waves are called sea. At the upwind end of the fetch the waves

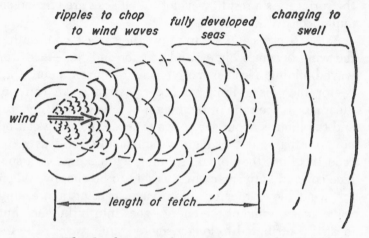

FIG. 16. The development of waves (conceptual). The fetch, within the dashed line, is the area of water on which a wind blows to generate waves. (After Richard Silvester)

are small, but with distance they develop—their period and height increase and eventually they reach the maximum dimensions possible for the wind that is raising them. Then the sea is said to be fully developed; that is, the waves have absorbed as much energy as they can from wind of that velocity. An extension of the fetch or a lengthening of the time would not produce larger waves.

The modern description of how the wind transfers its energy to the waves derives from the work of Harald Sverdrup and Walter Munk of the Scripps Institution of Oceanography. During World War II their attention was attracted to the problem of predicting the waves and surf that would exist on an enemy-held beach during amphibious landing operations. In *Wind, Sea and Swell* they gave the first reasonably quantitative description of how waves are generated, become swell, and move across the ocean to a distant shore.

SEA WAVES

Waves in a sea do not have the regular and precise properties of waves generated in a wave channel. The height of the crests and the depths of the troughs are irregular. The length of each crest is short. In a sea, waves are merely individual hillocks of water with changing shapes that move independently. The limits of a wave in a sea are indefinable. Each mass of water which the eye selects as a wave has a different shape, a different speed, and a slightly different direction from the other waves in the sea. The words period, velocity, and wave length have lost the meaning they had in the orderly environment of the wave channel. Try to decide on the wave length of the waves in Plate 1. The spacing between waves is exceedingly irregular and demonstrates why statistical methods must be used to describe the properties of waves in a sea. Wave heights are nearly as irregular, but fortunately waves rise from a ready reference (mean sea level) and there is somewhat less difficulty in defining wave height. For descriptive purposes, it is customary to use

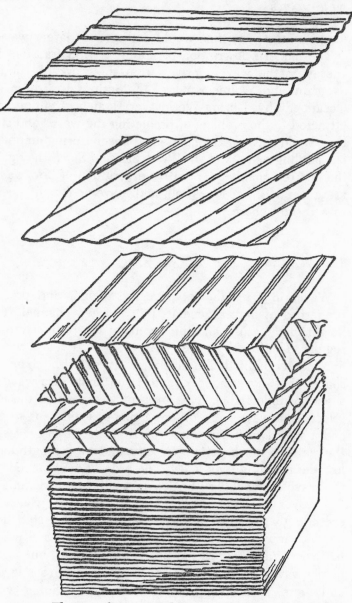

FIG. 17. The sum of many simple sine waves makes a sea. (After Willard Pierson)

the average of the highest one-third of the waves (called
the "significant height") and the average of the highest
one-tenth of the waves. These are sometimes noted as H_3
and H_{10}.

Thus a sea is the result of superimposing a number of
sinusoidal wave trains one on top of another, as shown in
the accompanying conceptual diagram. Each layer represents a series of regular sine waves, as alike as those on a
sheet of corrugated iron. Each layer has its own characteristic height, wave length, and direction. Individually
the waves in these trains are as true to the classical for-
mulas as those in the model tank.

The real sea surface is made up of all these layers
added together. Where a number of crests coincide, there
will be a high mound of water—but it will not last long,
for the component waves soon go their own way. Similarly a coincidence of troughs creates an unusually low
spot, also of short duration.

Since there are small wave crests in the large troughs
and small depressions in the tops of the high mounds, on
the average the troughs and crests of the many layers of
waves tend to cancel themselves out. The more layers of
waves, the more random the sea surface and the lower the
average wave height.

The need to reduce these complicated irregularities to
a form that would be usable by the Navy in wave
forecasting led Willard Pierson and G. Neumann, at New
York University, to a method of describing waves by
means of their energy spectra. In this scheme a value is
assigned to the square of the wave height for each frequency and direction. Then, after the portion of the spectrum where the energy is concentrated has been determined, it is possible to approximate average periods and
lengths and use these in wave forecasting. In other words,

TABLE II
WIND SCALES AND SEA DESCRIPTIONS

Beaufort scale	Seaman's description of wind	Wind velocity knots	Estimating wind velocities on sea	International scale sea description and wave heights	International code for state of sea
0	Calm	Less than 1 knot	Calm; sea like a mirror.	Calm glassy 0	0
1	Light air	1 to 3 knots	Light air; ripples—no foam crests.	Rippled 0 to 1 foot	1
2	Light breeze	4 to 6 knots	Light breeze; small wavelets, crests have glassy appearance and do not break.	Smooth 1 to 2 feet	2
3	Gentle breeze	7 to 10 knots	Gentle breeze; large wavelets, crests begin to break. Scattered whitecaps.	Slight 2 to 4 feet	3
4	Moderate breeze	11 to 16 knots	Moderate breeze; small waves becoming longer. Frequent whitecaps.	Moderate 4 to 8 feet	4
5	Fresh breeze	17 to 21 knots	Fresh breeze; moderate waves taking a more pronounced long form; mainly whitecaps, some spray.	Rough 8 to 13 feet	5
6	Strong breeze	22 to 27 knots	Strong breeze; large waves begin to form extensive whitecaps everywhere, some spray.		

Force	Name	Speed	Description	Sea State	Sea	Height
7	High wind (Moderate gale)	28 to 33 knots	Moderate gale; sea heaps up and white foam from breaking waves begins to be blown in streaks along the direction of the wind.			
8	Gale (Fresh gale)	34 to 40 knots	Fresh gale; moderately high waves of greater length; edges of crests break into spindrift. The foam is blown in well-marked streaks along the direction of the wind.	6	Very rough	13 to 20 feet
9	Strong gale	41 to 47 knots	Strong gale; high waves, dense streaks of foam along the direction of the wind. Spray may affect visibility. Sea begins to roll.			
10	Whole gale	48 to 55 knots	Whole gale; very high waves. The surface of the sea takes on a white appearance. The rolling of sea becomes heavy and shock-like. Visibility affected.	7	High	20 to 30 feet
11	Storm	56 to 63 knots	Storm; exceptionally high waves. Small and medium-sized ships are lost to view long periods.	8	Very high	30 to 45 feet
12	Hurricane	64 and above	Hurricane; the air is filled with foam and spray. Sea completely white with driving spray; visibility very seriously affected.	9	Phenomenal	over 45 feet

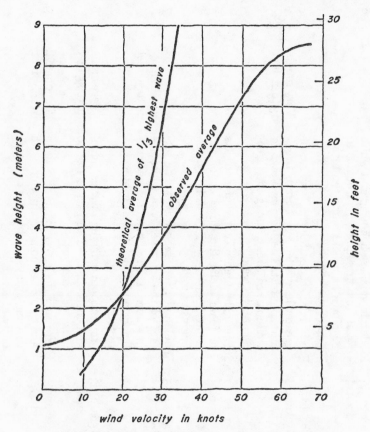

FIG. 18. Wave heights as observed by ten German weather ships in the North Atlantic (average of 70,000 observations). (After Roll)

a wave spectrum gives a statistical description of how wave energy is distributed among various wave periods.

Some of the properties of wind waves are illustrated by Figure 19, in which wave period is plotted against the amount of energy contained for three wind velocities. Each curve (spectrum) represents the distribution of en-

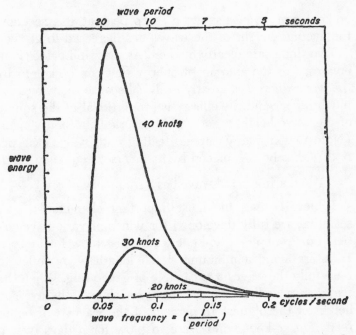

FIG. 19. Wave spectrum for fully arisen seas caused by winds of 20, 30, and 40 knots. (After Pierson, Neumann, and James)

ergy between various periods in a fully developed sea; the area under each curve represents the total energy. Consider first the 20-knot wind. (A knot is a nautical mile per hour.) This relatively modest wind raises waves whose average height is 5 feet and whose energy is spread over a band of periods ranging from 7 to 10 seconds.

If the wind increases to 30 knots the waves become substantially higher and the periods longer. There is more energy available and these longer waves store it better. Now the average height is 13.6 feet and the maximum energy is centered around a period of 12 seconds.

The uppermost curve of the energy spectrum of

40-knot wind waves shows a sharp peak at 16.2 seconds; the average height of the waves has increased to 28 feet.

Two things are clearly evident. As the wind velocity increases, (1) the amount of energy that can be stored by the waves increases greatly (this is because the waves are much higher and the energy is proportional to the square of the wave height), and (2) the periods become longer. (Note that in many papers dealing with waves, the period, T, has been replaced by its inverse, frequency. Thus $f = \dfrac{1}{T}$ and a 10-second wave has a frequency of 0.1.)

Table III gives the most important characteristics of seas that are fully developed for winds of various velocities. For example, a 20-knot wind must blow for at least 10 hours along a minimum fetch length of 75 miles to raise fully the waves it is capable of generating. When the sea from a 20-knot wind is fully developed, the average height of the highest 10 percent of the waves will be 10 feet. If a 50-knot wind were to blow for 3 days over a 1,500-mile fetch, the highest tenth of the waves would average about 100 feet high. Fortunately for ships, storms rarely reach such dimensions or durations.

Even in storms with lower-velocity winds there is always a statistical chance of a very high wave. No one can predict when or where or how high, but superwaves must exist because of the random nature of waves. For example, if 1,000 waves were observed on 20 different occasions, on one of those occasions the highest of the thousand waves will be 2.22 times the significant height. Thus, if the significant height were 44 feet, as it would be in a fully developed 40-knot sea, the exceptionally high wave could be 97 feet high.

Such a wave could exist only momentarily in a storm and there it would be very unstable. It would tower over twice as high as most of its fellows, reaching upward into

TABLE III

CONDITIONS IN FULLY DEVELOPED SEAS

| Wind | Distance | Time | Waves | | | |
Velocity in knots	Length of fetch (nautical miles)	(hours)	Average height (feet)	H_3 significant height	H_{10} Average of the highest 10% (ft)	Period where most of energy is concentrated (sec)
10	10	2.4	0.9	1.4	1.8	4
15	34	6	2.5	3.5	5	6
20	75	10	5	8	10	8
25	160	16	9	14	18	10
30	280	23	14	22	28	12
40	710	42	28	44	57	16
50	1420	69	48	78	99	20

a mass of air moving at forty knots. The crest would then be blown off, forming a breaking wave in deep water. It is these breaking storm waves—and they need not be super-waves either—that do the serious damage to ships that are unlucky enough to be hit. The thousands of tons of violently moving water contained in the torn-off crest of even a moderate-sized breaking ocean wave can wipe the superstructure right off a ship.

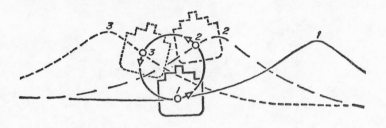

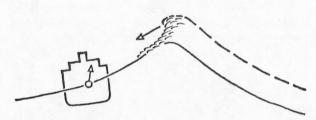

FIG. 20. Ship in breaking and non-breaking waves: *Top:* Ship and water particles in a large wave describe orbits of about the same size so that there is little relative motion. *Bottom:* Water in the crest of a large wave has broken free of the orbit and will collide violently with the ship.

The vast difference in the destructive power of breaking and non-breaking waves in deep water is worth examination since it illuminates a fundamental property of waves. Objects in the water, such as ships, tend to make the same motion as the water they displace. A ship at sea in large waves will describe orbital circles that are roughly the same size as the water in that part of the wave. There is little relative motion between the bulk of the ship and the surrounding water. This motion of a ship may be uncomfortable, but it is safe.

If the crest breaks off a wave, the water moves faster than the wave form and independently of the orbiting water (and ship). While moving in different directions the two may collide with disastrous results.

GREAT STORM WAVES

When sailors talk about the sea it is not long before they are on the subject of storms, great waves, and ship disasters. They speak of wave crests that are "mountainous" and troughs "like the Grand Canyon." However, when asked to assign dimensions to these features that can be used to test wave theory, their numbers are mostly guesswork—and likely to be on the high side to make their original story sound plausible. Since the heights assigned often do not seem to agree with theory, the question arises whether the eye has been deceived or the theory is inadequate. Moreover the statistical explanation of wave variability makes it hard to say that any observation is wrong.

Newspaper accounts of exceptionally large waves encountered by ships on stormy passages are likely to relate to the deluge that occurs when the vessel drives her bow head-on into a wave. For example, if the water goes over the navigating bridge and the bridge is one hundred feet above the waterline, a hundred-foot wave is reported. The unexpected impact of even a few tons of broken or "white" water at that level is no doubt a fearsome occurrence worthy of mention, but it is not evidence of wave height. Even if the water were part of a wave (green water) the bridge is well forward of the ship's center, so that when the bow is down it is well below its proper level. The true wave height would be much less than one hundred feet.

When visibility is good and a large ship is on a reasonably even keel, accurate estimates of wave height, even in a violent storm, are possible. The observer simply watches the distant horizon; when the crest of a wave obscures the horizon, that wave must be higher than the vertical distance between the observer's eye and the ship's waterline.

Stories of big waves at sea can be exciting. Vaughan Cornish, a British author who spent nearly half a century traveling the world on ships to collect data on waves, concluded that in North Atlantic storms waves over forty-five feet high were fairly common; he reported several well-authenticated examples of much larger ones. In his collection of data on wave length, he had many examples of storm waves six hundred to eight hundred feet from crest to crest, and swells two or three times that long.

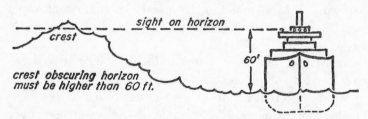

FIG. 21. Observing waves greater than sixty feet high from the SS *Ascanius*.

In October 1921, the captain of the twelve-thousand-ton SS *Ascanius,* en route from Yokohama to Seattle, reported an extended storm of hurricane force in which the barometer went off the low end of the scale. He hove-to (stopped the ship) to ride it out and noted in the ship's log that when the ship was in the trough on an even keel, his eye was sixty feet above the water level alongside the ship. He was certain some of the waves that obscured the horizon were greater than seventy feet high.

On December 29 of the following year, the SS *Majestic,* a large passenger liner, encountered a prolonged storm in the North Atlantic with winds of hurricane force and constant fierce rainsqualls. The ship was barely maintaining steerageway but "riding easily among waves of remarkable regularity and phenomenal size." Under these favorable observing conditions the ship's officers judged the waves and reported that the average height of a considerable number was around seventy-five feet and that individuals as high as ninety feet were seen.

Dr. Lawrence Draper of the National Institute of Oceanography in England reports that on September 12, 1961, when the ship *Weather Reporter* lay close to the track of the dying hurricane Betsy, the recording pen of the shipboard wave recorder hit the stops, top and bottom, on the chart paper. The period of this wave was 15 seconds, which meant that the weather ship was lifted over 60 feet in 7.5 seconds and then dropped almost as far in the succeeding 7.5 seconds. The wave was reconstructed later and found to be not less than 67 feet high. Using statistical techniques for the time when the recorder was inoperative, he estimated the highest wave from that storm was probably 80 feet from crest to trough.

A Russian stereophotograph of the Antarctic sea surface during a storm was used to estimate the vertical dis-

tance between highest and lowest points of the water surface at 82 feet. Since these are not an adjacent trough and
crest, that is not a wave height but a maximum roughness
figure.

There have been many reports of great waves at sea,
but the one seen by the officers of the USS *Ramapo* and
reported by Lieutenant Commander R. P. Whitemarsh in
The Proceedings of the U. S. Naval Institute tops all the
others by far. The *Ramapo*, a Navy tanker 478 feet long,
was proceeding from Manila to San Diego, California,
when it encountered a weather disturbance lasting seven
days that "was not localized as in the case of a typhoon,
but reached all the way from Kamchatka on the Asiatic
continent to New York. This permitted an unobstructed
fetch of thousands of miles with winds from a constant direction, all contributing to extremely high seas.

"By 2200 on February 6, 1933, there was a whole gale
of 58 knots with mountainous seas. We maintained our
easterly course with the wind almost directly astern. It
would have been disastrous to have steamed on any other
course.

"The storm reached its greatest height early the next
morning when winds up to 68 knots were clocked with
the anemometer. Although the vessel was dwarfed in
comparison with the seas, the conditions for observing the
seas were ideal. There was practically no rolling and the
pitching was easy; the moon was out astern. The period
of the largest sea wave was 14.8 seconds as determined by
stopwatch."

Among a number of separately determined observations, that of Lieutenant (j.g.) F. C. Margraff, the watch
officer on the bridge, was selected as the most accurate.
He declared that "while standing watch on the bridge he
saw seas astern at a level above the main crow's nest and

that at the moment of observation the horizon was hidden from view by the waves approaching from astern. Mr. Margraff is 5 feet 11¾ inches tall. The ship was not listed and the stern was in the trough of the sea."

On working out the geometry of the situation from the plans of the ship, as shown in Figure 22, the wave must have been at least 112 feet high!

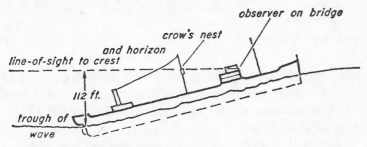

FIG. 22. How the *Ramapo* measured a wave 112 feet high. (After Whitemarsh)

How big can a wave get? If one makes a set of assumptions about weather conditions that are extreme but possible and plugs the data into a computer model, a (theoretically) large wave looms high above the heads of ocean design engineers. Joseph Goldman, a research meteorologist, and his associates established the following set of conditions that they felt would produce the maximum wave:

1. The storm must be twelve to twenty-four hours old and the weather system must be dynamically stable over the same period.

2. The geographic area where the storm occurs must be able to support a very low pressure zone. (The North Atlantic near Iceland and the Gulf of Alaska qualify.)

3. There must be a long, undisturbed fetch that allows large waves to develop.

Goldman et al. used pressure gradients of 900 to 980 millibars over a distance of 150 kilometers (95 miles). This is a very steep gradient that can generate winds up to 150 knots. Both the waves and swell build up until the computer output shows that a maximum combined height of 219 feet is possible.

ROGUE WAVES

Eventually some of the great waves predicted by statistical methods encounter a ship. They may sink it, but if there are survivors they will describe with awe the collision with a "rogue wave."

These are great solitary waves whose crests tower above their fellows and scare the living daylights out of the luckless mariners in their path. Sometimes these waves express themselves as extra-deep troughs—"holes in the sea" into which a ship can fall to be overwhelmed by the next crest. It is a matter of debate which is more dangerous, but doubtless these super-crests and super-troughs account for many of the ships that have simply disappeared at sea with all hands.

An old Cape Horn sailor, Captain William H. S. Jones, once wrote: "It is strange but true that in high southern latitudes where seas 50 feet high and 2,000 feet long roll forward in endless procession, occasionally one sea of abnormal size will tower above the others, its approach visible for a considerable distance." It is easy to be impressed by a wave that towers over "ordinary" 50-foot-high waves.

Jones made his observations from large sailing ships,

but Miles Smeeton aboard the 40-foot ketch *Tzu Hang*
saw the same kind of wave in the Cape Horn region. He
was "running on bare poles before a moderate gale when
this wave loomed up astern, the wave front being a mass
of broken water cascading like a waterfall." The ketch
was "pooped" (covered by a wave over the stern) and
"pitch-poled" (tumbled end for end), pivoting on its bow.
Everything above deck was swept away. But the *Tzu
Hang* righted itself and under jury rig was sailed to
Coronel, Chile, where it was refitted and proceeded on its
voyage. At 48° south and 900 miles west of the Strait of
Magellan the incident was repeated; the yacht survived
again and this time was overhauled at Valparaiso before
continuing on to England. Mr. Smeeton noted that immediately after the passage of the rogue wave the sea re-
sumed its previous moderate condition.

In February 1883 the 320-foot steamship *Glamorgan* of
Liverpool was plowing through heavy seas at night on an
Atlantic crossing when it was "totally submerged by one
tremendous wave." This wave swept off the foremast, all
the deckhouses, and the bridge (with the captain and
seven seamen in it), stove in all the hatches, and flooded
the engine room. The ship sank the following morning,
but the forty-four survivors who escaped in lifeboats told
of the one great wave.

In late 1942 the 81,000-ton, 1,000-feet-long passenger
liner *Queen Mary* was serving as a World War II troop-
ship. On one occasion, while loaded with 15,000 American soldiers bound for Glasgow, she encountered a winter
gale 700 miles off the coast of Scotland. The seas seemed
very large, even to observers on a ship whose deck is some
60 feet above the still-water level. Suddenly "one freak
mountainous wave" struck the ship broadside. An eyewitness reported that the *Queen* "listed until her upper decks

were awash and those who had sailed in her since she first took to sea were convinced she would never right herself." (Nearly all who have been to sea have been aboard a ship that rolled so far they were convinced she was going over.) But then, after hanging balanced on the brink of eternity for a few seconds that seemed very much longer, the *Queen* righted herself again.

The *Mary*'s sister ship, *Queen Elizabeth,* while under way off Greenland, took a wave over the bow so large that it flooded the bridge, ninety feet above the waterline.

In 1966, only eight hundred miles off New York, the Italian liner *Michelangelo* was struck by a huge solitary wave amid a storm. Other ships in the same storm did not observe any especially large waves, nor did the *Michelangelo* encounter more than one. This seems to have been a very deep trough followed by a massive crest. The flare of the ship's bow was crumpled, the inch-thick glass of the bridge windows eighty feet above the waterline was smashed, steel railings on the upper decks were ripped away, and some bulkheads collapsed, allowing many tons of water to enter the ship. The liner was carrying hundreds of passengers, many of whom were injured, and three died. Their first terrorized thoughts were that the ship had struck a reef; many commented on the succession of shudders that vibrated through the ship. A few days later the curious onlookers standing on the pier in the calm of New York Harbor had a very hard time believing that a wave could be so large as to rip up steel eight stories above their heads.

In 1938 Andy Mardesich was at the wheel of the sixty-five-foot fishing boat *Standard II* headed for Entrada de la Tortuga, Mexico. Fishing had been good, and the rest of the crew was icing fish in a storage space below the afterdeck. They were about four miles offshore with light

winds and low following swell, perhaps three to four feet
high. Andy was thinking about making the bay entrance
before dark and he does not remember any unusual motion of the boat. But suddenly a crewman burst onto the
bridge soaking wet, hollering, "We thought you had us in
the breakers." He looked around. The sea was calm, but
the afterdeck was awash and the other three men who
had been below were on deck, sloshing about in wet
clothes and jabbering about the strange wave that came
over the bait tank and down the hatch to half-fill the fish
hold with water.

Although no one actually saw the wave, the geometry
of the situation and the combination of the boat's freeboard, the height of the rail, and the bait tank could only
have meant that a solitary wave more than ten feet high
suddenly rose from a low sea to break over the stern of
Standard II and startle its crew.

On July 22, 1976, the tanker Cretan Star sailed from a
Persian Gulf port loaded with 28,600 tons of light crude
oil. On July 28 the master reported that the ship had encountered very heavy weather that had caused some
damage and oil leakage. The last message received said:
". . . vessel was struck by a huge wave that went over
the deck and caused damage in the number 6 tanks across
—damage cannot be surveyed due to prevailing weather
conditions." The ship was not far from Bombay at the
time, and on August 2 searching aircraft from that port
reported a black oil slick 4 miles long and 1.5 miles wide.
That was all. A subsequent inquiry noted that when the
southwest monsoon blows it reaches its greatest strength
in July off Bombay and periodically piles up "episodic
waves of vast proportions."

The R/V Oceaneer, a 100-foot-long survey ship, had
completed some sonar experiments at sea about one hun-

dred miles west of Point Conception, California, in company with another vessel in 1971 and was heading homeward in rough sea. The swell was large, but the ship was running easily before it with dry decks. At 3 A.M. the skipper, Alex Winton, was at the wheel himself when suddenly "the bow dropped away as the ship seemed to fall in a hole." The next wave came high over the bow, smashed out all the glass in the bridge windows, and threw the captain back against the bulkhead, waist-deep in water. All this happened in total darkness, of course; while he was still trying to figure out what had happened the ship shook off its deckload of water and surfaced.

No more "holes" or wave crests of unusual size were encountered that night. The *Oceaneer* ran in behind an island and rigged plywood covers with viewing slots in them to cover the openings for the rest of the trip. In a dozen years of work in equally rough seas, that was the only time it lost the bridge glass.

Lawrence Draper has examined the probability of occurrence of large single waves using the "Statistics of a Stationary Random Process." Using this theory, it has been shown that one wave in 23 is over twice the height of the average wave, one in 1,175 is over three times average height, and only one in 300,000 exceeds four times the average height.

One part of the ocean is so well known for rogue waves that all mariners are warned in advance by the British Admiralty's book of sailing directions known as the *Africa Pilot*. The danger zone is off the "wild coast" of South Africa between Durban and East London. A few miles offshore the gentle slope of the continental shelf reaches 100 fathoms and then drops precipitously away into deep water, thus creating a wall-like barrier against which the Agulhas Current presses hard. This massive flow of water moves southwest at high velocity—often at 4 knots (1.2 meters per second) and sometimes 6—according to measurements made by the South African National Research Institute for Oceanology. The strongest current is in the main shipping lane moving south—a lane chosen by the ship operators themselves.

When a gale blows from the southwest and raises waves that move directly against this current, the wave length is shortened and the wave steepness greatly increases. Even when there is no local storm, large swell coming north from the Antarctic Ocean meets the south-flowing current head on and creates impressive waves called "Cape Rollers" or "Agulhas Swell." Under some circumstances the unusually swift current actually doubles the height of the waves.

The question is why. There are several explanations. One reason is that approaching waves are refracted, or bent, toward the higher current velocity, especially at an abrupt change in velocity such as occurs along the steep continental boundary. This concentrates the wave energy over the strongest current and perhaps traps certain waves there. In the case of a ship moving with the current, the ship's velocity causes an additional steepening of the wave (relative to the ship). Moreover, if the ship is moving at 18 knots (9 m/sec), aided by a current of 4 m/sec, and encounters a wave moving at 10 m/sec, the velocity of the collision is the sum of these, or 23 meters per second. Since the force of impact is proportional to the square of the velocity, the current nearly doubles that force. If the wave is twice as high as an ordinary storm wave, a ship is likely to be in trouble.

This phenomenon is the subject of recent scientific attention, but it was known for many years before Professor J. K. Mallory of the University of Capetown called attention to the concentrated loss of ships. Early Portuguese caravels were lost in this area, and the passenger liner *Waratah* with 211 persons aboard vanished there in 1909. (Off the Cape Hatteras coast of the United States, jets of the Gulf Stream seem to have caused the loss of ships in a similar manner.)

Some of the recent stories about ship losses are fascinating as well as instructive. In December 1969, the middle of the southern summer, the 102,000-ton Swedish tanker *Artemis* ran through a storm on its way down the "wild coast." Captain L. J. Tarp reported that one wave came over the ship's bow and continued rolling down the deck at such height that it hit and flooded the wheelhouse level five decks up.

In 1973 a new British cargo vessel of 12,000 tons, the *Bencruachan,* was moving southwest when suddenly the bow of the ship was seen to extend out over a hole in the sea. A large, closely following crest then smashed down on the bow with such force that it broke the ship's back. Similar incidents with equally bad results have been reported by the ships *World Glory* (45,000 tons), *Neptune Sapphire* (12,000 tons), *Wilstar* (132,000 tons), *Wafra* (70,000 tons), and the supertankers *Texanito* and *World Horizon.*

Ships standing offshore another twenty miles or so would be well outside the part of the current that caused the damaging waves. However, the temptation of a free ride on a current of four knots or more, with its substantial saving in time and fuel, is too great. Nor is it easy to tell if a ship is in the current. Generally the largest ships are hardest hit. Because of its great mass a supertanker responds to waves more like a seawall than a floating object and tends to resist rigidly instead of giving way as a smaller ship would do.

INTERNAL WAVES

The opening sentences of Chapter I described waves as undulating forms that can travel on the interface between any two fluids of different density. The surface of the sea is the obvious place to study waves; however, other waves, quite different in character, travel on the interface between layers of slightly different density within the ocean. These are *internal waves*. Because waves are driven by gravity it follows that if there is a substantial difference between the densities, as there is between air and water, the forces that tend to restore a flat surface are great. If the density difference is small, as it is between layers within the ocean, the restoring forces are much weaker. This means that the wave periods, lengths, and heights of internal waves can be very much greater than those of surface waves. Although the heights may be large (20 meters or more) the energy these waves contain is small and the typical velocity is low, averaging around 20 cm per second.

It is not essential to have an abrupt density interface; any stable density stratification can support internal waves. And since there is usually a relatively warm surface layer over much of the ocean, internal waves are a common phenomenon. Although the major part of these waves is well below the surface, evidence that they exist can often be seen, especially on calm clear days. This is because internal wave currents affect the reflectivity of the sea surface by producing alternating bands of slicks and (small-scale) roughness.

Internal waves are probably important in several ocean processes, although we are not certain about the details of how they act. For example, the cold dense water formed in polar regions sinks and spreads over the bottom of the ocean basins. Somehow it must be mixed with the waters above if a reasonably steady state is to be achieved. According to Walter Munk, internal waves are the most likely cause of this mixing. They may play an even greater role in the transfer of momentum, especially between layers of water that are moving in different directions. It seems likely that the intermittent uplift of phytoplankton (tiny plants that are the foundation of the oceanic food web) into the sunlit surface water by the passage of internal wave crests leads to increased biological productivity.

There are many hypotheses about how internal waves are generated by the addition of downward energy from external sources. In principle, they can be set in motion by moving atmospheric pressure fields (weather fronts), variable wind stresses, surface waves, tides, ships, and downward (or upward) moving currents.

Sensing the presence of these huge slow-moving waves requires a great many measurements. Gifford Ewing of the Scripps Institution of Oceanography recorded shoreward-moving bands of variable roughness by means of a time-lapse movie camera on a cliff top. A series of bathythermograph (temperature-depth) measurements or a towed thermistor chain (200 meters deep with a temperature sensor every meter, recording on shipboard) was extensively used by Woods Hole oceanographers and by Gene Lafond of the U. S. Navy Electronics Laboratory to obtain a reasonably detailed picture of internal waves as revealed by temperature variations. Various measurements have been made from anchored buoys, and on one occasion twenty sets of sensors were deployed in a 5 km depth off Bermuda for forty days.

Marshall Orr of the Woods Hole Oceanographic Institution uses high-frequency underwater sound to make marvelous picture-like acoustic records of internal waves. This is possible because "pings" of 200-kilohertz sound from the slowly drifting ship are backscattered by the billions of tiny animals (zooplankton) that are concentrated in layers of constant density or temperature. The returning echoes from depths to about fifty meters are recorded and, ping by ping, a graphic representation develops of the changing pattern as internal waves pass beneath the ship. The sensitive system sometimes detects water turbulence that does not have abundant animal life.

As a result of this kind of work, the main objective of which is to understand ocean mixing and biological productivity, the Woods Hole scientists discovered that when the summer tide comes into Massachusetts Bay it generates a packet of about ten internal waves as it passes Stellwagen Bank. Sometimes the surface influence of these waves (alternate bands of slick and rough water) can be seen on a radarscope.

OIL ON TROUBLED WATERS

The calming effect of oil on the sea surface was known for many centuries before the physics of the action was understood. First, all oils are not equally effective; experience has shown that fish oils or other viscous animal oils are best and that petroleum products have relatively little effect. Since the latter are much more likely to be available around a modern boat, in recent years there have been many attempts to use motor oils without success. As a result, the idea of using oil to calm the sea surface has fallen into disrepute, to be regarded as an old seaman's tale without foundation in physics. But, properly used, oil can be very helpful to the small-boat operator under emergency conditions. However, he does not "pour" it on the troubled waters; rather he "leaks" it.

The time-honored method is to put cod-liver oil, for example, in a canvas bag filled with old rags and hang the bag overside in the water. The oil oozes drop by drop through the canvas and spreads out on the sea surface. Even a small quantity—say, a half gallon an hour—will calm the area around the boat to a distance of as much as one hundred feet.

There is no doubt whatever that this method works, but one must not expect too much. A thin film of oil could hardly be expected to have any effect on large waves or swell, but it does quickly extinguish the small waves. Moreover, as the sea surface becomes slick, the wind has less effect on it, no spray is blown about, and the wave crests become more rounded. The boatman can see better and there is much less chance of a wave's breaking as its crest is blown off by the wind.

This smoothing is caused by increasing the surface tension of the nearby area of sea. Surface tension is a property of liquids that makes them act as though they were covered by an elastic film—something like a toy balloon filled with water. The higher the surface tension of the liquid, the stronger this invisible membrane acts. But since engineering handbooks give a surface tension for water twice that of oil, it is not readily apparent how the addition of oil can help matters.

The answer is that the surface tension of the oil increases as its thickness decreases. The thinner the film the better, for oil can act like an elastic membrane even when it is only a millionth of a millimeter thick. Thus, as the oil spreads away from the boat it becomes more effective, opposing any motion that tends to increase the surface area. At a distance from the boat depending on the velocity of the wind, the elastic limit of the increasingly thin film is exceeded. It breaks up and blows away, making it necessary continually to add more oil at the center.

Other materials that are mixed in the water or are floating on it also tend to reduce wave action. Extremely muddy water will cause waves to decay rapidly; so will masses of floating debris.

For a hundred miles along the Southern California coast there is an almost continuous kelp bed parallel to the shore a few hundred yards off the beach. The large waves coming from far at sea pass through it unchanged, but the small waves caused by local winds are quickly dissipated, and the water surface is nearly always glassy just inside the kelp beds.

Fields of sea ice also reduce wave action; as waves move through the ice pack the shorter ones are "damped out" and there is an apparent increase in wave length.

SWELL

As waves move out from under the winds that generated them, their character changes. The original wind waves are said to decay. The crests become lower, more rounded, and more symmetrical. They move in groups of similar period and height. Their form approaches that of a true sine curve. Such waves are now called swell, and in this form they can travel for thousands of miles across deep water with little loss of energy.

In more formal language, these waves are "periodic disturbances of the sea surface under the control of gravity and inertia and of such height and period as to break on a sloping shoreline."

The usual range of period of swell is from six to sixteen

seconds, but occasionally longer periods are clocked. The average period of the swell arriving at the U.S. Pacific Coast is slightly longer than measured in the Atlantic. This difference arises partly from the much greater size of the Pacific, in which more long waves can be generated in larger storm areas, and partly from the greater distances the waves must travel across the Atlantic continental shelf before they reach the shore—in which the longer-period waves are attenuated.

As swell, the waves have relationships conforming rather closely to the simple equations that applied in the wave channel. That is, their wave length is about $5.12T^2$ and they move at a speed of $\sqrt{\dfrac{gL}{2\pi}}$.

Table IV gives the range of wave lengths and velocities that swell in deep water would have if it were truly a sequence of regular sine waves. It is not, but this approximation seems to be the best that can be done at this time. The longest swell ever reported, with a period of 22.5 seconds, came out of the South Atlantic and was measured by Vaughan Cornish on the Dover coast of England. These waves must have had a wave length of 2,600 feet and a velocity of 78 miles an hour.

For a rough estimate of wave lengths in deep water one can multiply the square of the period in seconds by 5; to estimate the velocity (in miles per hour) multiply the period by 3.5.

Swell moves across the open ocean between the generating area and the distant shore in "trains" made up of groups of waves. These trains are bundles of energy. Although any wave in the group moves at a velocity that corresponds to its length as indicated above, the velocity of the group as a whole is only about half as fast. The explanation is: as the wave train moves into an undisturbed

TABLE IV

APPROXIMATE LENGTHS AND VELOCITIES OF SINUSOIDAL
SWELL IN DEEP WATER

(The final column, $d/L = 0.5$, is the depth at which each
becomes a shallow water wave.)

T	$L = 5.12\,T^2$	$C = \sqrt{\dfrac{gL}{2\pi}}$	C	$d/L = 0.5$
Period in seconds	Wave length, feet	Velocity, feet/sec	Approximate velocity, miles/hr	Water depth, feet
6	184	30.5	21	92
8	326	40.6	28	163
10	512	51.0	35	256
12	738	61.0	42	369
14	1000	71.5	49	500
16	1310	82.0	56	655

area it must use some of its forward-moving energy to set
new water particles orbiting; this energy is contributed
by the leading waves, with the result that these constantly disappear from the front of the advancing wave
train; since new waves constantly form at the rear of the
train, the number of waves and the total energy remain
about the same, but the velocity of the group as a whole
is reduced.

It is easy to see that the understanding of group velocity is most important to those who forecast the arrival of
waves from distant storms. A wave group whose period
averages twelve seconds will take two days to cross one
thousand miles of open ocean instead of half that long,
the speed of an individual twelve-second wave.

This phenomenon was first reported by J. Scott Russell
in 1844, and it can be observed in a long wave channel if
the wave-making machine is operated for only a few

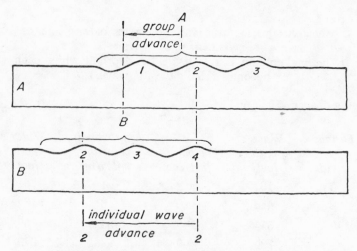

FIG. 23. Wave group advance. As the center of the wave group advances from A to B, wave number 1 dies out and wave number 4 forms behind. Since waves number 2 and 3 are moving at normal velocity, the velocity of a group of waves is only half that of the individual waves.

strokes. The observer, walking alongside the tank, focusing his attention on the first wave generated, will see it decrease in height and finally disappear altogether into the undisturbed water ahead of the group. The last wave in the group is usually not so clearly defined as the first, but sometimes a wave can be seen to develop behind the last wave generated.

Thus the composition of a group of waves is constantly changing and the individual waves observed at a shore are but remote descendants of those actually generated by a distant storm.

The energy possessed by a wave is of a twofold nature. In part it is kinetic energy, due to the motion of the water particles in their orbits; the remainder is potential energy due to the elevation of the center of gravity of the mass of

water in the crest above sea level. For swell, the two energies are equal.

Eventually the deep-sea swell approaching a coast
moves into the shallow water of the continental shelf, and
when the depth of water is less than half the wave length,
these waves feel bottom and undergo some radical
changes in length, velocity, and direction.

IV

Waves in Shallow Water

WE HAVE DEFINED SHALLOW-WATER WAVES AS THOSE THAT are traveling in water whose depth is less than half the wave length. Thus, whether a wave is in shallow water or not depends on the basin as well as on the wave. In a wave channel with water 2.5 feet deep, waves with pe-

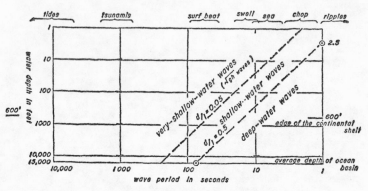

FIG. 24. Shallow-water waves.

riods longer than one second are shallow-water waves; in six hundred feet of water at the edge of the continental shelf a sixteen-second wave is in shallow water, and in the deep ocean basin (average depth fifteen thousand feet) all waves with periods greater than eighty seconds are shallow-water waves.

Therefore, this chapter deals with the entire range of wave periods as illustrated in Figure 24. On the continental shelf, large ocean swell moves predominantly as shallow-water waves, and in the deep ocean, tsunamis and tides are very-shallow-water waves.

As these various waves approach shore and move across shallow water they react in special ways. They reflect, diffract, and refract—which means that they are turned back by vertical obstacles, spread their energy into the water behind projecting rocky promontories, and bend to fit a gradually shoaling bottom. The great low waves of the deep sea may move up an estuary with an abrupt steep-front or they may break down into a dozen smaller waves. On entering a bay or harbor they may excite it in such a way as to cause a sloshing motion.

In short, shallow-water waves have just as complicated characters as deep-water waves, and they are likely to be more interesting, because it is in shallow water that they most affect mankind.

REFLECTION

When a wave encounters a vertical wall such as a steep rocky cliff rising from deep water or the vertical end of a wave tank, it reflects back upon itself with little loss of energy. If the wave train is regular in period, a pattern of standing waves may be set up in which the orbits of the waves approaching the cliff and those reflected by it modify each other in such a way that there is only vertical water motion against the cliff and only horizontal motion at a distance out of one quarter wave length, much as shown in Figure 25. Regular wave trains are rare in na-

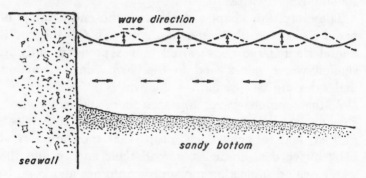

FIG. 25. Wave reflection (*clapotis*) from a nearly vertical wall. Standing wave patterns may be set up in which the water particles move as indicated.

ture and this unusual circumstance is called *clapotis*. The point is that as long as the wave is roughly sinusoidal, it exerts relatively little force on the structure that reflects it. Therefore, when possible, breakwaters are constructed in water too deep to cause waves to break. The forces that would be imposed on the same structure by breaking waves are far greater, as we will see presently.

Virtually any obstacle will reflect some part of the wave energy. An underwater barrier such as a submerged coral reef will cause reflections, even though the main waves seem to pass over it without much change. If the light is right, the reflections can be seen from the air as a halo of small waves surrounding the reef, bucking the main swell. Or, a steep beach may reflect waves to a remarkable extent—and as the reflected waves move outward and encounter the incoming waves head-on, thin sheets of water may shoot upward twenty feet or so. If the two meet at a slight angle a "zippering" effect is observed as the point of impact races along at as much as a hundred feet a second. The author has observed the waves of translation (foamlines) from large breakers strike steep cobble beaches and return seaward as reflected waves six feet high. When translatory waves of this size collide, there is a roar and much water is thrown about in confusion.

DIFFRACTION

Imagine that a train of waves (swell) moving across the ocean suddenly encounters a steep-sided island rising abruptly from the depths. Anyone would expect the waves to be lower on the lee side, and a boat seeking calmer water would run in behind the island. But exactly where would the boat stop rolling as it moved into more protected water?

Would the island cast a clear "wave shadow" in which the water is perfectly calm? The answer is no; the reason is that waves diffract. That is to say, as the waves pass the island some of their energy is propagated sidewise as the wave crest extends itself into the area apparently sheltered by the island.

Figure 26 shows what happens. When a train of regular waves passes an island whose geometric shadow is indicated by the dashed line B, some of the wave energy from the region between B and C flows along the crest into the region between B and A. The numbers given are approximate diffraction coefficients for this hypothetical case. That is, at C the waves are full height, at B they are only half the original height, and at A they are one tenth the height of C. The phenomena of wave diffraction must be taken into account by engineers who design breakwaters. Otherwise, ships moored inside, apparently in a safe lee, might be damaged by wave action.

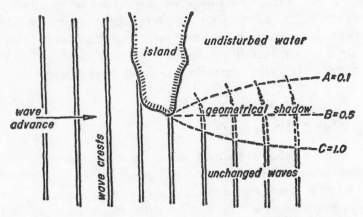

FIG. 26. Wave diffraction. As a train of waves passes a steep-sided island the wave energy originally concentrated between B and C is spread between A and C.

Diffraction need not be a shallow-water effect. This example specifies a steep-sided island rising abruptly from the depths. If the same waves had approached the island over a gently sloping underwater topography, the result would have been entirely different because of wave refraction.

REFRACTION

Refraction simply means bending. As waves move into shoaling water the friction of the bottom causes them to slow down, and those in shallowest water move the slowest. Since different segments of the wave front are traveling in different depths of water, the crests bend and wave direction constantly changes. Thus the wave fronts tend to become roughly parallel to the underwater contours.

A simple example, shown in Figure 78, is that of a set of regular waves approaching a straight shoreline at an

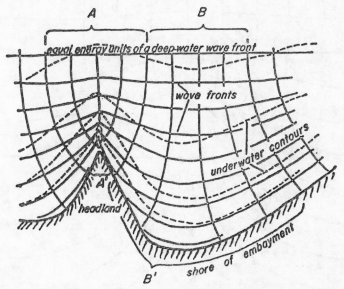

FIG. 27. Wave refraction causes a straight wave front in deep water to be bent until it almost parallels the shoreline. Equal energy units in deep water *A* and *B* are concentrated on the headland and spread along the bay shore. (Waves are moving toward the shore.)

angle. The inshore part of each wave is moving in shallower water, and consequently moves slower, than the part in deep water. The result is that the wave fronts tend to become parallel to the shoreline. Thus an observer on the beach always sees the larger waves come in directly toward him even though some distance out from shore they are seen to be approaching at an angle. The effect of refraction is to concentrate wave energy against headlands as shown in Figure 27; consequently it is a process

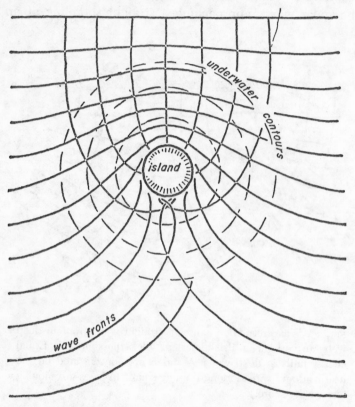

FIG. 28. Wave refraction around a circular island. (Waves are moving down the page.)

of considerable geological significance. It is a modern expression of the old sailor's saying, "The points draw the waves." Figure 6 in Chapter I shows the result of wave refraction acting over a long period of time.

Even on a circular island (with a gently sloping underwater topography on all sides) a wave train from one direction will "wrap itself" around the island so that the wave fronts arrive nearly parallel to the beaches on all sides, although of course the waves are substantially higher on the side facing directly into the deep-sea swell.

As train of swell becomes a shallow-water wave group where the depth is less than half the wave length, the effects of refraction begin. One can compute the velocity of a wave in shallow water, and it is possible to make a diagram showing how far the various parts of a wave advance during a series of equal time intervals. Such refraction diagrams are very useful in visualizing how waves of various periods and directions will influence a shoreline or a proposed coastal structure.

There are several methods of drawing refraction diagrams; all begin with an accurate contour chart of the bottom configuration out to a depth of half the longest wave that will be considered. Then the period and direction of the waves to be diagramed must be selected. The practicing coastal engineer will prepare diagrams for waves of many periods and directions, but usually he will also make a statistical wave hindcast. That is, he will make estimates of wave heights and periods based on historic weather maps to obtain statistics on what waves have arrived in the past and are likely to arrive in the future. One of these waves is likely to be predominant, and he will start with it—on much of the U.S. West Coast it is often a twelve-second wave from the northwest. Now he proceeds by drawing a straight line representing a wave front in deep water, or using another method, a wave ray (perpendicular to the wave front) that shows the direction of wave advance. In the wave-front method it is customary to calculate the new, somewhat reduced wave

length for each contour depth and to use these to step off
the advance of the wave front. The resulting diagram
shows the successive positions of the wave front at time
intervals equal to the period. As the wave slows down the
wave fronts get closer and closer together.

The principal question answered by a refraction diagram is: How is the wave energy distributed when it
reaches the coast? If the deep-water wave front is divided
into equal parts and wave rays are drawn through these
perpendicular to each wave front, the energy distribution
is readily seen. These wave rays separate areas of equal
wave energy and are called orthogonals. The ratio of the
length of the wave crest between orthogonals in deep
water to that at the beach is the refraction coefficient.
With it, one can compare the amounts of wave energy
reaching various points along the coast and determine the
effectiveness of proposed breakwaters.

A case history illuminating this method of using swell
hindcasting and refraction diagrams to determine how
waves damaged a shoreline structure is the study made
by M. P. O'Brien in 1947. During the period April 20–24,
1930, large breakers damaged a short segment of the tip
of the Long Beach, California, breakwater. This incident
was unusual because the breakwater had withstood wave
attack for years; at the time of the failure local winds
were light and the sea offshore—observed from gambling
ships anchored just beyond the three-mile limit—was
calm. At the San Pedro breakwater, only a few miles to
the north, there were no breakers; on the beaches to the
south, lifeguards noticed no unusual wave activity. Nev-
ertheless the waves breaking against the tip of the breakwater dislodged stones ranging in weight from four to
twenty tons. Observers had estimated the period of these

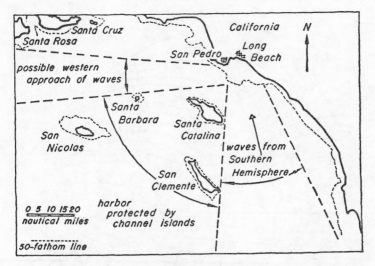

FIG. 29. Wave approaches to Long Beach, California.

waves at twenty to thirty seconds—a very-long-period swell.

Seventeen years later O'Brien set about finding out why. Historical weather maps were consulted, and it was found that at the time two storm centers in the Northern Hemisphere existed that might have been capable of producing long-period waves; one was to the west, the other to the northwest. No weather data from the Southern Hemisphere were available. The configuration of the coast and the protection of the channel islands immediately excluded the northwest storm as a possible wave source; a refraction diagram for twenty-second waves for the storm from the west showed that its waves could not have produced the observed effect either. Thus both the known storms were ruled out, and it was concluded that the source of the waves that damaged the breakwater

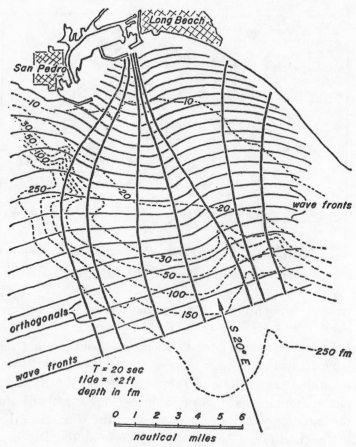

FIG. 30. Refraction diagram for destructive waves at Long Beach, California, showing how underwater topography several hundred feet deep and a dozen miles offshore focused wave energy on the breakwater.

must have been somewhere in the Southern Hemisphere, outside the area covered by the weather maps.

To the southeast the harbor area does not have the protection of offshore islands, and so a refraction diagram was constructed for twenty-second waves from various southerly directions. It was then discovered that a hump in the underwater topography, 180 to 600 feet deep and 10 miles away, acted as a lens to focus waves coming from S 20° E on the breakwater tip; that is, a special refraction condition for that particular wave period caused the wave energy of several miles of crest to converge. Waves only 2 feet high in deep water had been concentrated in a narrow zone as breakers over 12 feet high, and they caused the damage.

TRAPPED WAVES

One effect that refraction can have where the nearshore undersea topography slopes rather steeply toward deep water is to trap waves that strike the beach at an angle. As shown in Figure 31, which illustrates a wave front approaching a beach at an angle, the first part of the wave front to strike the beach is reflected and already moving seaward when the next part of the front reaches the sand. The figure shows successive positions of a single wave at intervals of about five seconds.

Trapping is evident in the dashed orthogonal line; this line shows the direction of motion of the wave energy and thus is always perpendicular to the wave front. A is a bundle of energy moving with this wave; at A′ it is reflected and we see the orthogonal start out to sea but then bend around and eventually strike the beach again at A″. A great deal of the energy is lost when the wave breaks and swashes up the sand, but, depending on the circumstances, up to about 30 percent of the energy could be reflected to continue on. At the outer edge of the reflected wave (stages 7, 8) the wave front stretches and more of the energy radiates off into deep water by diffraction. But much of it follows the orthogonal so that the wave at stage 12 is similar to that at stage 5 but much smaller.

Of course, one can directly observe this only in very special circumstances because of the presence of many other waves. The diagram shows only a single wave in

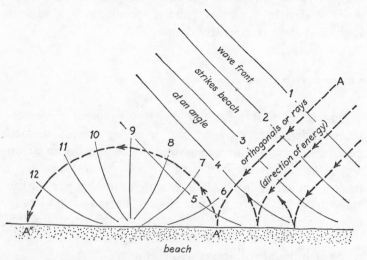

FIG. 31. When waves strike the beach at an angle, part of the energy that is reflected is "trapped" by refraction and moves along the beach. Numbers indicate successive positions of a single wave front.

successive positions because if all the other waves present were shown the diagram would be hopelessly complex. Trapped waves were discovered not by observation but by studying the implications of refraction, and the first description of them was given by Professors John Isaacs and Carl Eckart of the Scripps Institution of Oceanography in 1952. Later, Dr. Walter Munk, also of Scripps, and one of his students provided a more detailed mathematical treatment of what he called "edge" waves.

Because a reflected wave crest sometimes returns to sea as several smaller waves of shorter period, it is not quite clear how one should draw the refraction diagrams for these waves that move edgewise along the coast; Figure 31 is intended only to show the principle of trapping. It may be that this process is most important in the alongshore propagation of the energy of surf beat. That is, the bundle of energy in a package of several higher waves, which cause a short-term rise in water level on a beach, may be passed along. It would be difficult to draw meaningful orthogonals for this long-period disturbance (T is about half that of surf beat) to determine where the next bounce would come.

Probably there are some useful implications for geologists in this unusual type of waves when they are better understood. In certain areas they may be responsible for special conditions of erosion or deposition. Some geologists think they may be responsible for the location or existence of cusps.

STORM SURGES

During a violent storm there may be a substantial rise in the sea level along a coast that is known as a "storm tide" or surge. When this happens the wind-raised storm waves are superimposed on this surge, and sometimes the land is invaded with disastrous effect. This rise in water level is often the combined result of an atmospheric low pressure area surrounded by high pressure areas offshore; that is, the differences in air pressure cause a hump in the sea surface under the low pressure area. As the storm moves toward land this hump of water invades coastal areas. In addition, the strong winds create large waves and drive them across shoaling water, piling them on the shore. These steep, breaking waves are driven so hard, one upon another, that they create a general landward-flowing surface current (mass transport plus translation) that moves faster than the surplus water can return seaward along the bottom. The result of both factors is a flooded coast. The battering waves atop the general flood cause the serious destruction, for shoreline structures are now in the surf zone.

Some case histories of the great destructive effect of such surges serve to remind us of how quietly the ocean usually lies in its basin and how damaging a small change in sea level can be.

Probably the most famous example of a storm surge was the Galveston, Texas, "flood" of 1900. On that occasion a hurricane with winds of one hundred and twenty miles an hour raised the water level along that shore of the Gulf of Mexico fifteen feet above the usual two-foot tidal range. The storm waves, probably another twenty-five feet high, rode in atop the storm tide and demolished the city; some five thousand people drowned. A similar situation was created by Hurricane Carla of 1961, which also struck along the Gulf coast. But in the intervening years progress in weather and wave research made it possible to predict such surges. The area was evacuated in advance of its arrival so that there was no loss of life and minimum destruction.

On February 1, 1953, a strong gale swept down the North Sea and piled its waters against the Dutch coast. The storm surge rose ten feet above the highest high-tide level; the waves topped the dikes. The overflowing water eroded gulleys in the unsheathed inner side of the dikes until they were breached in sixty-seven places. In a short time channels as deep as one hundred feet and fifteen hundred feet wide were cut in the dikes. As the sea defenses collapsed, the North Sea poured in, and a steep-fronted wave advanced across the low country. The result was that 800,000 acres were flooded, 1,783 people drowned and the damage exceeded $250 million. But in a few years the Dutch had repaired the dikes, reclaimed their land, and were extending the dike system to include new lands. This super-gale was later determined by

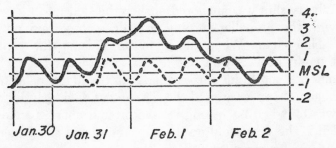

FIG. 32. Storm surge record made by tide gauge at Rotterdam, Holland, compared with the predicted tide. On February 1, 1953, the water level reached 2.75 meters (9 feet) above high tide and was largely responsible for the breaching of the dikes.

Dutch engineers to have been a "four-hundred-year storm." That is, the chance that all the unfavorable circumstances (high winds of long duration in that direction) would occur at one time was such that there was a likelihood of similar occurrence only once in four hundred years. Almost nobody expected the occurrence of such a storm.

India's low flat shores along the Bay of Bengal are densely populated and have at various times been invaded by great storm surges which have taken a terrible toll of

life. In 1876 the rising water accompanying a single storm
caused more than two hundred thousand deaths. More
recently, on October 31, 1960, at Chittagong, Pakistan,
near the mouth of the Ganges, a cyclone and storm surge
caused much damage but not without some amusing side
effects. At its worst, the winds were one hundred and
twenty miles an hour and the sea surface suddenly rose
twenty-two feet—inadvertently recorded by means of a
high-water mark left on the wall inside a lighthouse
tower. Three small islands were completely inundated;
thousands of lives and houses were lost. When dark fell, a
Liberty ship was anchored offshore headed into the wind
with the propeller turning to reduce the strain on the
anchor chain. When the main surge came, the captain
thought he was well out to sea, possibly as far as four
miles. Much to his surprise, later in the night, palm trees
began to appear around the ship and at daybreak the ship
was found to be resting on the ground about a mile inland. The ship could not be moved and was subsequently
cut up for scrap.

The captain of another ship recorded the storm in his
log in some detail, including: "At 1407 a tidal wave estimated to be forty feet high bore down on this vessel and
swept completely over her from bow to stern. The flood-
lights on the foremast and the fashion boards on top of
the flying bridge wheelhouse washed away. In the midst
of the mountainous seas this tidal wave was a distinct en-
tity, operating as a separate unit." He closes, "Why did I
ever sell the farm to go to sea?"

Khalilur Rahman, a Pakistan meteorological observer
stationed at the airport, also noted the surge in his log:
"Tidal bore opened the door and entered the observatory
room at 1314 filling it with sea water. Giving up all hope
of life I shut the door, otherwise the properties of the

Government would go away with the current of sea water. Whole night I was standing on a chair, placing it on the table to read the barometer. It was impossible to read the barometer after 1400 as I could not move with four to six feet of water on the ground. I like to mention here that the lower portion of the barometer was under water for some time."

The New England coast has had many serious storm surges and sixty-three hurricanes have been recorded since the Pilgrims landed. Of these, twelve (one every twenty-five years) have caused serious tidal flooding and major losses of life and property. The most spectacular example in recent history is that of Hurricane Carol, in August 1954. On that occasion the water level at Providence, Rhode Island, rose sixteen feet above normal, flooding the downtown business area eight feet deep and causing losses of $41 million. Providence officials decided to take action and build a protective tidal barrier rising 22.5 feet above mean sea level across the upper end of Narragansett Bay. Although the structure cost some $17 million, that has now been made up by the savings in storm surge damage.

V

Tides and Seiches

THE STUDY OF THE TIDES IS A LARGE AND COMPLICATED SUB-ject, most of which is beyond the scope of this book. The tides, however, are an important form of long-period wave, and it would be illogical to ignore them entirely. Besides, they play an important part in beach and coastal processes because they constantly change the depth of water in which waves approach the coast and the level at which waves strike the beach. Therefore, we shall touch lightly on the main points and encourage the especially interested reader to dig into the references for more detailed information and a fuller explanation.

THE TIDES

On all seacoasts there is a rhythmic rise and fall of the water which is called the tide, and associated with this vertical movement of the water surface are horizontal motions of the water known as tidal currents. Together they are known as the tides.

Tides are the longest waves oceanographers commonly deal with, having a period of forty-three thousand seconds (twelve hours and twenty-five minutes) and a wave length of half the circumference of the earth. The crest and trough of the wave are known as high tide and low tide. The wave height is called the range of tide, but since it is measured only in places where it is influenced by the shape of the shore, it varies greatly from place to place.

The gravitational attraction of the moon and the sun on the earth and the waters cause tides. Long before a word for gravity existed, the ancients must have realized vaguely that there was some connection between the moon and the motion of the water. But our civilization developed on the shores of the Mediterranean, an essentially tideless sea. Not until a number of explorers had ventured beyond the Gates of Hercules into the Atlantic and observed tides in England, where the range is large, was the relationship between the phases of the moon and the height of the tide established. Then some fifteen hundred years passed before Johannes Kepler wrote of "some kind of magnetic attraction between the moon and the earth's waters"—and Galileo scoffed.

It remained for Isaac Newton to discover the law of gravity, which holds that the gravitational attraction between two objects is directly proportional to their masses and inversely proportional to the square of the distance between them. From this relationship it can be shown that the gravitational attraction of the sun for the earth is about one hundred and fifty times that of the moon. The tremendous mass of the sun more than makes up for its much greater distance. But the moon is the primary cause of tides. Why?

The answer is that the difference in attraction for water particles at various places on the earth is far more impor-

tant than total attraction. That is, because of the moon's
very nearness (average only 239,000 miles) there is a big
difference in the gravitational attraction from one side of
the earth to the other.

The water on the side of the earth nearest the moon is
some four thousand miles closer to the moon than is the
center of the earth; the water on the far side is four thousand miles farther away. The sun, however, is ninety-
three million miles away, and a few thousand miles one
way or the other make comparatively little difference.
Thus, the sun's gravitational force, although far larger,
does not change very much from one side of the earth to
the other. So the moon is more important in producing
tides. For the sake of simplicity much of the following
discussion speaks only of the effect of the moon, but the
sun's effect is similar.

The result of these differences in gravitational attraction is that two bulges of water are formed on the earth's
surface, one toward the moon, the other, as we shall see,
away from it. The earth rotates on its axis once a day, and
it is not difficult to imagine that it turns constantly inside
a fluid envelope of ocean whose watery bulges are supported by the moon. This concept considers the tide wave
to be standing still while the ocean basin turns beneath it.
Thus, most points on earth experience two high tides and
two low tides a day.

It is easy to see why the gravitational attraction of the
moon should raise a bulge of water on the side of the
earth toward the moon, but it is not quite so easy to understand why there should be a similar bulge on the opposite side, away from the moon. Let me try to clarify
that point.

If the earth vanished, leaving three particles in space at
distances corresponding to the center and opposite sides

of the earth, the moon's gravity would act on them just the same. If we draw vector arrows from each point toward the moon, with lengths representing the intensities of gravitational attraction, the one nearest the moon is longest and the one farthest away is shortest.

But the three points are in fact part of the earth, which remains at a fixed distance from the moon because of the centrifugal effect of the rotating earth-moon system. If this force is represented at each point by an arrow equal in length but opposite in direction to that at the center of

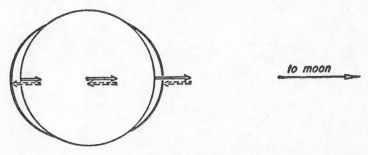

FIG. 33. Tide-producing forces.

the earth, the remaining force and direction will be equivalent to the tide-producing force. The differences in length between each of the pairs of arrows shown in Figure 33 correspond in magnitude and direction to the forces producing the tidal bulges on opposite sides of the earth.

The moon rotates about the earth (in the same direction as the earth's rotation) completing an orbit once a month. This motion of the moon requires any point on earth to go slightly farther than one revolution to come beneath the moon again; thus, the tidal day is twenty-four hours and fifty minutes long.

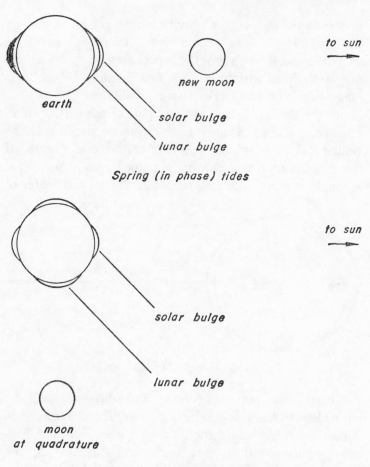

Neap (out of phase) tides

FIG. 34. Spring and neap tides.

One further complexity is that the bulge does not come directly beneath the moon but is slightly ahead of it, as shown in Figure 35. This positioning is the result of the friction of the earth as it rotates beneath the water. The rough-bottomed ocean basins tend to drag the bulges along; the gravitational effect of the moon tends to hold the bulge beneath it. The result is a compromise position at which these two forces are in equilibrium. In consequence a point on earth passes beneath the moon *before* high tide.

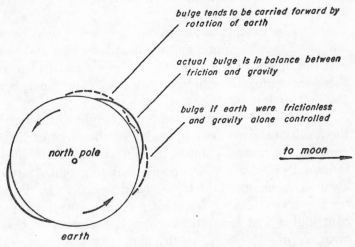

bulge tends to be carried forward by rotation of earth

actual bulge is in balance between friction and gravity

bulge if earth were frictionless and gravity alone controlled

north pole

to moon

earth

FIG. 35. Equilibrium position of the tidal bulge.

The sun tides, though much smaller, are important because of the way they increase and reduce the lunar tides. The two most important situations are when the earth, sun, and moon are aligned (in phase) and when the three make a right angle (out of phase).

In the in-phase case the solar bulge rides on top of the lunar bulge to make spring tides. During spring tides, which have nothing to do with the spring season but occur about every two weeks, the water level rises higher and falls lower than usual. This large range of tide lasts two or three days; then the two bulges get progressively further out of phase until, a week later, the high and low tides are about 20 percent less than average. These are neap tides; in effect, the sun's gravitational force reduces the moon's bulges.

Between these two extremes the solar bulge adds in a way that warps the shape of the main bulge, and the high and low tides come a little earlier or later, slightly varying the length of the tidal day.

Armed with this information, we are much better equipped than ancient man to look at the moon and forecast the height of the tide. At new moon and full moon there are spring tides; neaps come when the moon is in the first or last quarter.

Another important variation in the height of the tide is the result of the moon's elliptical orbit about the earth. At perigee, the nearest point in its orbit, the moon is fifteen thousand miles closer; at apogee it is that much farther away. This change in distance (and therefore in the attractive force) causes tides that are, respectively, 20 percent higher and lower than average. Perigee is reached once an orbit (once a month) and only rarely does this coincide with the in-phase alignment of sun, earth, and moon. But at least twice a year both effects exist at the same time—that is, a full moon or a new moon exists at perigee. Then the perigee tides add to the spring tides to produce the highest tides of the year.

Having considered the main forces that produce tides, we now can think about how these curious waves behave. Many shores, including the U.S. Atlantic Coast, experience two tides a day of about equal heights; these are called semidiurnal (semidaily). A few places in the world have only one high and one low a day. And most of the Pacific and Indian oceans have mixed tides; that is, the heights of high and low waters are unequal, as at Seattle or Ketchikan.

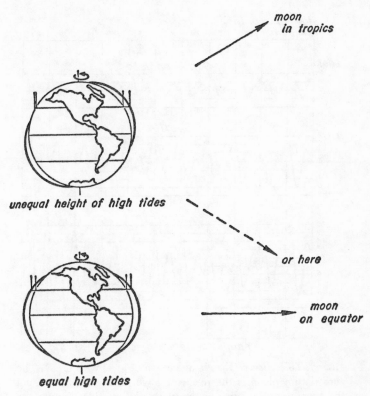

FIG. 36. Tidal inequality.

The cause of this changing inequality is shown in Figure 36. When the moon is opposite the equator the highs and lows are about equal. But when the moon is "in the tropics"—that is, above the tropics of Cancer or Capricorn —different thicknesses of bulge move past points away from the equator.

One of the most important influences on the height and character of the tide is the shape of the basin where it is observed. No good measurements have yet been made of the height of the tide in the deep ocean. There the range

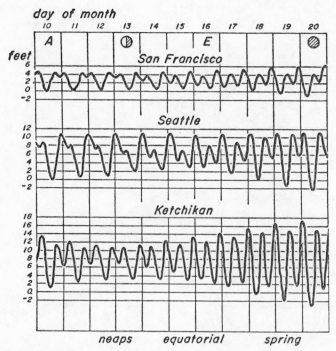

FIG. 37. Tide curves (the change in water level with time). The zero datum plane is the mean of lower low waters, meaning the average of the lower of the two daily low tides. Notice the large inequality in the heights of low tides in the same day except when the moon is on the equator. The large range of tides indicates spring tides; the small range, the neaps.

is believed to be small, perhaps a foot, as it is on small mid-ocean islands.

But as the solid earth turns beneath the tidal bulge, the shallow continental shelf acts as though it were a wedge driven under the wave front. The result is that the deep-water tidal range is much exaggerated at the shore. Estuaries with wide funnel-like openings into the ocean tend to amplify the tide range further. The width of the tide wave that enters the opening is restricted as the channel narrows; this constriction concentrates the wave energy and increases its height. Of course, if the estuary is very long, the frictional effects of sides and bottoms gradually reduce the height of the tide wave until it vanishes.

The importance of coastal configuration is illustrated by the difference in tidal height between Nantucket Island (about a foot) and the Bay of Fundy (over forty feet), which are only a few hundred miles apart. The opposite ends of the Panama Canal are only about fifty airline miles apart, but there is a great difference in the tides at the two terminals. At Colón, on the Caribbean side, the tide is generally diurnal and the range is about a foot; at Balboa, on the Pacific side, the tides are semidiurnal with an average height of fourteen feet and the locks are built to withstand spring tides of as much as twenty-one feet. This difference will create some interesting problems when a sea-level canal finally is built.

Although the tide doubtless advances across the ocean like a sine wave, there are only a few places on earth where this pattern can be observed directly. One such location is Chesapeake Bay. There the troughs and crest (the high and low tides) move up the bay as a series of "progressive" waves traveling slowly at "square root of gd" velocity. Usually there are two high-tide zones within its 150-mile length at the same time, with 50 miles of low-tide water in between.

It is interesting to speculate on the tide waves that must forever circle about Antarctica. From such speculation the "progressive wave" or "southern ocean" tide theory originated. The idea is simply that the Antarctic Ocean is a continuous belt of water extending completely around the earth, six hundred miles wide at its narrowest point. The tidal bulges must act as a forced wave into which energy is constantly being added by the tide-producing forces. As each high tide passes the openings into the Indian, South Atlantic, and South Pacific, waves are initiated that travel freely northward and modify the local tides as they go.

Accompanying the rise and fall of the tide are substantial horizontal motions of water known as tidal currents. Like the vertical changes they have little significance in the open sea, but in harbors and narrow estuaries they are of considerable importance. On a rising tide the currents are said to be flooding; on a falling tide, they ebb. The direction of flow is the set of the current.

When there is no flow, the current is slack; thus the time of slack water is usually within an hour of high or low water. The maximum current velocity comes about at the same time as the maximum change in the height of the water. Since these relationships depend largely on the local conditions, no general rule applies.

Tidal currents of ten knots in Seymour Narrows, Alaska, and four knots in the Golden Gate to San Francisco Bay are normal. Such currents have little influence on open beaches, but they may have considerable effect on sand movements in and near harbor mouths. For example, the combined effect of these currents and of ocean wave forces often causes a sandy bar (harbor bar) to form just outside the harbor entrance. This barrier will cause large waves to break and endanger small craft entering or leaving the harbor, thus explaining the many allusions in literature to sailors' fears of a breaking or moaning bar.

Tidal or other currents will cause waves to break or shorten their wave length. It is this change in the texture of the sea surface that permits the Gulf Stream and other great currents to be recognized from the air.

PLATE 11. Swell estimated as six to eight feet high bends around Rincon Point in the Santa Barbara Channel. In such conditions a lucky surfer can get a ride of half a mile. *Steve Bissell / Surfing Magazine*

PLATE 12. When low swell moves into very shallow water on this coral reef at Apra Harbor, Guam, each wave becomes several smaller waves to conserve energy. *U. S. Navy Photo*

PLATE 13. One beautiful unspoiled bay-mouth beach is at the Nestucca River entrance on the Oregon coast. Refraction produces an unlikely pattern of small waves perpendicular to each other. *Willard Bascom*

PLATE 14. Plunging breaker on the north side of Maui, Hawaii. There is no beach here, so the surf crashes directly against a rocky shore. The photographer took considerable risk when he shot this picture from a surf mat. *Dan Merkel/ Surfing Magazine*

PLATE 15. When a wave reflected from the breakwater at San Pedro, California, meets an incoming wave the result is an explosion of water about five meters (fifteen feet) high. *Willard Bascom*

PLATES 16 A & B.   High and low tide at Alma, New Brunswick, on the Bay of Fundy. The difference in water level between the photos is about seven meters (twenty-two feet). *Sid Bahrt*

PLATE 17. Tidal bore at Moncton, New Brunswick, on the Bay of Fundy. This is the front of the entering tide wave after extreme low tide. *Sid Bahrt*

PLATE 18. On a very flat beach such as this one at Cape Grenville, Washington, the shallow backrushing water flows out over the shallow incoming water to create a standing wave about 20 cm high that lasts five to ten seconds. *Willard Bascom*

PLATE 19. As this tsunami front rages across a coastal road, two cars (right arrow) are rolled over while a man (left arrow) dashes for higher ground. *Honolulu Advertizer*

Sea level is the height that the sea surface would assume if it were undisturbed by waves, tides, or winds. But because these disturbances do exist, the technique of averaging all possible sea levels has been adopted. The result is mean sea level (MSL), a convenient datum plane from which heights of tide or depths of water on a chart are measured. Charts and tide tables for the U.S. Pacific Coast refer to another datum: mean of lower low waters (MLLW)—the average height of the lowest of two low tides a day.

TIDAL BORES

There are a number of places in the world where rivers enter the ocean via long funnel-shaped bays. In such estuaries, especially during high spring tides, the broad front of the incoming tide wave is restricted by the narrowing channel and the shoaling water so that it abruptly increases in height and a visible wave front or bore exists. Most bores are dull (except to the ardent wave researcher) and are regarded merely as a local curiosity, but in a few places they are respected or even feared.

Sir George Airy, one of the founders of wave theory, observed the bore in the Severn River in England and wrote that he was thrilled by "the visible advancing front of that great solitary wave," the tide.

Actually, on entering shallow water the solitary wave front often breaks down into a series of small waves. Photos of the Severn bore show a series of about six or eight short steep waves about a foot high and ten feet long moving up a small glassy-surfaced river. In other places the entry of the tidal water causes the river surface to heave upward with an almost imperceptible front; in the space of two minutes the water level rises by three feet or more.

A few famous bores have steep breaking fronts that connect the original water surface with a new surface at a substantially higher level. That of the Chientang River in northern China has been described by Commander W. U. Moore, R.S.: "At Haining, where there is a sudden contraction of the channel, the bore is eight to eleven feet high, extending in a nearly straight line across the river which is rather more than one statute mile in width, traveling between twelve and thirteen knots, its front a cascade of bubbling foam falling forward and pounding on itself. The slope of this traveling cascade is uniform at any particular part of the front, but varies in different places from 40° to 70°, being highest and steepest over the deep parts of the river."

Visitors to the Hankow waterfront have been amazed to see the local boatmen suddenly paddle frantically for the riverbank and apparently without cause pull their boats out of a placid stream. In a few minutes the breaking bore passes, the boats are returned to the river at its new, higher level, and work resumes.

The bore of the Amazon is even more spectacular and is said to attain a height of twenty-five feet. Seen from the high dikes near the river mouth it has the appearance of a several-miles-long waterfall traveling upstream at a speed of twelve knots for three hundred miles. The roar can be heard for fifteen miles.

SEICHING

If the surface of an enclosed body of water such as a lake or bay is disturbed, long waves may be set up which will rhythmically slosh back and forth as they reflect off opposite ends. These waves, called seiches, have a period that depends on the size and depth of the basin. They are a rather common phenomenon, but because the wave height is so low and the length so long, they are virtually invisible, and few laymen are aware of their existence.

Seiches can be regarded as standing-wave patterns or as the reflection of trapped waves. A pattern of standing waves (in contrast to the progressive waves of the open ocean) is composed of nodes, at which the height of the water surface stays the same, and loops, where the surface moves up and down. The nodes and loops maintain a fixed position, as do the surface particles of water, but beneath the surface there are swift currents as the water shifts to support the changing wave form.

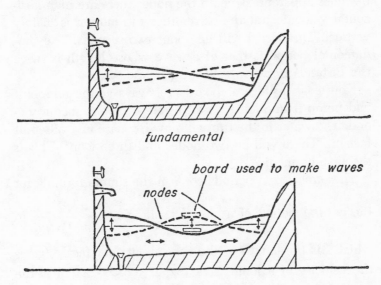

fundamental

first harmonic

FIG. 38. Seiching in a bathtub.

Natural basins are so irregular in shape and depth that it is best to begin by thinking about the nice clean situation that exists in a bathtub. A tub is nearly rectangular and has almost vertical frictionless sides—thus fulfilling the requirements of simple theory. If you put about six inches of water in your tub you can make model standing waves or seiches.

First set the mass of water rocking with a fundamental wave that reflects back and forth off each end. The midpoint of the tub is a node and the water depth there will remain the same (six inches) while that at each end will vary from, say, four inches to eight inches. If you add some neutrally buoyant marker, such as small wads of paper that float at middepth and move with the water particles, the motion of the water in these standing waves becomes apparent. Beneath the nodes there are high horizontal velocities; at the extremities the motion is mainly vertical. The period will be about two seconds. The fundamental period is that of a wave whose length is twice the distance between reflecting boundaries.

Now float a piece of board crossways at the midpoint and pump it up and down at a rate of about once a second. The water in the tub will now resonate in a different fashion. There will be two nodes and three loops. This is the first harmonic.

These measured periods confirm the simple formula for the natural period of a closed basin. $T_n = \dfrac{2l}{(n+1)\sqrt{gd}}$ in which l is the length of the tub—about four feet, $\sqrt{gd}$ is the velocity of a long wave ($\sqrt{32 \times 0.5} = 4$); n is the "order" of motion (fundamental $= 0$, 1st harmonic $= 1$, etc.).

Thus the natural period of the tub is 2 seconds and its first harmonic is 1 second. For a harbor a mile across averaging fifty feet deep the fundamental period is 264 seconds and the first harmonic 132 seconds. Other, higher harmonic orders may also be present at the same time.

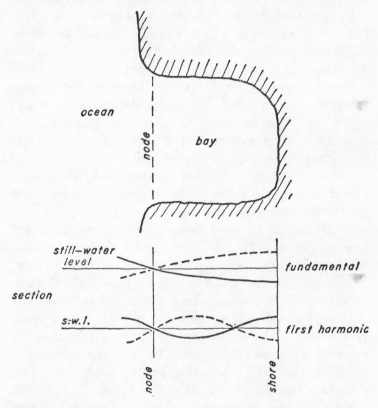

FIG. 39. Seiching in an open-sided bay. Natural period
$$= T_n = \frac{4l}{(n+1)\sqrt{gd}}$$ (Note that an independent set of seiches may reflect back and forth across the bay in the other direction.)

Since few harbors have the neat boundaries of a bath-tub, the waves do not reflect evenly and it might be ex-pected that long wave patterns would be difficult to es-tablish. Not so. Even harbors with exceedingly irregular shapes seem to rock with remarkable regularity, which is recorded on the tide gauges. Moreover, many harbors and bays have a large part of one side open to the ocean. This has two major effects: (1) The laws governing the seich-ing are different and (2) disturbances from the ocean can easily enter and start the harbor seiching.

If one side of the bay is open to the ocean, the missing reflecting surface is replaced by a nodal line, as shown in Figure 39. Then the fundamental mode of oscillation is that in which the opening is at the first node; the first har-monic has the second node at the opening.

Tidal recordings made on open coasts also show seiche-like motions of the water surface that can be interpreted only as oscillations of the water masses on the continental shelf. These are believed to exist because the shelf acts like an open bay. Thus we discover that neither the bath-tub nor the bay is necessary for this kind of wave to exist.

The question now arises as to the source of the disturb-ance that causes seiching. In a lake or other completely enclosed basin a sudden change in atmospheric pressure, such as would be caused by a windsquall passing over one end, is the most likely cause. But seiching in bays that open into the ocean is almost invariably caused by the ar-rival of a long-period wave train. A Pacific tsunami will usually succeed in exciting all the bays and harbors around its rim. Often these will oscillate for days, produc-ing tide-gauge records similar to that shown in Figure 40 of Pago Pago, Samoa, on May 22, 1960.

Once the water is set in motion by the first arriving

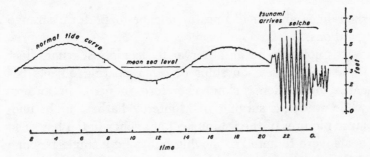

FIG. 40. Seiche in Pago Pago, Samoa, excited by the tsunami of May 22, 1960.

wave, seiching at the natural period of the harbor is likely to mask subsequent wave arrivals, thus making it difficult to obtain the period of the tsunami itself from the tide gauge. At Pago Pago, for example, the natural period of the harbor is twenty-two minutes and its precise rhythmic motion is quite unlike that of other harbors disturbed by the same tsunami. If, by coincidence, the period of the tsunami is an even multiple of the natural period of the harbor, then the seiching motion is amplified by each new wave that arrives, and the water motion inside the harbor may become more violent than the motion outside. The fact that tsunamis are relatively rare suggests that long-period waves from other causes are responsible for creating most seiches.

The phenomenon of seiching is rarely troublesome to man, the exception being a situation in some harbors that is known as surging, in which moored ships are moved about by these long low waves. For long waves of the same height (these waves are usually less than a foot high) the amount of horizontal water motion is in proportion to the period. Thus seiches with a period of several minutes can cause large ships tied to piers to strain at their lines and small ones at anchor to perform strange gyrations.

It is not easy for an observer to decide just what effect these waves have on ships or other floating objects because the motion is slow. Therefore, in 1946, the author, while studying surging in Monterey harbor, took time-lapse pictures of the fishing fleet at anchor in the bay. The boats were tethered to moving buoys by a single bowline and thus were reasonably free to move. A rigidly supported motion picture camera set up on the bluff over the harbor was used to take pictures of the boats at the rate of one frame per second. When these photographs were projected at sixteen frames per second the surging motion was speeded up sixteen times. Clear patterns of water motion became evident as the previously indiscernible three-minute surge was compressed into eleven seconds. Later on, boats in the relatively quiet Noyo River and Santa Barbara harbors were similarly photographed on days when no surging motion could be observed. To our surprise, when the film was projected and the boat motion speeded up, a substantial surge could be seen. The boats would strain on their lines in unison first in one direction and then in the other with remarkable regularity.

In most harbors the surging is more a scientific curiosity than a serious problem, but Los Angeles harbor is an exception. There, even when the water surface appears calm, large ships tied up may move as much as ten feet, snapping heavy mooring lines, breaking piles, and damaging the ships themselves. These invisible surges have periods of three, six, and twelve minutes, corresponding to the natural periods of the basin.

When the tsunami of April 1, 1946, arrived with a period of about fifteen minutes, this was close enough to the

natural period so that each new wave that arrived added
to the height of the existing ones in the harbor. Fortunately there were not many waves in the series, and,
somewhat surprisingly, no unusual damage was reported
by the larger vessels.

VI

Impulsively Generated Waves

WHEN A FORCE IS SUDDENLY APPLIED TO A WATER SURFACE, waves are generated. The impulse of a pebble tossed into a puddle sends out a train of waves in concentric circles. In the ocean an earthquake, a volcanic eruption, a landslide or a nuclear explosion may produce the same effect on a much larger scale. The train of waves leaving such an event often contains a huge amount of energy and moves at high speed. As a result the waves may be tremendously destructive when they encounter a populated shore.

The general public has long referred to these waves as tidal waves, much to the annoyance of American oceanographers who are acutely aware that there is no connection with the tides. In an effort to straighten out the matter they adopted the Japanese word tsunami, which now is in general use. Later they discovered that tsunami merely means tidal wave in Japanese, but at least the annoyance has been shifted overseas.

SEISMIC SEA WAVES

A somewhat more descriptive term that applies to waves caused by earthquakes is seismic sea waves.

There are several mechanisms by means of which earthquakes can generate seismic sea waves, two of which are illustrated. The first is a simple fault in which tension in the submarine crustal rock is relieved by the abrupt rupturing of the rock along an inclined plane. When such a fault occurs, a large mass of rock drops rapidly and the support is removed from a column of water that extends to the surface. The water surface oscillates up and down as it seeks to return to mean sea level, and a series of waves is sent out. If the rock fails in compression, the

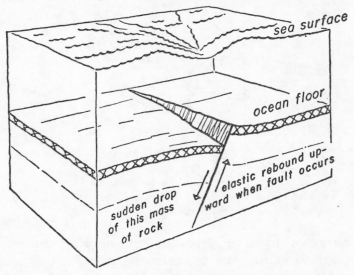

FIG. 41. Origin of a tsunami. A fault in the crustal rock causes part of the sea floor to drop rapidly. The water surface above also falls and a series of seismic sea waves is generated.

mass of rock on one side rides up over that on the other, and a column of water is lifted, but the result is the same: a tsunami.

A second mechanism is a landslide, which is set in motion by an earthquake. If the slide begins above water, abruptly dumping a mass of rock into the sea, waves are made by the same action as the plunger in the wave channel. An example of such an event will presently be cited. If the slide occurs well below the surface, it creates

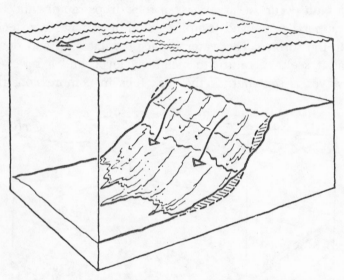

FIG. 42. Origin of a tsunami. A landslide of loose sediment accumulated on the brow of a steep submarine slope is set in motion by a nearby earthquake.

waves, as shown in Figure 42. Both drawings are much exaggerated in order to make the point. Actually the water surface may fall only a few feet in water many thousands of feet deep, but that would not show at this scale.

The waves so created are very long and very low. Their period is of the order of a thousand seconds; their wave lengths may be as much as one hundred and fifty miles; their height, only a foot or two in deep water. The slope of the wave front is imperceptible and ships at sea are unaware of their passage.

Because the wave lengths are so long, tsunamis move as shallow-water waves, even in the deepest ocean. As such their velocity is controlled by the depth.

$$C = \sqrt{gd}$$

Thus, if $g = 32$ and $d = 15,000$ feet (average depth of the Pacific basin), the velocity of a wave in the deep Pacific is 692 feet per second or 472 miles an hour. Fortunately the Pacific is large enough so that waves moving at even that speed take considerable time to cross it, and a seismic sea wave warning system has been established to warn coastal inhabitants of approaching tsunamis.

The events so far mentioned usually take place out of sight of man where they can do little harm. It is when these waves approach a coastline that they are at their spectacular worst. There the influence of the bottom topography and the configuration of the coastline transforms the low waves of deep water into rampaging monsters.

The first tsunami of which there is a record wiped out Amnisos, Crete, about 1470 B.C. A thousand years later, according to Pausanias, an ancient Greek, "the town of Helice perished under the waters of the Gulf of Corinth where the population was drowned to a man." In that millennium perhaps ten tsunamis were recorded. Now two or three a year cause local catastrophes. Certainly there is no change in the activity of undersea earthquakes; the reason for the apparent increase is mainly that the world's population has grown so that people and wealth are now spread along once deserted shores. Since this trend is certain to continue, the danger to mankind from great sea waves is increasing.

A list of two hundred and seventy seismic sea waves from antiquity to 1940 was compiled by N. H. Heck of the U. S. Coast and Geodetic Survey. In reading them one easily envisions great walls of water suddenly towering above frantic crowds; harbors being swept clear of ships; soaked and terrorized survivors of the first wave racing the next wave to high ground. Table V contains some choice samples.

TABLE V
SOME GREAT SEISMIC SEA WAVES

September 14, 1509 — Turkey. Sea came over the walls of Constantinople and Galata following earthquake.

December 16, 1575 — Chile. Intense wave in the inner port of Valdivia. Two Spanish galleons wrecked.

March 25, 1751 — Chile. City of Concepción was extensively damaged for the fourth time in a century by earthquakes. Sea withdrew and returned at great height several times. Disastrous effects at Juan Fernández Island.

November 1, 1755 — Portugal. Great Lisbon earthquake. Waves fifteen to forty feet high along Spanish and Portuguese coasts. Very high at Cádiz, where eighteen waves rolled in.

December 29, 1820 — Celebes, Makassar. A wall of water sixty to eighty feet high swept over the fort of Boelekomba. Great damage at Nipa-

	Nipa and Serang-Serang. A similar great wave at Bima, Sumbawa, carried ships over houses.
August 13, 1868	South Peru (now North Chile). USS *Wateree* carried a quarter mile inshore by a wave with a maximum height of seventy feet. Receding wave uncovered Bay of Iquique to a depth of twenty-four feet and then returned with a forty-foot wave, covering the city of Iquique.
June 15, 1896	Northeast Japan. Sea waves nearly one hundred feet high at head of bay; elsewhere, ten to eighty feet; 27,000 lives lost along 320 kilometers of coast; 10,000 houses swept away.
March 16, 1926	Palmerston Island, Cook Group. Island submerged and natives lost their means of sustenance.
November 21, 1927	Chile, Aysén River region. Sea invaded land along twenty-five miles of coast. Boat *Mannesix* with crew flung into treetops of forest.
November 18, 1929	Newfoundland, Burin Peninsula. A tidal wave from the Grand Banks earthquake swept up several narrow inlets to a height of fifty feet, destroying villages and causing heavy loss.

On reading Heck's notes my first reaction was that their very terseness tended to make them more exciting than reality by stimulating the reader's imagination. However, upon examining the more extended accounts from which he took his data, I concluded that it would take a rare imagination to equal the actual circumstances. For example:

The USS *Wateree*, a Civil War side-wheeler gunboat, was stationed at Arica, Peru, in August 1868, when the tidal wave referred to by Heck occurred. According to a witness, it was "carried by an exceptionally heavy wave completely over the town, scraping the tops of the highest buildings and was safely deposited on some sandy waste-land about a mile inland. Thanks to her flat bottom she fetched up on an even keel and although it was impossible to get the ship back into her accustomed element she was in no danger structurally. The ship was therefore left in full commission for several months until sold. Service routine continued but with certain readjustments. Sanitary facilities were erected ashore and a vegetable garden was started. The most unusual modification was the substitution of burros for boats. If the captain wanted to go 'ashore,' the bosun's mate would pipe and call, 'Away brig.' Thereupon the coxswain would run out on a boom, slide down a pennant to a burro, cast off and come alongside to the ladder which had been lengthened to reach the ground. The captain would mount and ride off into the dunes."

The author well remembers how his own interest in tsunamis was generated. On April 1, 1946, our field party returned to the Berkeley campus of the University of California after five months of daily observation of the waves and beaches of the north Pacific coast and was greeted by: "Did you see the big wave?" It sounded much like an April Fool's Day joke, but, sadly, it was not. There had been a landslide in the Aleutian Trench early that morning and its waves were wreaking havoc around the Pacific basin. After the bad luck of missing the actual arrival of the waves by a day we set about collecting whatever data we could.

The next few days were spent questioning people who had seen the wave, surveying high-water marks, and photographing wrecked houses and stranded boats. Some of the stories were amusing and each contained some useful fact that could be applied to the understanding of seismic sea waves. For example, we found that the first arriving crest is often so small it is unnoticed, but it is soon followed by a major recession of the water.

This happened at Half Moon Bay, where a surveying party was mapping the shoreline at the site of a proposed breakwater. The rodman's instructions were to hold the rod at the water's edge. As the water retreated with the first trough, he followed instructions. Just as the engineer on the transit was beginning to wonder how he could be reading five feet below sea level on the rod, the direction of the water movement changed; rodman and rod inadvertently surfboarded in on the first large crest.

Areas of bottom or rocks never before seen may be exposed. The first trough suddenly stranded the Half Moon Bay fishing fleet on a sandy bottom in an anchorage where it normally floated at the lowest range of the tide. But not for long. Before another ten minutes had passed the boats had refloated, dragged their anchors several hundred yards, and were stranded again—this time on a paved road thirteen feet above the original water level.

The arrival of the trough of one of these great waves should serve as a warning, but instead it attracts the curious, who often follow the receding water out to pick up flopping fish and look at the newly exposed bottom instead of running for high ground. When the next crest arrives it may come fast—in some cases it is a huge breaking wave—and the curious pay for their folly. This drop in water level over a period of several minutes without change in the appearance of the usual waves is something like the rapid ebbing of the tide. In a similar way the incoming crests may be seen only as a rapid rise in the general level of the water without any observable wave front. Doubtless this tide-like action, which occurs in twelve minutes instead of twelve hours, is partly responsible for the usual misnomer "tidal wave."

On the same occasion in the cove at Pacific Grove, California, a man was dozing on a bench fifteen feet above the normal water level. He awakened when one dangling hand was wet by the gently rising water and sat bolt upright on the still-dry bench to watch the surrounding water slowly recede again. At the same instant, in nearby Monterey harbor, marine biologist Rolf Bolin noticed unusual currents around his skiff but no important rise or fall of water level.

These incidents raised an interesting question. Why should there be this major difference in the height of the wave at two points only a mile apart? Part of the answer seems to be that Pacific Grove faced away from the wave, Monterey faced into it.

Later, over a period of years, I traveled to many Pacific shores asking about the effects of that tsunami. Remarkably often points facing into the waves and bays facing away from them were hardest hit. For example, Taiohai village at the head of a narrow south-facing bay in the Marquesas Islands four thousand miles from the earthquake epicenter was demolished. Hilo, Hawaii, only half as far from the disturbance and whose offshore topography seems precisely suited to funnel tsunamis toward the town, fared worse. There the captain of a ship standing off the port watched with astonishment as the city was destroyed by waves that passed unnoticed under the ship. Another ship, the *Brigham Victory*, was unloading lumber at Hilo when the tsunami struck. The ship survived with considerable damage but the pier and its buildings were destroyed. One hundred and seventy-three persons died and $25 million in property damage was done by the waves at Hilo that morning.

But the truly great waves of April 1 struck at Scotch Cap, Alaska, only a few hundred miles from the tsunami's source, where five men were on duty in a lighthouse that marked Unimak Pass. The lighthouse building was a substantial two-story reinforced concrete structure with its foundation thirty-two feet above mean sea level. None of the men survived to tell the story but a breaking wave over one hundred feet high must have demolished the building at about 2:40 A.M. The next day Coast Guard aircraft, investigating the loss of radio contact, were astonished to discover only a trace of the lighthouse foundation. Nearby a small block of concrete one hundred and three feet above the water had been wiped clean of the radio tower it once supported.

TSUNAMI WARNING SYSTEMS

Largely as a result of the Hilo disaster a seismic sea wave warning system has been developed by the U. S. Coast and Geodetic Survey. It works like this. Ten seismograph stations around the Pacific rim from the Philippines to Alaska and from Peru to Japan are equipped with automatic alarm systems and visible recorders. When the tremors from a large earthquake are received, the alarm sounds, alerting the local observers, who transmit the recorded data to a central station in Honolulu. If analysis there of the arrival times of the first earthquake shock at the various stations shows that the quake is located under the ocean, a radio message containing estimated times of arrival of a possible tsunami is sent to tide-measuring stations nearest the quake's epicenter. Each station is asked to report back whether or not such waves actually arrive. If unusual wave activity is reported, a warning is issued to

local authorities (civil defense and police) in coastal areas
that may be affected. At present no attempt is made to estimate the height of the waves to be expected, but that
may be possible after further research is done.

Walter Munk was an early consultant in the development of tsunami warning devices and on passing through
Hilo in 1950 could not resist the chance to ask about the
workings of the embryonic system. He found the instrument was mounted at the outer end of the Hilo pier and
was designed to detect waves in the one thousand second
band midway between the longer period tides and the
shorter period swell. The arrival of a tsunami at this finely
tuned instrument would actuate an alarm bell in the police station some distance inland and the city could be
warned in time to flee to higher ground.

However, the police chief, with a fine distrust of such
gadgets, passed the word that no warning would be given
until he telephoned a man at the end of the pier who
would visually inspect the standard tide gauge and
confirm the existence of unusual waves. Aside from the
obvious delay involved under the best of circumstances,
this procedure seemed to place undue emphasis on the
necessity for tsunamis to arrive during working hours.
Even then, if the phone on the pier was not answered, a
question would remain as to whether the pier, gauge, and
telephone had been swept away or whether the observer
was busy elsewhere. But the plan did eliminate false
alarms.

After a more recent trip, several tsunamis later, Professor Munk reports an increased mutual respect between
the ocean and the chief.

The need of Pacific-rim cities for a wave warning system was clear enough and over a period of years a combination of false alarms and small tsunamis made it possible

to "work the bugs out of the system." When needed for one of the greatest tsunamis of the past century, it was ready.

On May 22, 1960, a violent earthquake (magnitude 8.5) shook the coast of Chile. A volcano erupted; there was widespread faulting, subsidence, and hundreds of landslides. In a local disaster area five hundred miles long, four thousand people died, half a million homes were damaged, and $400 million worth of property was destroyed. There was also a major subsidence on the great undersea fault that parallels the coast, and this generated a tsunami that was felt on all Pacific shores.

In Chile itself dozens of waterfront towns were devastated. Coastal cities in New Zealand, Australia, the Philippines, and Okinawa were flooded by several feet of water. On the U.S. coast, Los Angeles and San Diego harbors suffered a million dollars worth of damage to piers and small craft. In Japan, nine thousand miles from the origin, the waves were as much as fifteen feet high. There, 180 people died and the damage was estimated at $50 million.

But Hilo, Hawaii, again took the worst blow, and although the property damage was more serious than in 1946, this time the population was warned and there were few deaths. The sequence of events abstracted from the log of the Coast and Geodetic Survey's Honolulu observatory is an interesting record of the progress of the wave:

0938   Alarm sounded by distant earthquake.

0959   Requested data from other stations.

1014, 1120   Seismograph stations at Berkeley, Tucson, Fairbanks, Suva report in.

1059   Requested tide report from Balboa, Canal Zone.

1159   Issued bulletin (not warning) to Honolulu police and military:

This is a seismic sea wave advisory bulletin. A severe earth-quake has occurred in Chile. It is possible a damaging sea wave has been generated. If so, it will reach Hawaii about midnight.

1204   Valparaiso reports tsunami on coast of Chile.

1340   Issued news bulletin reconfirming that a wave may be on the way.

1847   Issued official warning:
This is a seismic sea wave warning. The estimated time of arrival of the first wave at Hawaii is midnight. The danger may last several hours. The intensity of the wave cannot be predicted. [Arrival times estimated for Tahiti, Christmas Island, Samoa, Fiji, Canton, Johnson, Midway.]

1924   Balboa reports no wave; Christmas Island reports negative.

2223   Tahiti reports unusual wave activity [first actual tsunami report other than Chile].

2255, 0011   Samoa and La Jolla report tidal rise.

0035   Heard via broadcast band radio that unusual wave activities had begun in Hilo.

0611   All clear sounded by civil authorities.

The "unusual wave activities" that began almost exactly at midnight at Hilo included the arrival of a series of waves whose crests reached fifteen feet above the normal high-water mark. As these successive walls of water swept across the city, they carried before them virtually all the buildings on seven city blocks. The record of the Hilo tide gauge (Figure 43), which went off scale and was rendered inoperable by the second wave, shows the abruptness of the beginning of the large waves.

There is little practical action that can be taken to prevent property damage by such waves. Hilo's solution was to move to higher ground nearby and make the waterfront area into Tsunami Park. Doubtless this low area will be swept again and again by future waves.

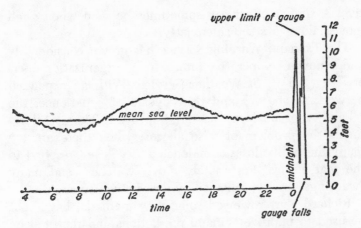

FIG. 43. Tsunami recorded on tide gauge at Hilo, Hawaii. Abruptly at midnight on May 23, 1960, a series of great seismic waves began arriving which wrecked the city. The gauge that ordinarily records tides with a four-foot range hit the stops at top and bottom before being smashed by the second wave.

In order to investigate the possibilities of protecting Hilo against such waves, the Corps of Engineers built a large hydraulic model of the undersea approaches to Hilo Bay that included a faithful reproduction of the nearly vertical cliff along the northern shore of the bay. When subjected to properly scaled tsunamis, the model unexpectedly showed that these large waves are made even larger by a Mach stem that forms against the cliff.

This phenomenon causes the wave height to nearly double for the following reason: as the wave crest is squeezed against the cliff by the narrowing bay, the extra water (from the extension of the crest that no longer exists) moves into the remaining wave crest. The crest now contains a second, internally reflected, wave. Because the extra water increases the depth somewhat, the higher wave may also move a little faster and be more destructive. A similar effect can sometimes be seen when swell moves along a steep-sided jetty.

The Tsunami Warning Service has grown considerably and is now a co-operative international organization operated by the U. S. Weather Service. With an expanded network of stations and thirty years of experience, the reliability of its forecasts has improved. There still remains the problem of false alarms; when there are too many the public loses confidence and will not respond to the real alarms. Fortunately most "watches" and many "warnings" are not followed by destructive tsunamis.

Richard Kerr reviewed some new methods that might be used to improve tsunami predictions and reported on them in *Science*. He notes that waiting for tide-gauge proof of a wave has obvious drawbacks, and points out that it would be better if the warnings could be issued solely on the basis of information from seismograph stations. In order to predict whether or not a tsunami has been formed, details of the location and magnitude of the earthquake must be known. As a general rule, destructive tsunamis are generated by earthquakes of 8 or stronger on the Richter scale, depending somewhat on the exact location of the quake. Thus any Pacific earthquake greater than 7.5 initiates a watch, but a warning is issued only after tide gauges detect a wave. (There have been about two watches a year in Hawaii but no warnings since 1967.)

One problem is that the magnitude estimates now come from seismographs that are particularly sensitive to seismic waves with periods of less than 20 seconds. Longer waves, which contain much of the energy, are excluded. This means the quake location is pinpointed by means of the higher-frequency seismic waves but the earthquake amplitudes are derived from the intermediate length, 20-second, waves. Some seismic researchers, including

James Brune and Hiroo Kanamori, think that 20-second waves do not accurately reflect the true magnitude of some earthquakes and that 100-second waves should be used instead. Otherwise much of the energy released by large earthquakes that may make tsunamis goes undetected.

For example, the Chilean earthquake of 1960 had a magnitude of 8.3 when calculated on the basis of 20-second waves, but its magnitude was 9.5 if the longer waves were included. The difference represents 10 times greater wave amplitude and 60 times more energy released. It seems possible that if seismographs were used that detected the long-period waves the warnings would be more realistically based. Tests of such instruments are now under way.

The remarkable thing about the ocean is how calm and stable its surface is. Considering its breadth and depth, the changes in height caused by waves and tides are insignificant, except to those who live at the water's edge.

A fascinating example of a seismic sea wave generated by an above-water landslide is the Lituya Bay incident. Lituya Bay on the Alaska coast is an active earthquake region. Two glaciers flow into the upper end of the steep-sided bay; near its center is Cenotaph Island; a sandspit across the mouth keeps out the big waves from the Gulf of Alaska so that fishermen regard Anchorage Cove, just inside the entrance, a safe haven.

On July 9, 1958, two fishing boats, the *Badger* and the *Sunmore*, were anchored just inside the spit when a major earthquake occurred. The shock started landslides which cleaned the soil and timber off the mountainsides at the upper end of the bay at eighteen hundred feet above sea level and at the same time caused great masses of ice to fall from the front of the glaciers into the water.

An eyewitness account by the skipper of the forty-foot *Badger* gives a vivid picture of the result. He felt the earthquake, and looking inland saw the first wave building at the head of the bay. As it passed Cenotaph Island he estimated its height at fifty feet (measurements made later indicated it probably was much higher). It swept through Anchorage Cove, carrying the *Badger* over the spit at an altitude of about a hundred feet and dropping it in the open sea. There the boat foundered, but the boatman was able to launch a skiff and he and his wife were picked up by another fishing boat. The fifty-five-foot *Sunmore* was not so fortunate; it was swept against a cliff and no trace of it or its crew was ever found.

This wave, although very high, was very localized. The somewhat unusual circumstance of its origin leads one to muse on the great waves that must have been generated in billions of years of geological time. One can visualize the walls of water that must have raced outward when whole mountains suddenly slid into the sea, or when a continental perimeter abruptly shifted, or when a great meteorite landed in the sea—a pebble in earth's puddle.

EXPLOSION-GENERATED WAVES

Tsunamis may also be generated by large violent explosions; fortunately such an origin is much less likely than an undersea earthquake. The classic example of an explosion-generated wave is the eruption of the volcano Krakatoa in the Sunda Straits, Dutch East Indies. This story is best told by excerpts from the words of the original report:

"Krakatoa erupted with the most violent explosions of recorded history. The entire north portion of the island was blown away and in place of ten square miles of land with an average elevation of 700 feet, there was formed a great depression with its bottom more than 900 feet below sea level. Apparently pent-up superheated vapor exploded and ruptured the throat of the volcano allowing cold ocean water to 'freeze' a crust on the rising molten magma there. Then, as with a safety valve tied down, the pressure began to build up. On the morning of August 27, 1883, this crust let go.

"Over four cubic miles of rock was blown away; the sea was covered with masses of pumice for miles around—in many places of such thickness that no vessel could force its way through. Two new islands rose in the strait, the lighthouses were swept away. A column of dust rose 17 miles and spread out so that at Batavia, a hundred miles away, the sky was so dark that lamps had to be burned in the houses at midday. Eventually this dust was distributed by stratospheric winds over the entire earth. The sound of the principal explosion was heard 3,000 miles away and the atmospheric shock wave reflected off itself at the antipodes of the earth.

"But the most damaging effect was that of the waves which inundated the whole of the shores of Java and Sumatra which border the strait. Many villages were carried away including Tyringin and Telok Betong where the water reached heights of 60 and 72 feet. The town of Merak, at the head of a funnel-shaped bay, was struck by a wave variously estimated at 100 and 135 feet high. More than 36,000 people were drowned and many vessels were washed ashore including the man-of-war *Berouw* which was carried 1.8 miles inland and left 30 feet above sea level.

"How the wave was formed, whether by large pieces of the island falling into the sea; by a sudden submarine explosion, by the violent movement of the crust of the earth under water; or by the sudden rush of water into the cavity of the volcano when the side was blown out, must ever remain, to a great extent, uncertain."

The waves radiated westward from the straits into the Indian Ocean, around the Cape of Good Hope, and northward through the Atlantic. Tide gauges in harbors at South Africa (4,690 miles from the source), at Cape Horn (7,820 miles), and Panama (11,470) clearly traced the arrivals of a series of about a dozen waves, which had traveled at an average velocity of about four hundred miles per hour. The period of the waves taken from tide stations nearby the explosion is about two hours; at great distances it is closer to one hour. No explanation can yet be given, but a similar decrease in period with distance is noted in the records of the May 1960 tsunami.

In early 1952 the author was given the job of measuring the waves from Mike, the first large thermonuclear explosion. It was to be exploded on the wide reef at the northern end of Eniwetok atoll, in the Marshall Islands. Somehow it would make waves, but by what mechanism, and how large would the waves be? The best guide was the Krakatoa report of the Royal Society of London, and I prepared an extensive abstract of it from which the preceding account has been taken. We guessed that the energy released by Mike would be about the same as that of the main explosion at Krakatoa.

Six years earlier, in the preparations for the first underwater nuclear test inside Bikini lagoon, many wave-generating experiments had been made in an attempt to forecast the size and period of the waves and the means by which they would be generated. Explosives were shot in ponds and circular steel plates were dropped into basins that contained models of the entire atoll. There was a lot of splashing and countless rolls of data were taken; there was an abundance of theories. But even after photos of the actual waves made by "Bikini Baker" had been studied, many uncertainties remained about how such waves were formed.

Mike was a different situation. It would be set off at sea level on a flat reef a mile wide. On one side was the shallow lagoon, nowhere deeper than two hundred feet. On the other side, the outer slope of the atoll dropped away into water over twelve thousand feet deep. We were nervously aware of the similarity of Krakatoa and we had to be sure that no large tsunami would be generated. If such a wave were released in deep water, it could cause damage all around the Pacific.

Mike would dig a large crater in the reef, but would it breach the outer edge of the reef? If so, the direct effect of the blast moving rock outward or the fast flow of water from the ocean back into the hole might start a wave. Experts were certain the crater would not be that large. Could the earthshock from the bomb start a landslide on the outer side of the atoll? Other experts were sure it could not because the outer slope was not quite steep enough. Could the rise in barometric pressure caused by the air shock start a wave? Yes, and although we could not estimate with certainty exactly how large it would be, we were sure that it would not be dangerous to people living around the Pacific.

The waves actually produced by Mike confirmed the advance opinions and although the hole in the reef was a mile in diameter and six hundred feet deep it did not breach the outer edge. A tsunami—a very small one—was generated. After much persuasion by me over a period of months during the preparations, a very inventive fellow named Bill Van Dorn, also of the Scripps Institution of

Oceanography, consented to set up instruments and measure the characteristics of the prospective tsunami at the distant islands of Wake, Guam, and Midway.

Over a period of years Dr. Van Dorn became increasingly involved in the measurement of tsunamis and is now probably the world's expert in the field. Years later when he was selected to measure long-period waves during the International Geophysical Year, he asked that I accompany him to the islands of the South Pacific to help install wave recorders. My obligation remained so intense I could not refuse and so had to spend that year in Tahiti and the pearling islands.

WAVES PRODUCED BY SHIPS

Any disturbance of the water surface, including the passage of a ship, creates waves. But the waves made by ship are of a different kind and are studied for a different reason than we study the natural waves we have considered. Much of the power expended in propelling a ship goes into wave-making and anything that can be done to reduce these waves results in increased efficiency and is of direct economic importance. Consequently some of the greatest names of hydrodynamics are associated with the ship-wave problem, including Bernoulli, Lord Kelvin, Rankine, and the Froudes.

A ship moving through the water is accompanied by at least three pressure disturbances on each side, which produce not one but several trains of waves. In addition, the movement of the ship sets up an unusual traveling undulation that is not a wave in the ordinary sense because it stays with the ship and is nonrepeating. This undulation, sometimes visible to a practiced eye if a ship is moving at slow speed through glassy water, is called the Bernoulli contour system. It consists of two low mounds of water, one ahead of the bow, the other abaft the stern, and a broad amidships depression. This special form of a standing wave seems to be an inescapable result of ship motion if Bernoulli's theorem is satisfied.

Lord Kelvin investigated analytically the pattern of waves generated by a pressure disturbance concentrated at a point and moving in a straight line. A thin stick drawn vertically through quiet water or even a small boat on a large expanse of smooth water will create such waves. This Kelvin wave system is characterized by (1) diverging waves—a series of curved crests, concave outward and lying in echelon position; (2) transverse waves —convex forward and perpendicular to the direction of motion; (3) a line of crest intersections, where the diverging and transverse waves meet, forming a constant angle with the direction of motion. These are illustrated in Figure 44, in which the crest segments that are visible normally are indicated by heavy lines.

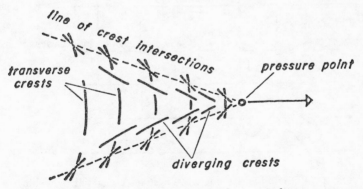

FIG. 44. Kelvin wave pattern generated by a traveling pressure point or a small boat.

For large ships, whose hull would occupy a substantial part of the pattern just described, the mathematically ideal Kelvin system is replaced by the more realistic Velox wave system. Since various points along the hull generate waves—usually at changes in curvature along the waterline—there are usually at least four Velox systems present on each side. In fact, the wave-generating intensity is related to the abruptness of change of direction. These four generating points, shown in Figure 45, are the bow, the forward shoulder, the after shoulder, and the stern. Note that bow and stern create positive pressures and the waves begin with a crest; at the shoulders negative pressures create wave systems, beginning with a trough. When the vertical displacements of the water surface are added algebraically the answer is an approximation of the resultant wave alongside the ship. Fortu-

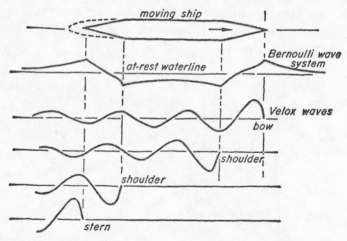

FIG. 45. Bernoulli and Velox wave systems generated by a ship and its parts. (These add in a complicated way depending on the speed of a ship.)

nately the waves made by ship models in a towing tank are accurate predictions of those that will be created by the full-size ship they represent and check the theoretical calculations so the designer knows what a ship will do in advance of actual construction.

These various sets of waves adjust their dimensions according to ship speed and consequently interfere with each other in a complicated way. As the ship's speed increases, the waves lengthen. Of course the ship remains the same length and each wave group still originates at the same point of curvature. But now the second and third crests in each system move farther aft; at some speed these will cancel (or reinforce) the waves of the following system. Thus the pattern of waves made by a ship changes as its speed changes.

A slightly submerged streamlined body such as a submarine at periscope depth also generates surface waves. It creates a Bernoulli system and transverse Velox waves above its bow, midships, and stern points. Thus even a submarine, if it is moving at a shallow depth, spends some of its power in making waves.

It is much less difficult to make waves than to avoid making them. Since a large part of a ship's power goes into unintentionally making waves, a good deal of thought has been given to methods of reducing this wasted power. This is not the same as streamlining a ship to reduce its hydrodynamic drag. However well a ship is streamlined, its passage will still give the impulse that creates the various kinds of waves just discussed. This led Admiral David Taylor to express the wish that the sea could be covered with a phantom sheet of ice through which a ship could move but by which all waves would be suppressed. Somewhat later a large ship actually ran trials in an area covered with about three inches of ice; it did indeed make trial speed with less power and slower rotation of the propeller.

Of the waves produced by a ship the bow wave is the largest, so attention first centered on how to reduce it. In the late nineteenth century the British warship *Leviathan* was built with a large projecting underwater bow for ramming in the ancient Greek tradition. The ship's "superior performance" was attributed to this bow, and in 1907 David Taylor designed a similar bow for the USS *Delaware* in which the ram bow was enlarged and placed farther beneath the surface. Thus the bulbous bow was born. Its primary advantage is, of course, that the wave crest created by the movement of the bulb through the water coincides with the trough of the bow wave and the two mostly cancel each other out.

Subsequent warships were fitted with such bows, but without great success because the design rules were inadequately known. So in the early 1930s a ship model was towed without a bulb; then the bulb was towed without the model; finally the model was towed with the bulb attached. Even though the bulb was crudely attached to the hull (not streamlined) there was a substantial reduction in resistance. This was developed by a British hydrodynamicist named W. C. S. Wigley into the basic theory for the bulbous bow. He found that at low speeds the total resistance of a ship increased because of the additional frictional and form drag of the bulb. At high speeds the reduction in wave resistance (because of the interference between bulb and hull waves) overcomes the increased drag and there is a net reduction in total resistance.

Wigley concluded that (1) the farther the bulb projects forward of the stem, the greater the reduction in resistance; (2) the bulb should be as low and wide as possible and still permit proper fairing into the hull; (3) the top of the bulb should not be too near the water surface; and (4) the useful speed range of a bulb is when the ship's velocity divided by the square root of its length is from 0.8 to 1.9.

For a modern bulk cargo ship 900 feet long moving at 30 feet per second this comes out to be 1.0, and the bulbous bow is useful. The ship's resistance is reduced 10 to 15 percent and the propulsive efficiency is increased 4 to 5 percent; thus a reduction of 20 percent of the shaft horsepower in smooth water is possible. For the Greek trireme 120 feet long rowed at 9 feet per second the corresponding number is 0.8.

Over the last fifty years it has been repeatedly suggested that enemy submarines (every unidentified submarine is an enemy) could be tracked by means of their wakes. They must make waves, or leave a trail of slightly warmer water or a trace of oil or some other evidence behind, as they cleave silently through the sea. A great deal of effort has been spent on studies and experiments to test the possibilities of so detecting them. Aside from the obvious problem that there is a huge natural background of waves, temperature variations, and surface slicks, there are many other ships at sea that are also making waves and leaving other kinds of wakes. Figure 46 shows one estimate of the distribution of the positions of merchant shipping on the North Atlantic on an average day. A few years ago the number of ships present at any given moment was said to be eight hundred. Clearly it would be very difficult, if not impossible, to pick out a submarine wake.

If, however, you have any other suggestions for finding submarines in that maze of ships the Navy will be glad to hear them.

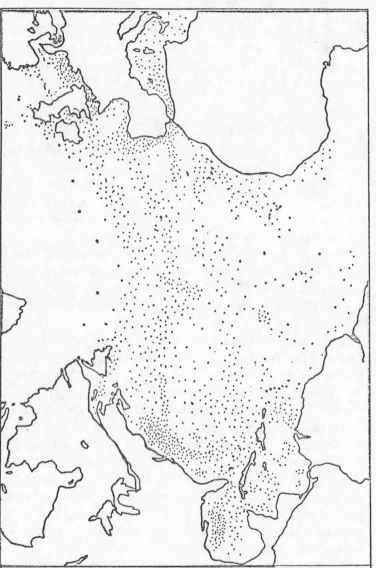

FIG. 46. Usual distribution of merchant shipping in the North Atlantic.

Ships also may generate unseen internal waves on the interface between two layers of water of different density. In regions of rapidly melting ice or near the mouths of large rivers, a layer of fresh water often rests on the heavier oceanic salt water with little or no mixing. When this layering happens the progress of slow-moving ships is retarded because most of their propulsive energy goes into generating waves on the boundary between the fresh and salt water. These subsurface waves may be much higher and move much slower than the visible surface waves generated at the same time.

This phenomenon is known as the "Hall effect" after two brothers who studied it intensively in an Edinburgh

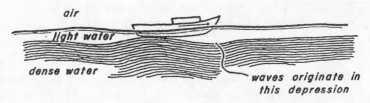

air

light water

dense water

waves originate in this depression

FIG. 47. The Hall effect. Slow-moving small craft generates waves on the interface between fresh and salt water.

wave tank in 1830. Much later V. W. Eckman, investigating strange tales of Norwegian fishermen who claimed their boats got "stuck" in the "dead water" of fjords, gave the following explanation:

The deep and still salt water of the fjord is "flooded" with fresh water. The bow of a fishing boat moving in the lighter-density upper layer causes a rise in pressure that depresses the fresh-salt interface just as though a thin flexible membrane separated the two. This sets a train of waves in motion on the surface of the salt water which move at about one eighth the speed of those on an air-water interface. These waves in effect "capture" the boat that creates them so that waves and boat move together as a unit. Then the resistance of the slow internal waves adds to that of the ship. This is the reason why, once a ship is slowed down and caught in the position shown in Figure 47, escape is difficult. Eckman suggested that fishing craft could avoid this difficulty by maintaining a speed above five knots.

RIDING THE WAVES

Surfboards, small craft, and animals (including porpoises and body-surfers) can take energy out of the waves to propel themselves by sliding down the forward surface of an advancing wave. The surfboard is thrust forward by a downhill force or slope drag, shown in Figure 48 as a vector connecting the gravity force to the buoyancy force (which always acts perpendicular to the water surface). When the slope drag is greater than the hydrodynamic drag (water resistance) the object moves at wave-crest speed. The trick of surfing, of course, is to get the board moving and the weight properly balanced so that the slope drag can take over the work of propulsion at the moment the wave passes beneath. If the surfboard is also moving sidewise across the face of the wave, it may move at a considerably higher velocity than the wave itself.

Dukws—amphibious trucks used for surveying the surf zone—not only can assume the proper slope, but also can take advantage of an additional effect to "surfboard" on large breaking waves. Their front axles hang down so as to offer a vertical surface for the orbiting water particles

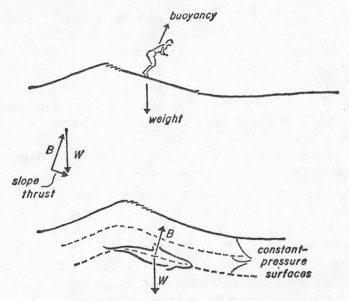

FIG. 48. Slope thrust drives the surfer and the porpoise. (After Harold Saunders)

to press against. Body-surfers who hold their hands down beneath their bodies can get the same kind of boost.

The air-water interface is a surface of constant pressure; beneath it are other parallel surfaces of constant pressure that move with imaginary waves that are subsurface reflections of the visible waves above.

Porpoises are neutrally buoyant and with a little practice learn to tilt themselves at the proper slope to take advantage of the slope drag to surfboard on some underwater constant-pressure surface. These animals can ride beneath the bow wave of a ship indefinitely without appearing to exert any effort at all. Apparently a porpoise can do this because the skin drag of his curious hide is less than the slope drag on the invisible surface.

It is possible to surfboard on the waves made by a ship. As boys on the Hudson River we used to paddle frantically to get a canoe into the proper position behind a ferryboat as it pulled away from the pier so we could get a free ride across the river, merely steering to hold position on the steep slope of the first transverse wave in its wake.

And it is also possible for boats to surfboard on their own waves. In the days when canal barges, drawn by horses on a towpath, were widely used for transportation, the horses soon discovered that if they temporarily speeded up on approaching a narrow stretch of canal, they could then relax while the boat rode the waves of its own creation. So reported Benjamin Franklin in 1768 after traveling on the canals of France. Many years later Scott Russell studied "fly boats" on the Scottish canals where the same "advantageous principle was employed to reach high speeds in the passenger trade."

The canals were very shallow (probably less than four feet) so that the waves moved at $\sqrt{gd}$ velocity or about ten feet a second (7 mph). One can imagine that when the canal suddenly narrowed and the height of the bow wave increased, a wise horse (or driver) would smile to himself at the prospect of surfboarding his load for a while.

In 1946 an interesting accident to an integrated barge flotilla on the Mississippi River reminded modern barge operators of the importance of these waves. This flotilla was made of eleven sections twelve hundred feet long pushed by the towboat *Harry Truman.* On one occasion, after many successful trips, the bow unit (one hundred feet long and fifty-four-foot beam) suddenly jackknifed and lifted twelve feet out of the water, breaking up the flotilla. It was apparent that the bow had not hit bottom and investigation subsequently showed that the bow had passed over a shoal that had caused the bow wave to peak up abruptly. So a ship (or at least a train of barges) can destroy itself with its own waves.

VII

Ship Motions and Ship Losses

BASIC MOTIONS AND STABILITY

Now CONSIDER THE MOTIONS OF A SHIP IN RESPONSE TO THE movements of the sea surface. A ship can make six basic motions, three of translation (surge, sway, and heave) and three of rotation (roll, pitch, and yaw). *Surge* means the ship moves directly ahead or astern along the line of its keel; *sway* means it moves broadside as though being pushed sideways to a pier by a couple of tugs; *heave* means it moves vertically up and down. If you push a toy boat in the bathtub directly downward and then release it, the excess buoyancy will cause it to heave upward and it will bounce up and down a few times at the water surface with its natural period of heave.

As for the rotational motions, *roll* means the deck tilts to one side and then the other; *pitch* means the deck tilts fore and aft with the bow down and then up. When a vessel *yaws* it rotates about a vertical axis, as, for example, when it is overtaken by a wave not directly astern. Then for a moment the stern will move sideways a bit faster than the bow—something like the rear of a car skidding on a wet pavement.

Once started, three of these motions (surge, sway, and yaw) tend to continue indefinitely; the other three (roll, pitch, and heave) encounter a restoring force. In the latter case, as the motion and the restoring force alternately move the ship it oscillates with a periodic motion. The up and down oscillation in heave of a toy boat has been mentioned. In that case the restoring force is explained by Archimedes' principle: a floating body displaces a weight of water equal to its own weight. In pushing the boat down, an excess of water was displaced. When that force heaves it up the inertia carries it too far, but after a few oscillations it uses up the inertia in each direction and comes to rest. The periods of roll and of pitch are usually of more interest to the ship designer; they also involve excess displacement and inertial overrun.

Again using a toy boat in the bathtub, or perhaps a dinghy alongside of a pier, push down on one side and then let it freely rebound. It will rock back and forth several times; the time in seconds to complete each cycle is the period of roll. A similar experiment on the end of the boat will give the natural period of pitch. With large ships these periods are discovered in a more complicated way but the principles are the same. Every ship has its own natural periods that derive from its shape and the way its weight is distributed. (Thus a change in cargo loading changes the characteristics.) There are good reasons for wanting to know these natural periods; the stability and steadiness of the ship depend on them.

Stability is the tendency of a ship to return to its original upright position after it has been tilted (rolled) by external forces. *Steadiness* is the tendency of a ship to minimize motion caused by the sea. These two factors conflict with each other and nearly every ship design is a compromise between the two. That is, most people want a ship that is steady (moves so little they are not likely to get seasick) but at the same time they want to be quite sure it is stable (will not roll over). The word "stability" is frequently misused by persons meaning "steady."

Compare the response of a shingle and a wooden cylinder to small waves. The shingle is very stable; it cannot be turned over, but it follows the shape of the sea surface instantly with a series of snap rolls. The cylinder in the same waves is very steady; it presents the same shape to the waves in any position and so it does not respond. For the same reason it could be easily overturned.

The measure of (initial) stability of a ship is its metacentric height, commonly known as GM (see below). A large GM (the shingle) means a very stable ship; the disadvantage of this is a fast response or quick (short-period) roll, which causes severe racking stresses in the ship, the likelihood of cargo shifting, and uncomfortable passengers. Such a ship is said to be "stiff."

On the other hand a small GM (the cylinder) produces a "tender" ship, which is comfortable because it has a poor response to waves and a long slow roll. The disadvantages are less safety if a compartment is flooded and a greater chance that large waves will break over the decks. As you have doubtless guessed by now, passenger liners have small GMs (plus high decks and lots of watertight bulkheads) and drilling ships have large GMs.

Figure 49 shows how the GM, or transverse metacentric height, of a ship is determined. Three key letters (G, B, M) need definition. G is the center of gravity of the ship—a single point at which all the downward forces of the ship can be considered to act. B, the center of buoyancy, is a single point at which all the upward forces

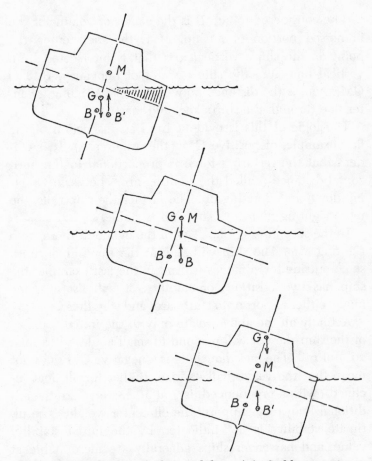

FIG. 49. Conditions of ship stability. (1) Stable: positive
metacentric height. B outside G. The buoyancy of the shaded
section will restore the ship to an even keel. (2) Neutral:
Tilting and restoring forces act along the same line. Ship will
remain at this angle until changed by some outside force. (3)
Unstable: When G is outside of B, the ship will remain in a
tilted position but will not tilt farther. (After J. La Dage and
L. Van Gemert)

can be considered to act. It is the center of volume of the immersed portion of a ship. M is the metacenter—the point on the ship's vertical axis that is intersected by a vertical line from the ship's center of buoyancy, B. The GM, then, is the distance between G and M along a center line through the ship's keel and mast.

The logic of this is evident from an inspection of the first example, of positive GM (the usual case). It is evident that the restoring force is proportional to the horizontal distance (called the righting arm) between G acting down and B acting up. The farther the ship rolls, the more righting moment. The ship is stable.

In the second example, as with the cylinder, there is no righting arm. The ship will stay at the same angle until some outside force moves it. And in the last example, the ship has two positions of stability; it will list at some angle, either to port or to starboard, and stay there.

Actually all the above relate only to the initial stability of the ship—how it will respond to small angles (less than 20°) of roll. The fact that there is a negative GM does not mean that the vessel will capsize. Rather it will float inclined (with a pronounced list) at an angle where the additional buoyancy supports the off-center weight. The ultimate stability is not indicated by the initial stability value, and passenger ships generally are more stable at very large angles than freighters. A number of ships have, as a result of cargo shifting or collision damage, listed as much as 55° or even 90° and stayed there for quite a while without capsizing.

Passenger liners with small GMs generally have a roll period of around twenty-eight seconds; freighters (not superships) often have a roll period of about fourteen seconds. As a rule of thumb passenger ships have a GM that is 2 percent of their beam. (If they will go through the 106-foot-wide Panama Canal the metacentric height is about 2 feet.) GMs of freighters are likely to be 5–8 percent of their beams. The supertankers and bulk cargo ships are long enough to bridge several wave crests and massive enough to have a slow response. Their periods are proportional to the sixth root of their displacement tonnage.

Among the reasons for concern about the natural period of the ship and wanting it to be longer than the period of most waves is that this reduces the chance that the ship's period will be the same as that of the waves. A ship with a roll period of, say, twelve seconds would roll violently if it ran parallel to the crests of a group of twelve-second waves because each roll would be reinforced by the next wave. Ships are more likely to run at an angle to the waves, which are not very regular anyway; this makes the effective wave period longer. The ship's speed can make the effective period longer or shorter, depending on whether the waves are coming toward the ship or moving with it. Captains do not like to encounter waves head on and they generally reduce speed if encountering large head seas. The reason, of course, is that the force of impact increases as the square of the velocity of the collision between ship and wave. The result is often that the bow "slams" and great vibrations or shudders run through the ship. In Kipling's words: "The ship goes wop with a wiggle between."

Depending somewhat on the size of the ship and its purpose, the designer may treat it as a rigid beam. That is, he will give it enough strength so that it would not break if it were supported at only the midpoint or only at each end. In both cases the ship would bend because steel is very elastic. With a single wave crest under the mid-

point, the ends droop a bit; this is called "hog." If the
bow and stern are supported by crests the center section
"sags."

One ship has been built that sacrificed all other consid-
erations to decouple it from sea motions. This is FLIP
(Floating Laboratory Instrument Platform) of the
Scripps Institution of Oceanography, largely the brain-
child of physicist Noel Spiess and naval architect Larry
Glostens. FLIP has two positions of stability: it can lie on
the water surface much like a ship (it is not self-
propelled) or it can flip to a vertical position to avoid
wave motion. This oddly shaped platform is 350 feet long
with 12 feet beam (or 12 feet long and about 294 feet
draft when upright).

The objective of FLIP was to get a quiet and virtually
motionless seagoing laboratory with a long heave period
(twenty-eight seconds) so that careful measurements of
underwater sound could be made at the bottom end.
Those who have lived aboard say FLIP is as steady as a
house.

During a violent North Pacific storm of December 1–5,
1969, when FLIP was five hundred miles north of the Hawaiian Islands, its capability for ignoring waves was
tested. The winds were forty to fifty knots; the fetch was
very long, perhaps one thousand miles; and a great swell
arose. FLIP held steady, but its crew temporarily took to
life rafts when green water entered ventilators twenty-
eight feet above the waterline and knocked out the generators. They observed this super wave staff (wave measuring board) in midocean and saw some of the waves reach
forty-four feet above the waterline and equally far below
it. These skilled and intensely interested observers reported later that the hourly extreme wave height was
eighty feet and that the average height of the upper one

PLATE 20. An alert photographer aboard the *Brigham Victory* took these photos of the April 1, 1946, seismic sea wave destroying warehouses on the pier at Hilo, Hawaii. The unlucky longshoremen (arrow) died a moment later. *Wide World Photo*

PLATE 21. The tsunami of May 23, 1960, cleared off several blocks along the Hilo waterfront, depositing the wooden houses like driftwood at the high-tide mark. *Ichii, Honolulu Advertizer*

PLATE 22. Lighthouse at Scotch Cap, Alaska, before the great wave. The light is 92 feet above mean low water. The foundation of the radio mast is 103 feet; the upper mesa is 115 feet.

PLATE 23. The tsunami of April 1, 1946, swept away the lighthouse and other buildings; the radio mast is gone and debris has
been deposited on the mesa.

PLATE 24. The amphibious trucks (Dukws) used by John Isaacs and the author to survey the beaches of the U.S. Pacific Coast (1945–50) on the beach at Cape Grenville, Washington. *University of California*

PLATE 25. Dukw surfboarding on a twelve-foot plunging breaker during a beach survey. High point is author's head. *University of California*

PLATE 26.   One is not often privileged to see inside a beach. Here a bulldozer has cut a trench some three meters deep across a beach at low tide. This was in the search for diamonds in South Africa; diamond-bearing gravels are exposed at knee level. *Willard Bascom*

PLATE 27.   On the beach north of the Quillayute River, Washington, the driftwood is impressive. The Dukw, nine feet high, seems diminutive beside the root of this Douglas fir. The rest of the tree, beyond, was nearly two hundred feet long. *Willard Bascom*

PLATE 28. This array of cusps on the beach at El Segundo, California, has a wave length of about twenty-five feet. *U. S. Navy Photo*

PLATE 29.   Swash marks. *Willard Bascom*

third of the waves was forty-nine feet. FLIP's actual heave during that great storm is believed to have been about six inches.

It is evident that a ship is less likely to survive a storm at sea if it is overloaded. Insurance companies and ship classification societies naturally want to be sure that the ships for which they are responsible are not overloaded for the wave conditions likely to be encountered. There is an easy way for an inspector to determine proper loading, devised by Samuel Plimsoll when he was a member of the

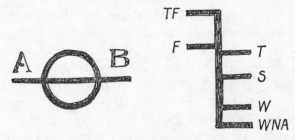

FIG. 50. Plimsoll mark (left) certified by the American Bureau of Shipping. Load lines for various conditions at the right: WNA is for winter North Atlantic, W is for winter, S is for summer, T is for tropical, F is for fresh water, and TF is for tropical fresh water.

British Parliament (1868–80). It is a paint line identified by a circle on the side of every ship that shows the waterline for allowable loading in summer seas. This line and circle is known as the Plimsoll mark. Usually it is identified by the initials of the classification society (A and B, for example, denoting the American Bureau of Shipping) that has approved that position of the line.

Alongside the Plimsoll mark there are other qualifying marks, all related to wave conditions at sea. (See Figure 50.) As one would expect, the ship is required to have the

most freeboard, or distance between the waterline and
the top of the hull, during winter conditions in the North
Atlantic (WNA) and the least in tropical fresh water
(TF).

WHY SHIPS SINK

It is apparent from Chapter III that many ships, including large modern ones, have been sunk or nearly sunk
by great storms and huge solitary waves. This raises questions in one's mind about how many ships have been sunk
and what other reasons there are for ships to sink. In
Deep Water, Ancient Ships I reviewed the why and
where of ancient ship sinkings in considerable detail from
the point of view of the marine archaeologist. It is a fascinating subject, and a recapitulation of the points that
relate to wind and wave losses is not out of place here.

The principal statistics on ship sinkings can be stated
quickly: (1) Of all the ships that have ever existed, about
95 percent were wooden sailing ships. The modern steel-
hulled ship driven by engines and propellers has been
around only about one hundred years of the six thousand
years of known seagoing activity. (2) Of those wooden
sailing ships (if we use statistics from the British sailing
navy of the 1700s and 1800s) about 40 percent ended
their careers by running aground on reefs, rocks, and
beaches. This is a fantastic number of ships, perhaps as
many as three hundred thousand per century for the
world's oceans. Another 10–20 percent (say one hundred
thousand per century) sank offshore, usually with all
hands.

Ships are relatively safe when they are in deep water,
well offshore. They are most likely to be lost, as the above

statistics indicate, by running ashore (usually at night) or being driven ashore by high winds. Consequently, when large ships are in small harbors and a great storm is forecast they will often put out to sea, preferring to take their chances in open water to the possibility of dragging anchor and going aground.

The reasons for peacetime ship sinkings in open water have changed somewhat with the changes in the kinds of ship. Collisions with icebergs and other ships are still frequent, and explosions account for many of the large ship losses these days.

In the last decade a number of superships, including some of the largest ships ever built, have disappeared at sea. For example, on December 30, 1975, the three-year-old combination carrier *Berge Istra,* 224,000 tons, en route from Brazil to Japan, suffered a series of explosions east of the Philippines and sank in very deep water. Its fate might never have been known except that two crew members, picked up in a life raft nineteen days later, described how this huge ship (314 meters overall, 50 meters beam) sank in a few minutes. The inquiry tentatively ascribed the cause to "undetected gas pockets detonated by sparks from missiles or machinery."

But we are more concerned here with ships sunk by the violence of the sea. If they were wooden sailing ships the following additional factors contributed to their loss.

Some ships have been lost because they were poorly designed or not built exactly as designed. In an effort to make ships go faster, they are made slimmer—which may also mean that they roll over easily. The position and height of the mast, the size of the sail, the weight and location of the ballast—all are important in how well a ship survives at sea.

Virtually all merchant sailing ships were ballasted with

material heavy enough to drag down a water-filled hull that might otherwise have stayed afloat. Since the ballast was usually made up of many small rocks not cemented in place, it was possible for ballast to shift position if the ship rolled hard, readjusting itself downward toward the lee side. This, of course, prevented the ship from returning to an even keel and no doubt contributed to numerous sinkings. The famous Swedish warship *Wasa*, salvaged from the bottom of Stockholm Harbor in 1961, apparently rolled over because it was underballasted (presumably, the naval architect's plan was not followed carefully).

Wooden ships are generally built of bent planks nailed to rib timbers or, in ancient times, mortised edgewise to each other carvel-style. A nail could corrode through or a tenon rot so the planks would come free of each other and pull away from the rib. Instantly, there can be huge leaks, far beyond the capacity of hand pumps to stem. Since sailing ships were rarely compartmented with transverse bulkheads, as modern ships are, the hull could rapidly fill with water and sink.

A more serious variation of this mishap could arise if the whole ship structure were so weak that the ship flexed as waves passed beneath it. With a wave crest at the center and the bow and stern relatively unsupported (or vice versa) there is always minor bending of the ship's structure. But if the ship flexes too much it can come apart; the deck crumples or pulls in two, the ribs spread, the seams open, the mast falls, and its stays rip out the shear strakes. The ship can quickly become a mass of kindling wood.

Wooden ships caught fire with remarkable ease. At night or belowdecks, oil lamps were used for light; it is easy to imagine that these could be spilled in such a way that blazing oil could run down the ribs and planking into the bilge or other areas where it would be hard to extinguish. Cooking fires could be an even more efficient cause of disaster. Glowing coals, usually restrained by cooking tiles and grating, would be thrown onto the deck by a lurch caused by a sudden large wave or by the ship coming about on the other tack. The dumping of red-hot coals must have happened fairly often on every ship that cooked. If this was not noticed because the men were busy elsewhere or if a blaze got out of control, the ship might have to be abandoned. Or so much water might be applied to put out the fire, it could sink the ship.

A ship can be overwhelmed by the conditions at sea. Winds at whole-gale force, with velocities of fifty knots or more, can, by brute force, blow a ship over. Even if all the sails have been taken in (or blown out) and the ship is running before the wind on bare poles, the rudder can fail or the helmsman make a mistake and the ship can broach (turn sidewise to wind and wave) and capsize. Or a ship may be low in the water because of leaks or overloading. With low freeboard, the lee rail easily goes under; then perhaps the cargo will shift or the deck will leak and the list will increase until the ship cannot right itself again. Or a ship blown hard before the wind, perhaps built with a sleek bow for speed, will drive into the back of a huge wave and be taken by the sea in one gulp. On other occasions, not necessarily in very high winds, a ship running on one tack will suddenly pass through a weather front into winds coming from exactly the opposite direction. Then the square sails will flatten back against the masts and the ship will be blown over backward in a matter of seconds. Open hatches or scuttles, now on the low side, let the sea pour in and the ship is gone.

For example, HMS *Eurydice,* a British sailing warship

of the last century, moving up the English Channel under all plain sail at the end of a four-month cruise to the West Indies, stood close inshore to signal her safe arrival. Watchers on the cliffs at Spithead, admiring the *Eurydice* and the *Emma*, which followed it, noted that the glass was falling rapidly and that there was an "ominous stillness" as the west wind decreased. At ten minutes to four, the wind suddenly veered to the east. Both ships disappeared into a snow squall with violent east winds. By four o'clock the cloud bank lifted again but now, to the amazement of the distant observers, the *Eurydice* had disappeared and the *Emma* continued on as before. In those few minutes, a ship had vanished into the sea. The *Emma* picked up 5 men of the 368 aboard the *Eurydice*, who reported that one sudden, violent blast of wind had blown the ship over so that it filled with water through open ventilators and sank.

In July 1932 the German sail training ship *Niobe* had an experience similar to that of *Eurydice* while operating not far from its home port of Kiel. A sudden line squall capsized it, and although this time there were no open ports, it sank in four minutes—before boats could be launched.

During the Napoleonic Wars, which lasted twenty-two years, the Royal Navy lost over three hundred ships by mishap but fewer than a dozen by enemy action. This is at a time when the total of vessels in the Navy was about two hundred and fifty; the figures suggest that the fleet was completely rebuilt every twenty years if the entire shipbuilding program only replaced ships lost to the sea.

Relying on Lloyd's statistics once more—this time for merchant ships in the last days of sail, when ships were probably better designed, built, and sailed than ever before—we have the following shocker: in the five years from 1864 to 1869, ten thousand sailing ships insured in England were lost in various parts of the world, nearly a thousand without a trace!

Of the 130 vessels that left European ports for the Pacific in the summer of 1905, 53 had vanished in Cape Horn waters by the end of July.

The Danish ship *København* was a splendid five-master of 3,900 tons bound for Melbourne. It last reported its position by radio, on December 22, 1928, as several hundred miles east of Tristan da Cunha, after which all radio signals ceased. To this day, no one knows what happened, although there were guesses that the ballast had shifted, that it struck an iceberg, or that a sudden squall caught it with all sails set.

The most recent loss of an auxiliary training ship was the four-masted barque *Pamir*, en route from Argentina to Germany in September 1957. The ship encountered hurricane Carrie somewhere south of the Azores, and through heavy radio interference came a series of ever more ominous messages: "Foremast broken by heavy seas," "All sails lost," "Listing 45 degrees, in danger of sinking." Eventually, five survivors were picked up in a swamped and split lifeboat. The explanation given for the loss was that "a sudden veering of the wind in the center of the hurricane caused the sails to beat back and cause serious damage to the rigging and further damage to the hull by falling pieces of rigging."

Small ships are still lost at a remarkably high rate. For example, a news dispatch from Tokyo datelined April 2, 1972, reported thirty-three small ships sunk or capsized in the waters around Japan in three days of squalls and high winds. Small shipping companies and fisheries were accused of kamikaze (suicide) practices because they sent the ships to sea in the face of adverse weather forecasts.

In December 1944, during World War II, when U.S.
naval might in the Pacific was at a maximum, the fleet in
the vicinity of the Philippine Islands was caught in a typhoon. Three destroyers reported by radio that they were
experiencing violent rolls of as much as 70°. At that angle
water must have poured down the stacks; none of the
three ships was heard of again.

An astonishing number of modern steel ships will disappear at sea this year. Even in these days of careful inspection by insurance companies, no pirates, radioed
weather broadcasts, and voyages measured in a few days
instead of weeks, some will be declared to be "missing
without a trace." No one can ever be sure why those ships
were lost.

In a piece by John Fairhall in the British *Guardian* of
June 22, 1971, he reported that 70 ships were "missing" in
the previous ten years out of 2,766 ships lost. The total
was made up of various categories: foundered, burned,
collided, wrecked, lost for other reasons, and missing.
Wrecked was the largest category (1,136 ships). Next was
foundered: 771 ships were overwhelmed by the sea alone,
without the aid of rocks, reefs, or other ships.

Lloyd's of London posts a ship as "missing" if it disap-
pears without known cause, leaving no survivors and no
substantial wreckage. "Posted as missing" is the formal
death certificate of the crew and the clearance for the insurance claim to be paid. Consider a few "missings" from
the files of Jim Dawson, a well-known Lloyd's broker.

In March 1973 the 13,000-ton Norwegian bulk carrier
Anita sailed from Hampton Roads, Virginia, for a German
port and encountered a severe gale. Nothing was ever
heard of the *Anita* again, so it was listed "missing." The
Norse Variant, on a similar voyage at the same time with
a cargo of coal, broke in two during the same gale and

sank very quickly about 130 miles southeast of Cape May, New Jersey. This ship would also have been listed as missing, and the possibility of a collision considered, except that a lone survivor was picked up a few days later who was able to tell what happened.

Later in the same year a 13,900-ton bulk carrier, the *Theodore AS*, sailed from Norway for Spain with a cargo of iron ore. In crossing the North Sea the ship encountered fierce gales and disappeared, thus taking away from the *Anita* the dubious distinction of being the largest ship to be declared missing—until the *Grand Zenith* of 18,700 tons vanished off Cape Sable, Nova Scotia, in December 1978.

Hashlosha, of Haifa, an Israeli motor vessel with 1,800 tons of clay in bulk from Kimlos Island for Marseilles sent a *m'aidez* (May Day) on January 24, 1967, as its last contact with the shore. It was believed to be eighty miles west of Naples in an area lashed by gales. Two overturned lifeboats were picked up off Sardinia on the twenty-seventh.

Oostmeep, a Dutch ship with a cargo of steel billets from Brussels for Monfalcone, on the Adriatic Sea, reported passing Gibraltar on October 29, 1968; it was last seen off Cape Bougaroni on the thirty-first. This 1,134-gross-ton ship had been recently surveyed, and the only suggestion as to why it was lost was that there were gale-force winds and generally heavy seas in the lower Adriatic. Nothing more. A new steel ship, well manned, simply disappeared.

The above stories produce a mental picture of ships unexpectedly getting into trouble, mostly from storms, and suddenly disappearing. Most of these seem likely to have "foundered"—that is, they were overwhelmed by the sea, took on water, and sank. If the statistics for all oceans

hold good outside the period studied—when 771 ships
foundered for 70 missing—the ratio of foundering (with
some survivors) to missings (with no survivors) is about
11:1.

In a ten-year period in the Mediterranean, five large
ships were cited as missing (although undoubtedly there
were more), which would mean that fifty-five more foundered, or a total of sixty ships went down in deep water in
the ten-year period. This is equivalent to six hundred in a
century or six thousand in a thousand-year period. The
small craft—fishing boats, yachts, ferries, etc., which are
much harder to get statistics on—must have been lost in
far greater numbers.

Anyone who still has any doubts about the kinds of
troubles ships can get into at sea need only read the following paragraph on the subject. This is the "Perils" paragraph of the American Institute Hull Clauses, dated January 18, 1970, commonly used in insuring modern ships at
sea.

PERILS
Touching the Adventures and Perils which the Un-
derwriters are contented to bear and take upon them-
selves, they are of the Seas, Men-of-War, Fire, Lightning,
Earthquake, Enemies, Pirates, Rovers, Assailing Thieves,
Jettisons, Letters of Mart and Counter Mart, Surprisals,
Takings at Sea, Arrests, Restraints and Detainments of all
Kings, Princes and Peoples, of what nation, condition or
quality soever, Barratry of the Master and Mariners and
of all other like Perils, Losses and Misfortunes that have
or shall come to the Hurt, Detriment or Damage of the
Vessel, or any part thereof, excepting, however, such of
the foregoing perils as may be excluded by provisions
elsewhere in the Policy or by endorsement thereon.

Do very large modern ships have problems with the winds and waves that sink these relatively small ones? The following is a quote from a letter I received in 1976 from Vice Admiral Bob Cooper, Commander of the U. S. Pacific Fleet. "While literally surfboarding in an aircraft carrier down the fronts of truly mountainous seas in a mistral [winter storm] I wondered how many land lubbers would believe that the peaceful Mediterranean could ever look like that!"

The most recent data available come from Lloyd's Register of Shipping, reporting on ship accidents in 1977. In that year the merchant marine lost 330 ships (1,073,127 gross tons) as follows: 129 founderings, 112 wrecks, 57 fires, 32 collisions. "Founderings" means "overwhelmed by the sea."

VIII

Measuring Waves and Making Waves

SCIENTIFIC PROGRESS IS LARGELY DEPENDENT ON THE ABILITY to make better measurements. Therefore much wave research of recent years has been directed toward the development of new kinds of instruments and techniques for measuring waves. The understanding of how and why measurements are made as they are gives one a much better insight into the nature of wave motion.

Until the early 1940s direct observation, the photograph, and the tide gauge were the principal means available for studying waves. The observer would watch the sea surface and make notes. He would record the number of seconds between wave crests passing a piling (or the bow of his ship) and estimate the height of each one. This was not very satisfactory at night or when the ship was moving; besides, with this method, the sea has to be watched constantly or unusual events will be missed. Moreover, the dynamic quality is lost in a series of uncertain tabulations: wave crests cross each other; secondary crests ride on the flanks of large waves; the crests a little way off are aligned with the trough being observed. Except near the shore, where the effect of the bottom tends to "organize" the waves, a thoroughly confusing situation exists, too complicated to be retained or analyzed by the human mind. Only a general impression could be obtained. Clearly, measuring and recording instruments were needed.

WAVE OBSERVATIONS

The first step was to stop the motion and "freeze" the shape of the sea surface by photographing it. Then the instantaneous situation could be studied at leisure. From single still-photos the photographic technique evolved to stereo-pairs taken from a ship's mast so that wave height could be obtained and the sea surface contoured. Then came motion pictures of waves under many conditions—at sea in storms, breaking waves on the beach, slow-motion movies of waves in tanks, and fast-motion (time-lapse) movies of waves in harbors. Sometimes, in order to give scale to the photograph, markers were introduced; these included floating disks and spar buoys graduated in feet. A spar buoy is a slender buoyant pipe that floats vertically; often it is attached by a rubber cord to a horizontal damping disk that hangs far beneath. This reduces its vertical motion to a minimum as the waves pass.

Aerial photography for wave research explored a whole series of possibilities. By analysis of precisely timed wave photographs, techniques were developed for measuring the depth of water in the approaches to an enemy-held beach. The Waves Project field party made radio-controlled photo sequences in which pictures of the surf zone were taken simultaneously from an aircraft at twelve thousand feet, the top of a cliff and the beach. From analysis of these pictures it was possible to determine what waves were arriving and how they were affected by the underwater contours. Walter Munk used the "Cox lens" (lens removed from camera) to record the sun's glitter pattern on the sea surface and determine the average slope of the waves and the power spectrum of the sea under various wind conditions.

In addition to the photographic methods of measuring and recording ocean waves, sound beams and radio beams also have been tried. Aircraft in level flight at low altitude above the water can use a recording radio altimeter to get wave height. Submarines can point an echo sounder upward and record changes in the distance to the water surface above as waves pass. Or, in shallow water, a recording echo-sounder in a small boat that is hove-to will give an approximate picture of the waves that raise and lower the boat relative to the bottom. Most of these were tools rather than instruments; they made wave observations more convenient and reduced the demands on estimation and memory. But a true instrument does something more. It amplifies sensory perception and makes it possible to learn things that could never be discovered by the ordinary human senses. Most of the present instrumentation had its beginnings in the later days of World War II, when research was driven by the expected need to forecast or otherwise determine wave conditions on enemy-held beaches where amphibious landings might have to be made.

The development of an instrument begins with an analysis of the properties of the subject. What qualities of waves can be sensed and measured?

Table VI summarizes wave properties and lists instruments that have been used most generally. Although there are quite a few, the list is by no means complete and perhaps the reader will be able to think of still other means of measuring waves. More than likely he will reinvent some previously tried instrument, for by now virtually every possibility seems to have been explored. Somehow the existence of many varieties of instruments, instead of satisfying the demand, seemingly has challenged wave investigators to devise new forms that employ different principles.

Mrs. Kaye Steele accepted the challenge and invented a device that would make use of parrots for transducers, and would sense the wetting property of waves. The parrots are spaced at one-foot vertical intervals on a pole in the surf, so that, as the wave passes, the wetting effect of the wave is transformed by the parrot into sound energy in the form of a loud squawk. The scientist (on shore) has only to count the squawks to learn the height of the wave. Mrs. Steele's ingenuity seems to have laid the conceptual groundwork for the step resistance gauge of the U. S. Corps of Engineers, which came later.

The simplest way to measure waves is to observe them passing a wave staff—a vertical board on which a scale in feet or meters has been painted.

This is not the place for any detailed description of wave-measuring devices, but it seems worthwhile to describe a few of the major forms of instruments that have contributed substantially to modern wave theory.

TIDE GAUGES

The oldest instrument is the tide gauge, invented by Lord Kelvin in 1882 and brought to a high degree of reliability by the U. S. Coast and Geodetic Survey. It is usually set up on a pier in the quiet waters of a harbor or protected bay—not in the open ocean. A pipe, perhaps a foot in diameter, open at both top and bottom extends from near the harbor floor to well above the highest tide

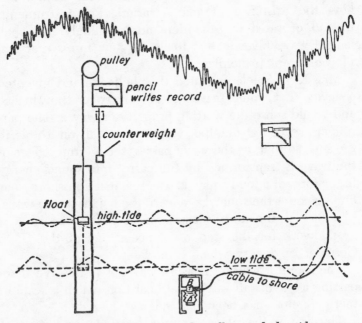

FIG. 51. Record of both tide and swell is made by tide gauge (pipe open at bottom) or by absolute pressure transducer, which measures the pressure of A relative to B.

level. Inside the pipe (sometimes called a stilling well) is a float; from the top of the float a wire extends up around a drive shaft and down to a counterweight. A clockwork mechanism keeps chart paper moving slowly beneath the drive shaft and attached to the latter on a lead screw is a pencil. As the tide—and the float—rises and falls, the pencil position moves back and forth, tracing out the height of the water on the paper.

When Lord Kelvin, who is best known for his abstract formulation of the second law of thermodynamics, presented his scientific findings with this instrument to the Institute of Civil Engineers, he was roundly criticized for having used a pencil instead of a fountain pen (which had just been invented). In answering the derogatory comments Kelvin said, in part, ". . . the ink marker has been tried for tide gauges and has hitherto been found unsuccessful on account of the slowness of the motion, but there is ample power in the tide gauge to drive a pencil." He further remarked, ". . . good workmanship is too often required to overcome the evils of a poor design."

Tide gauges are usually set up in the quiet waters of a harbor, where they are not exposed to any swell and their pipes extend deep enough so that the small waves generated inside the harbor do not affect the float. If the same device were attached to a pier extending out into the ocean, the float would rise and fall with each passing swell. This is because the open lower end of the pipe would permit the water to flow in and out rapidly and the water surface inside would be at the same level as that outside.

However, a small change in the instrument converts it into a long-period wave recorder. If the bottom end of the pipe were completely sealed off, the water level inside would not change. But if this seal has a small hole in it, the pressure created by the passage of a wave crest will cause water to flow through the hole and raise the level inside the pipe slightly. Short-period waves and even ocean swell go by too quickly to permit enough water to flow through the hole to appreciably change the water level in the pipe. But long waves with periods of several minutes maintain the pressure long enough for the water level inside to respond. Therefore, even though these long

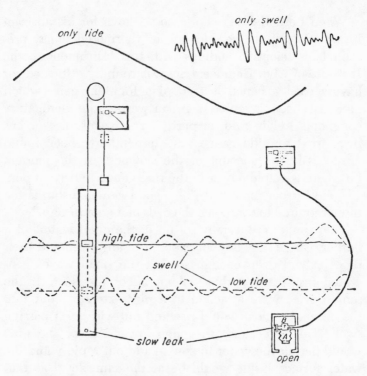

FIG. 52. Tide-gauge pipe, sealed at bottom except for small hole which lets water leak slowly in and out, draws smooth record of the tide. Differential pressure transducer measures pressure at A relative to that at B. The small tube allows water to leak slowly in and out of chamber B so that only swell is recorded.

waves are only a few inches high in the midst of a turbulent zone of waves five feet or more in height, this instrument measures only the low long-period waves and ignores the much higher swell.

The hole restricts the flow to a slow leak and its size can be computed to "tune" the instrument to the desired period. Such was the principle of Walter Munk's long-period (tsunami) recorder on Scripps pier which first recorded surf beat.

WAVE RECORDERS

In the late 1940s the author headed a field party of the Waves Project of the University of California that installed twenty or thirty wave recorders off the California, Oregon, and Washington coasts, usually just outside the surf zone. These operated on various principles as we experimented with one scheme and then another to find the best way of measuring the deep-sea swell. Some operated for several years; others were knocked out in a few hours —the Pacific Ocean is a tough proving ground. But we did get results, and the effort produced miles of chart paper covered with good records of waves, enough to form a sound basis for the first statistical summary of Pacific swell.

These measuring-recording systems were generally similar. A differential pressure pickup on a steel tripod rested on the sea floor in thirty to sixty feet of water; an armored submarine cable encasing three or four electrical conductors led ashore to a recorder in a shack on the beach. As the waves passed over, the sensor detected the changes in pressure at the bottom caused by the differences in the height of water above the instrument. The signals were electrically transmitted ashore, and on a moving chart a pen traced a red line representing the crests and troughs of the passing waves.

In most cases the transducer, a device that changes pressure into an electrical signal, was actuated by the motion of a bellows. (A bellows is a small metal cylinder

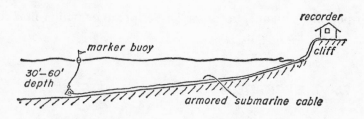

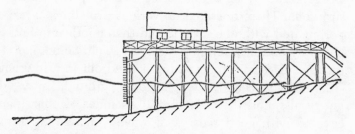

FIG. 53. Shore-based wave recorders. *Top:* Pressure-sensing pickup mounted in tripod on ocean floor. *Bottom:* Step-resistance wave meter mounted on pier.

with corrugated sides that can expand and contract as the pressure changes.)

In the tsunami recorder described earlier the problem was to get rid of the effect of swell and record only long-period waves. But in these recorders we wanted to look only at the swell and eliminate the effect of the long-period waves and tides.

An absolute or total pressure recorder would measure all waves (including swell and tides), superimposed one on another, plus the weight of the water above the instrument and the atmospheric pressure. Obviously the chart required to record eight-foot waves atop an eight-foot tide is twice as wide as that required for the wave alone. Moreover, it is more convenient to analyze a wave record that is made relative to the straight line of instantaneous sea level than relative to the changing curve of the tide. So the differential pressure sensor is designed to remove the effect of the tide.

The differential pressure instrument measures the rapidly changing pressure of the passing wave relative to the slowly changing pressure of the average sea level. In the long-period wave recorder the water level inside the pipe remained almost at average sea level, moving only slightly up and down in response to waves with a three-minute period. This relative stability was attained by allowing the water outside the pipe to leak in and out slowly through a small hole. The swell recorder makes use of the same technique to obtain a reference pressure. In it the instantaneously changing pressure in A caused by the waves with period of up to twenty seconds flexes the bellows in and out. Chamber B is sealed except for a very small hole so that it maintains a reference pressure equivalent to that of average sea-level at the moment. Then the transducer T measures the instantaneous wave pressure in the bellows A relative to average sea level pressure.

Most subsurface wave-measuring instruments work in a similar manner; the differences usually are in the kinds of pressure transducer used.

The bottom-mounted wave-pressure recorder has both advantages and disadvantages. Since it is installed usually in water thirty or more feet deep, the higher frequency waves are filtered out by the depth and do not confuse the record. That is, chop and small wind waves do not affect the pressure pickup on the bottom (because it is deeper than half their wave length). This is a disadvantage only to those who are interested in the small waves.

The bottom recorder requires no special installation offshore and can be placed almost anywhere on the bottom. On the other hand, it is harder to service and may be covered with sand in some seasons and thus rendered inoperable.

A pressure record is not a precise reflection of the sea surface. It ignores the small waves, and the indicated

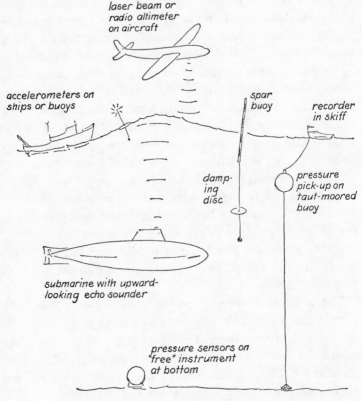

laser beam or
radio altimeter
on aircraft

accelerometers on
ships or buoys

spar
buoy

recorder
in skiff

damp-
ing
disc

pressure
pick-up on
taut-moored
buoy

submarine with upward-
looking echo sounder

pressure sensors on
"free" instrument
at bottom

FIG. 54. Deep-water wave-measuring methods.

heights of large waves must be modified according to the calibration curve of the instrument.

In order to overcome these objections the Beach Erosion Board of the Corps of Engineers developed a step-resistance wave gauge. The gauge consists of a pipe twenty-five feet long mounted vertically on one piling of a pier so that its midpoint is about at mean sea level. At intervals of 0.2 of a foot along its length, pairs of contact points (modified spark plugs) project from the pipe. As the crest of a wave approaches, the salt water closes the circuit across the spark plug gaps; as it passes, the contacts are broken. Resistors in the circuit are so selected that when power is applied the variation in current flow is proportional to submerged length of pipe.

A record of the electric current flowing then becomes a direct record of the history of the height of the sea surface alongside the pier. Chop, wind waves, swell, and tides, each atop the others, are all recorded simultaneously in magnificent confusion.

There is also interest in measuring the waves in the ocean far from the shore where the depth of water is so great that a bottom recorder would see only the very long waves. It is possible to make use of this filtering effect of depth selectively to record tides and tsunamis. Another possibility once tried by the author is to mount a shallow-water type pressure recorder on top of a submerged buoy that is held about a hundred feet below the surface by a taut wire anchored to the bottom.

A more commonly used method of measuring waves in deep water is to mount accelerometers in a floating buoy and directly record the acceleration of the buoy caused by the passing waves. One version of this developed by

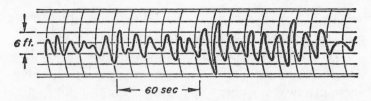

bottom-pressure record (water 40 feet deep)

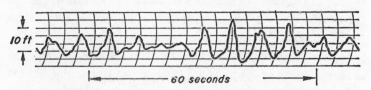

step-resistance record (surface height alongside pier)

FIG. 55. Recordings of waves in which wave height is plotted against time. Note that the record of bottom-pressure changes caused by swell is nearly sinusoidal whereas that of the wave surface (in a storm) shows long troughs and pointed crests.

the Navy is the Splashnik, which is intended to be expendable but has the disadvantage that the users often spend a good deal of time trying to retrieve it. Another accelerometer system has been developed by M. J. Tucker, of the British National Institute of Oceanography, into what is perhaps the most sophisticated instrument of all: the shipboard wave recorder.

The ship takes the place of the buoy, but because a ship is large compared to the waves, a combination of accelerometers and pressure pickups at the bow and stern is required. The instruments are mounted in the hull about ten feet below the normal water level. The pressure sensor measures the height of passing waves above this point, and the accelerometer measures the height of the pressure pickup relative to average sea level. The signals are fed into a central computer which sorts out the data and records the major waves.

There are some new techniques for studying and measuring waves from aircraft. One is the laser altimeter, which uses a laser (coherent light) beam pointed vertically downward and a reflection receptor to get precise wave heights. It has been used with some success to obtain data on wave growth within a fetch area.

Another is Side Looking Airborne Radar (SLAR), in which a long antenna is used to illuminate a narrow band of water extending outward and to one side of a low-flying aircraft. A series of pulsed radio emissions is back-scattered by the smallest waves (principally the capillary waves), whose wave length is about half that of the radio waves. The returning echoes from each pulse are received and translated electronically into light and dark lines, a series of which is accumulated to make an image of the sea surface. Duncan Ross of NOAA's Sea Air Interaction Laboratory has written extensively about the many complexities that are involved in making accurate SLAR measurements. This technique can, however, be used to obtain wave length (with a resolution of 10–50 meters) and wave direction to about two degrees.

WAVE FORCE MEASUREMENT

Another class of instrument makes it possible to measure the force exerted by waves on pilings, piers, and shoreline structures. Some instruments have been used to observe storm wave forces and obtain data that can be applied in the design of offshore structures, including large oil drilling and production platforms. Others are intended to determine the shock caused by the impact of a breaking wave on a breakwater or other very-shallow-water structures.

The measurement of wave forces on pilings is complicated by the continual reversal of direction of the water as the crest moves in one direction and the trough moves in the other. The water velocities in the various parts of the wave vary with time and with depth. Moreover, since the force is caused by the rush of water past the pile (the drag), the answer is sensitive to the square of the velocity as well as to the shape and size of the piling. There are so many unknown factors that it is best to determine the answers directly by experiment, first in the model tank, then at sea. In the early tests, specially instrumented pile sections were exposed to ocean waves under various sets of conditions.

As shown in Table VII, the forces imposed on pilings by swell are relatively modest, but as the wave begins to break and the water particle velocity increases, waves of about the same period and height cause substantially greater forces. One moral of this story is: when possible, build your structure in water too deep to cause waves to break.

No wave-direction recorder has ever worked very well, the reason apparently being that waves from so many directions are always present and the direction sensor is as confused as any human observer would be. There certainly ought to be a handsome reward offered to the inventor of a good one. So far, the most practicable direction sensor was devised by John Isaacs in 1949 and placed by the author a half mile off Point Arguello, the most exposed point on the Southern California coast. His direction sensor was a Rayleigh disk about a foot in diameter, which has the property that it always orients itself perpendicular to the water motion (in contrast to a wind vane, which stays parallel to the motion). This technique was used because the wave orbital currents change direction by 180° as a wave passes and a disk does not have to flip from side to side as a vane would. It was mounted on a tripod on the sea floor in about forty feet of water, alongside a wave-pressure sensor. A submarine cable brought the electrical signals from the two instruments ashore, where they were recorded on the same chart. The idea was to detect the direction from which the large waves and trains of waves were coming, at least to the nearest compass point. We hoped to be able to track shifting storm centers or at least to determine if the swell was coming from the Southern Hemisphere. Sometimes it seemed to work well; other times we were not so sure. Certainly the relationship between the pressure records and the current at the sea floor was more complex than we had expected.

Other schemes utilize three or more wave sensors and correlate the passage of wave crests by means of a computer to obtain wave direction.

Most oil platforms are built in sufficiently deep water to avoid shoaling breakers, but when great hurricanes sweep across the Gulf of Mexico the towers must withstand breaking waves at sea. Oil company engineers made measurements on the towers during such storms and obtained data roughly equivalent to those given here, but this left some of them unsatisfied. They believed that real ocean waves and the forces they produce on a structure might be substantially lower than those ordinarily used for design calculations. Moreover, actual waves have ran-

dom shapes and speeds; rarely are they uniform along a
crest. More realistic designs could ensure platform survival at less cost.

Thus in 1976 Exxon joined with six other oil companies,
and two ship classification societies to build a scaled-
down model of an oil production platform that could be
used to make direct measurements of storm waves. Engineer Robert Haring of that company reports that this test
platform is a one-sixth to one-third scale model, twenty
by forty feet on the sides, that rises over sixty feet above
water fifty-three feet deep. It is festooned with transducers and strain gauges; the structure as a whole serves
to measure overturning moments and total base sheer.
When it was complete the entire structure (roughly com-
parable to a twelve-story building) was calibrated by
pulling on it in the fabrication yard with side loadings up
to 120,000 pounds—equivalent to the magnitude of wave
forces expected in winter storm waves.

Following calibration, the structure was loaded on a
barge, towed out to the test site, and lowered into place
by a large crane. From then on, the wave-force transducers, current meters, total-load sensors, wave staff, and
atmospheric sensors were in action. There is no point in
recording the usual calm weather situation, so the recording mode is utilized only when waves are sufficiently high
to "trigger" the system. This happens when the significant
wave height exceeds ten feet on two of the wave staffs.
Then data is recorded on digital tapes for up to eighteen
hours while the large waves continue. From these data
one hundred large waves will be chosen for analysis.

The Corps of Engineers, which is responsible for the
maintenance of harbors and coastal structures, is especially interested in the large instantaneous pressures

TABLE VI

INSTRUMENTS FOR MEASURING WAVES

Property to be sensed	Means of sensing	How used
Light reflection	Visual	Too many ways to enumerate here
	Camera	
	Float in pipe	Standard tide gauge
	Spar buoy	In deep water with deep damping disk
	Aneroid barometer	Measures heave of ship
	Radio waves	Radio altimeter on low-flying aircraft
Height of water surface	Echo sounder	Pointed down from buoy in shallow water or up from submarine in deep water
	Step gauge	Water closes contacts between spark plugs
	Paired wires	For model tank experiments with very small waves
	Side-looking airborne radar	Scans sea surface
	Flexible bellows plus:	
	Bourdon tube	Uncoiling tube drives pen
Pressure at sea floor	Potentiometer	Bridge circuit to galvanometer
	Variable inductance	Measures change in magnetic field

Property to be sensed	Means of sensing	How used
	Thermopile	Measures adiabatic heating of air
	Strain gauge	Measures change in length of metal
	Air bladder	Directly drives pen via air hose to surface
	Vibrator	Changes frequency as pressure changes
Water motion (velocity or acceleration)	Accelerometer	Mounted on buoy to measure acceleration of waves
	Accelerometer-pressure comb.	Shipboard wave recorder that computes wave height for several sensors
	Rotor	Measures currents caused by waves
Drag	Strain gauge	Senses wave forces acting on special pile
Direction	Rayleigh disk	Orients itself parallel to wave front
Impact	Dynamometer	Sliding bar moves to show maximum force
	Diaphragm	Same as above plus hydrostatic force
	Piezoelectric disks	Electronic amplification of force

TABLE VII
WAVE FORCES ON PILING

Wave type	Wave period (seconds)	Wave height (feet)	Measured force (pounds)	Total moment (ft. lbs.)	Drag Coefficient
Swell	9.3	3.4	9	85	.32
Peaked-up swell	10.0	3.1	10	93	.49
Wave immediately before breaking	10.8	3.3	19	186	.86
Breaker	10.3	3.3	23	226	1.28
Foamline (wave of translation)	10.3	3.5	33	320	1.46

These data for waves of similar height and period were obtained with a 3.5-inch-diameter test piling ten feet long at Monterey, California, in 1953. Notice the substantial increase in force on the piling as waves change from swell into breakers and then foam lines.

created by the impact of water moving at high velocity in breakers. Over a period of years, it has conducted experiments to determine how great these shock pressures can be and how new structures might be designed to resist them. Anyone who has stood on a rocky coast in a storm has felt the ground shake under the waves and seen the water hurled high into the air, and will have some appreciation of the problem. The pressure required to project water into the air is about one half pound per square inch for each foot of height. Thus, water going forty feet into the air requires twenty psi or an impact load of nearly a ton and a half on each square foot of rock.

The shock-pressure gauge consists of a stack of thin plates of tourmaline crystal set in a strong metal case. When subjected to pressure, this gauge produces a small charge of electricity which can be amplified, measured with an oscilloscope, and recorded with a camera. In wave-channel experiments, waves only six inches high have produced pressures as high as eighteen psi—but lasting only a thousandth of a second.

MAKING WAVES

In an early chapter the simplest and most widely used form of wave channel was described. A paddle-type generator made waves in the simple sine pattern on which wave theory rests. There are many other kinds of wavemakers, however, and many other uses for model waves in controlled conditions. Experimental facilities range in size from tabletop ripple tanks to maneuvering basins much larger than a football field.

Why make experimental waves? There are many reasons, beginning with scientific curiosity about the nature of waves themselves. Better answers are needed to the questions: How are waves created? What shape are the orbits under various conditions? How are they propagated? What are the conditions under which waves of different sizes refract, reflect, diffract?

The shoreline engineer must know in advance of construction the effects of various kinds and sizes of waves on beaches, breakwaters, groins, jetties, seawalls, and similar structures. How effective will these structures be in protecting a harbor or stopping the drift of sand along the coast? How high should a new dam be to prevent storm waves from going over the top? What size rocks should be used in the breakwater?

The naval architect wants to tow ship models in wave conditions simulating a true seaway and determine the magnitude of the stresses in each hull. He can discover also how seaworthy a design will be and can estimate the speed that some future ship will be able to make into the teeth of a gale that will blow a dozen years hence.

Each of these areas of interest may require a special wave tank to duplicate properly the shape and motion of the natural water surface. Let us begin with the very shallow, glass-bottomed ripple tank used both for teaching students about waves of all kinds (including sound and light) and for simple model studies of harbors. Often these tanks are about four feet square and a few inches deep. A bright light, shining upward from beneath, projects images of the waves onto a screen above. The wave crests produce bright images because they act as converging lenses to concentrate the light; the troughs act as diverging lenses and appear dark. These patterns of light dance on the screen, responding within a second or two to changes in the tank. It is a very convenient arrangement, and with water less than an inch deep, waves can be

generated by very small motions such as dipping a finger
into the tank or, more systematically, driving an elongated paddle with a simple sine-wave generator. The
characteristics of wave motion can be observed and simple experiments conducted. Even this modest equipment
can be of help to the harbor designer, who can use rows
of dominoes to model possible breakwater arrangements
and watch the effect of any change as he makes it.

The four types of wave-makers in general use are
shown diagrammatically in Figure 56. Actually, no particular ingenuity is required to produce waves in a tank; in
fact, it would be a much more remarkable feat to do anything to the water without making waves. Each type has
advantages for special applications. The paddle, the
plunger, and the piston are all connected by a rigid arm
to an eccentrically located pin on a turning wheel and
thus directly produce mathematically satisfying sine
waves. One can see by inspection of the diagrams how
these work. It is evident that reducing the speed of the
driving wheel lengthens the wave period and increasing
the radius of the pin connection increases wave height.
These are commonly used in long narrow wave channels
to produce a large variety of wave sizes.

Pneumatic wave-makers are a more recent development; usually several of them are mounted side by side
along two walls of large square tanks. They create waves
by changing the air pressure beneath a hood so that the
water surface there rises and falls. As the water surface
inside the hood is depressed the pressure is transmitted,
by Pascal's law, to the water immediately on the other
side of the partition where the surface is raised. This disturbance will then travel the length of the tank. The
speed of the blower motor controls the amount of air
pressure and thus the amplitude of the waves; the speed

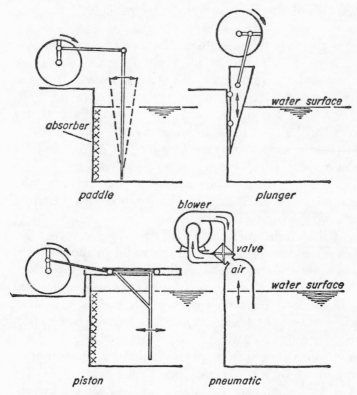

FIG. 56. Four types of model-tank wave-makers.

of the valve-operating motor controls duration of pressure and thus the wave length.

Once I saw a wave channel at the University of Kenya where there was no money for a mechanical wave generator. Instead one of the students rocked a piece of plywood, whose lower edge rested on the tank bottom, back and forth between two chalk lines on the tank rim, timing the action with the second hand of a watch. As far as I could see, it worked about as well as most other generators and, of course, it was instantly variable at the professor's request.

It is also easy to generate capillary waves and compare their mechanics with those of gravity waves. A very small drop of water landing on a still water surface will generate surface wrinkles (capillary waves) that radiate outward. As the size of the drop is increased, the capillary waves will be seen to be followed by tiny gravity waves that plainly have a longer wave length. An eyedropper and a bathtub are all the equipment needed.

For the measurement of capillary waves, Professor John Isaacs and David Sheres of the Scripps Institution of Oceanography use a "rotating teacup," a six-inch-diameter enclosed cylinder made of Plexiglas, which revolves 600 times a minute. At that speed, the water in the chamber forms a vertical cylindrical shell about half an inch thick against the tank wall. In this tank, gravity is radial and much greater than earth's gravity; this means that short gravity waves, not affected by surface tension, can be produced by a 60 cps wave generator inside the tank. Wave observations are made photographically, the motion being frozen by a 1/50,000-second strobe light.

This kind of an experimental setup has been used to obtain dispersion data on waves moving in each direction. It could be used to investigate waves in high-gravity environments (such as rocket fuels), impulsive waves, or gravity waves interacting with submerged flow.

The Coastal Engineering Research Laboratory at Fort Belvoir, Virginia, a modern descendant of the Army's old Beach Erosion Board, operates two 150-foot-long glass-sided wave channels with programmable piston-type generators. In these it is investigating scaling effects and run-up on beaches caused by variable waves. In its large concrete channel, 635 feet long, 15 feet wide, and 20 feet deep, a 500-horsepower generator makes waves 6 feet high that attack and overtop quarter-scale models of ocean breakwaters.

The CERL also has a shore-processes test basin 300 by 150 feet, with six 20-foot-wide piston-type wave generators. In it the engineers probe the fundamentals of along-shore sand transport. At Duck, North Carolina, they operate a research pier that extends 1,800 feet seaward to 20 feet of water. It is instrumented with various wave gauges and a radar that obtains wave direction—the principal object being to discover the changes in the character of waves as they cross the shelf.

The Waterways Experiment Station, another Army research group, located at Vicksburg, Mississippi, uses similar equipment to study more practical problems of waves and sand transport. Researchers often want to know about breakwater stability, or the best position for jetties at a specific tidal entrance, or how waves enter and reflect around a harbor. For this purpose, the Hydraulics Branch uses a 50-by-200-foot wave tank 6 feet deep with an L-shaped wave absorber.

It also has several three-dimensional basins, one of which (200 by 260 feet) had a model of Los Angeles–Long Beach harbor that was extensively tested (vertical scale 1:100, horizontal scale 1:400) at a cost of over $3 million. To date, over fifty models of U.S. harbors and coastal installations have been tested in the various basins at Vicksburg.

With such facilities, it is almost fair to say that ocean waves have been brought indoors for study.

Of the many other possible ways to make waves, one of the most imaginative was invented by W. G. Van Dorn, who wanted to create very long, very low tsunami-like waves in a small tank. His apparatus is a channel about a foot wide, a few inches deep, and one hundred feet long, so constructed that the bottom of the tank can be flexed by a series of motors which raise and lower the entire channel a few tenths of an inch in an undulating motion, generating micro-tsunamis as required. John Isaacs solved the tsunami-modeling problem in a different way by floating a light liquid on a denser one and making waves on the interface between the two. Such waves travel very slowly because of the small density difference. These are clever but bizarre experiments. Most of today's researchers are interested in directly duplicating a stormy ocean surface where the waves are casually described as confused. An understatement!

First it is necessary to find out what the surface is like by directly measuring the waves with a shipborne or other kind of wave meter. If the actual shape of the waves—also referred to as the "time-history of the height of the surface at a point"—is recorded on magnetic tape, it can be played back as often as desired. The next step is to devise a mechanism on which the tape recording can be played back—much as a tape of music would be played—except in this case it is reproduced on a wave-maker instead of a hi-fi set. If the height of the water at intervals of o.1 second is scanned from the tape and fed into a wave generator at the head of a channel, the waves created are almost exactly like the ones experienced and recorded by the ship, and ship models can be towed on a realistic sea surface. The narrow channel with its two-dimensional roughness did not, however, create sufficient confusion to satisfy some scientists, and basins have been built in Holland, France, and the United States with wave generators lining two sides of the tank, each producing different waves. With these, shorelines can be subjected to complex waves, and model ships can be towed at various angles to the seaway.

Another form of wave machine is in some ways even more realistic. If the wave channel or ripple tank is covered with a low hood and air is sucked or blown through the space above the water surface, model wind waves are created. Such an arrangement is fine for studying the mechanisms by which the wind raises waves, but it is of little use for most problems.

Most wave channels require "beaches" or wave absorbers to prevent reflections from the end opposite the wave-maker. In some cases these may actually be made of sand, but for ship-towing tanks there are more practical solutions. Many substances and surfaces have been tried, including metallic honeycomb, expanded metal, and meshes of various kinds. A gently inclined wooden beach with crosswise slots is often most satisfactory. The water runs up it and falls through the slots so that no reflection is possible.

With a choice of wave-makers that can duplicate natural waves in the ocean, the experimenter can select a tank shape that is suited to his problem and equip it to make waves of the complexity he desires. Tank shapes fall into several major classifications, each suited to a particular kind of model work. The long narrow channel is usually selected for experiments on the waves themselves, on ship models towed parallel to wave direction, for beach experiments in which the offshore-onshore motion of sand is under study, and for tests of breakwater sections. The large rectangular basins that are only a foot or two deep are generally favored for studies of the longshore transport of sand and for models of harbors. Large deep tanks are used for the maneuvering of "free" (radio-controlled) models as well as for towing large ship models at an angle to complex seas. The following descriptions of some of the largest and most elaborate wave tanks indicate how important this kind of research tool is to engineers and scientists working with oceanic problems.

E. V. Lewis of the Experimental Towing Tank at Stevens Institute of Technology seems to have been the first naval architect to inject planned realism into ship-model testing. On the assumption that a seaway never repeats itself, it is only necessary to re-create the statistical properties in order to reproduce any sea state. Since the sea surface is made up of an infinite number of sine waves randomly combined, it is possible to duplicate the surface by randomly programming the stroke of the wave-maker. On testing model ships in such waves it was discovered that the longitudinal bending moments on the ship's structure were greatly increased over the results from the regular waves previously used.

A year or so later, the ship-towing tank at the University of California at Berkeley (200 by 8 by 6 feet) was equipped with an even more ambitious irregular wave generator by Robert Wiegel and his associates. Their computer takes data from wave records and feeds them to a mechanical device that moves a piston-type or "bulkhead" generator to reproduce the sea surface originally recorded.

The Neyrpic laboratory in Grenoble, France, has developed the "snake type" wave-maker for the generation of complex seas. It is composed of a large number of small paddle-type generators side by side which can be oriented independently and operated. The line of generators is something like a vertical venetian blind and can be arranged in curves of various shapes (hence the name) to produce waves of nearly any complexity.

Some of the largest and most modern facilities are those at the Navy's David Taylor Model Basin in Washington, D.C., where channels and tanks permit hydrodynamic measurements of all sorts. Two of these facilities are worth special mention. The "deep water basin" is 2,775 feet long, 51 feet wide, and 22 feet deep. Its pneumatic wave-maker makes waves up to 2 feet high of any desired length. Ship models 32 feet long and weighing up to 5 tons can be towed at speeds up to 60 knots by a carriage running on heavy steel rails. These precise rails vary in height no more than two thousandths of an inch and actually take into account the curvature of the earth.

The new maneuvering and seakeeping basin, named after Captain Harold Saunders, who conceived it, is 360 by 240 feet and 20 to 35 feet deep. It is spanned by a 230-ton bridge, which supports a towing carriage and can be pivoted to tow the ship models at any angle relative to the wave system. Batteries of pneumatic wave-makers along two sides can create waves up to 2 feet high, 5 to 40 feet long, in accordance with taped instructions. When the water surface is still and the wave-makers along one side of it are started, the phenomenon of the disappearance of the first wave (mentioned in Chapter III) can be seen clearly. For some wave periods the first seven waves will disappear before a disturbance reaches the opposite end of the tank. In order to make certain that the waves in this huge tank would be satisfactory, a tenth-scale model (itself bigger than many experimental basins) was built, and Wilbur Marks practiced making waves for a year or more in advance of the construction of the main tank.

There are a great many more wave channels, test

basins, hydrodynamics laboratories, and experimental wave facilities. The examples given should permit appreciation of the great interest in the subject of waves and the cost to society of the effects of waves.

IX

Energy from the Ocean

IN RECENT YEARS THERE HAS BEEN MUCH INTEREST IN THE
search for new sources of energy to power our civilization. One sensible place to look is in the ocean, which is
famed for its constant motion and frequent violence. Most
of the ocean's energy is a secondary form of solar energy;
that is, the original radiation has been converted into heat
or motion or photosynthesis. The rest of the harnessable
energy comes from the celestial mechanics of earth rotation and gravitation.

The sun's radiation warms the earth's atmosphere and
its surface, which is 71 percent ocean. Because the air in
tropical regions receives more direct rays, it is warmed
more than the air at higher latitudes. The warmed tropical air rises and is replaced by cooler air from the north or
south. This movement, driven by the sun and guided by
the rotation of the earth, causes the major winds. Near
the equator the air is relatively still (the doldrums), but
not far to its north or south the trade winds blow steadily
to the west. At higher latitudes (40° to 50°) the winds
blow *from* the west.

These winds raise waves and provide most of the driving force for the great currents of the earth. The trade winds furnish the initial impetus to the equatorial currents. These flow close to the surface toward the west until they encounter a land mass that turns them away from the equator. The water masses flow to the north or south and eventually close the loop, forming huge eddies or gyres that rotate clockwise in the Northern Hemisphere and counterclockwise in the Southern. Each ocean has these great jets of water, those in the Atlantic being known as the Gulf Stream and Benguela Current; in the Pacific they are the Kuroshio (Japan) Current and the Peru-Chile (Humboldt) Current.

The storms that raise waves have similar origins. For example, the intense solar heating of a windless area warms the air, causing it to rise and bringing in cool air at the surface. Often a great whirlpool of air forms in which winds are driven by the difference in temperature. Thus great cyclonic storms form with winds that move at as much as 150 knots.

Tidal forces and motions have already been described. Solar heating of the ocean's surface waters is self-evident. All of these effects of solar heating and the earth's rotation are potential sources of power which we must figure out how to use.

This chapter goes into some detail on six possible ways of extracting energy from the sea. The first three are closely related to the rest of this book; the rest are included for the sake of completeness and comparison. All are technically feasible—which means they can be made to work if enough effort is put into them. The question is whether it is worth while, relative to other sources of energy, or to the costs of manpower and materials, to produce power by these methods.

In our society, energy and power have become virtually synonymous with electricity. We must remember, however, that if heat or mechanical power can be used directly, the efficiency may be very much greater than if the same energy is converted to electricity. For example, if the sun's rays are used directly to heat water, that is perhaps fifty times more efficient than using the sun's rays to make electricity, which would then be used to operate an electric water heater.

Figure 57 gives relative amounts of energy theoretically available from five potential ocean sources, according to Gerald Wick and John Isaacs.

Dozens of methods for extracting energy from waves have been proposed, and many have been patented in the last hundred years. The Patent Office calls these devices "wave motors" or "pump activated by ocean swell" or "apparatus for obtaining power from the sea." Many come from the nineteenth century, when amusement piers often extended out over the breaker zone. Apparently various inventive customers, impressed by all the energy they saw wasted in turbulence against the pilings below, dashed home to figure out a way to use it. At any rate, many inventions start with a pier.

From a pier one can suspend large flaps that move to and fro, driving pistons, pulling lines to weights and clutches, or pumping water to a higher level. Floats of various shapes were very popular. As a float moves up and down with wave and tide, it can be supported on the end of a lever or in vertical slides. Through various linkages the constantly moving float can be made to pump water, compress air, or lift weights. Many of these devices were invented before electric generators existed and so had to perform some work that was immediately useful. Still other kinds of wave devices have been invented

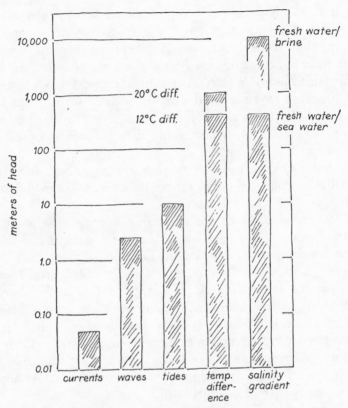

FIG. 57. Concentration of energy in different ocean sources expressed as meters of head. "Temperature difference" head is calculated on the basis of maximum theoretical efficiency; "currents" uses velocity head. (After Wick and Isaacs)

that sit on or under the sea bottom and make use of the pressure changes caused by the passing waves. There are schemes for letting wave crests directly drive large cams and for directly taking electricity from the succession of moving wave crests; after all, the sea water is a moving electrolyte cutting lines of force in the earth's magnetic field, so it must generate electricity. Then there are large buoys that have an eccentric weight and work like a self-winding watch. And a shiplike hull that would be moored parallel to wave crests, causing it to roll heavily; below-decks this hull would have a huge heavy pendulum that would swing with each roll to drive a gear train and thence a generator.

Several of these inventors have pointed out that it would be possible to focus waves on their shallow-water wave motors by changing the undersea contours and thence the wave refraction pattern. The available energy could of course be considerably increased if the wave directions remained steady. It may also be possible to make use of the mass transport of water by waves to do some kind of work—although this seems less promising than using the wave form.

All these ideas and others are now being re-examined by ocean engineers interested in finding the best way of harnessing wave energy. Let us hope that among them there are a few real gems that can be useful somewhere.

WAVE ENERGY

The thunder of a large wave breaking and the shudder of a beach in response impress the observer with the huge amount of energy in waves. One tends to forget that those large waves are likely to be followed in a day or so by small waves that contain very little energy. One of the problems of using waves to generate power is the extreme variability. However, a reasonably steady source of this power exists in the trade-wind seas just north and south of the equator. There, during most of the year, waves roll

steadily across the lower latitudes at an average height of
about nine feet and a period of about eight seconds.

In such trade-wind seas, the power expended by the
waves in raising and lowering a passing ship every eight
seconds is greater than the power of the ship's engines.
This has led many inventors to think about how to extract
power from the rise and fall of some buoyant object.
Many ways are possible, but one of the most successful
will be discussed here; it is the wave pump invented by
John Isaacs.

He began by noting that if a dam existed that were the
equivalent of the average height of trade-wind waves, it
would be so low that very little hydroelectric energy
could be derived from it. This meant that any wave device would have to amplify the low head of average
waves. It would also have to respond to (amplify) waves
of all lengths. Finally, it would have to be able to extract
power from small waves as well as survive in large storm
waves.

The wave-powered pump is illustrated in Figure 58. It
has the great virtue of simplicity; moreover, a seagoing
model of it works very well, even in low waves.

The pump has the following parts: a buoy (cork-
shaped, widening toward the top); a long vertical pipe (a
300-foot-long pipe magnifies the wave head twenty
times), with a simple check valve near the upper end; an
air-compression chamber into which the water from the
long pipe flows and from which the water is forced by the
compressed air; and a turbine atop the buoy that converts
the pumped water into electricity.

The system works in this way: as the buoy descends
into a wave trough, the open pipe slides downward
through the water. Relative to the pipe and the buoy, the
water in the pipe moves upward. Water spills out the

PLATE 30. Uprushing water carries sand up the beach face and deposits it on the berm. Then the water sinks down through the sand. Because there is little backrushing water to carry sand down the beach face, the beach builds seaward. *Willard Bascom*

PLATE 31. Fine flat sand ...ruptly changes to pebbles ...d then cobbles topped by a ...e of driftwood, at Tilla-...ook Head, Oregon. *Willard ...scom*

PLATE 32. An extreme low tide has exposed this classic example of a longshore bar and rip channel in the beach at Cape Meares, Oregon. The berm, wide and light-colored, slopes abruptly into the flooded trough.

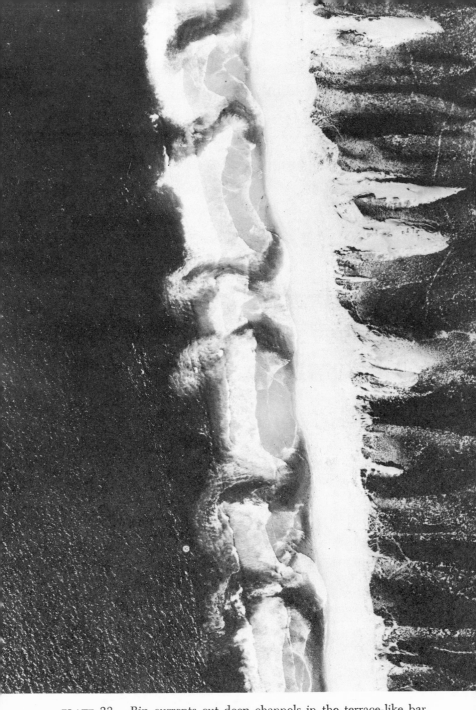

PLATE 33. Rip currents cut deep channels in the terrace-like bar at Ford Ord, California. *U. S. Navy Photo*

PLATE 34. A series of parallel ridges rise as much as forty feet above low water on the sandy plain behind the beach at Clatsop spit, Oregon. *Willard Bascom*

PLATE 35. Bars and ripple marks created in an experimental tank at the laboratory of the Coastal Engineering Research Center, Fort Belvoir, Virginia. *U. S. Army Corps of Engineers*

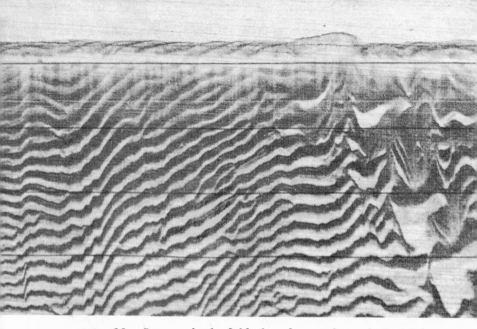

PLATE 36. Sonograph of a field of sand waves beneath Cook Inlet, Alaska, abruptly changing to dunes at the right. Black lines are 25 meters apart, so the wave length of the waves is about 5–6 meters. *A. Bouma, U. S. Geological Survey*

PLATE 37. Surfer "dropping in" on a large well-shaped wave at Bonzai Pipeline, north shore of Oahu, Hawaii. The photographer, swimming just outside the main break, used a Plexiglas-enclosed camera and a lot of know-how to snap this picture. *Dan Merkel/ Surfing Magazine*

PLATE 38.   USCGC *Taney* between huge breakers on an unidentified bar. *Cdr. W. A. Swansburg USCG*

PLATE 39. This Coast Guard surfboat started out through the jetties at the Quillayute River in Washington only to encounter a couple of surprisingly large breakers. *L. Thompson/U. S. Coast Guard*

upper end of the pipe into a chamber in the buoy, compressing the air therein as it does so. Then, as the next wave crest approaches, the buoy rises. This causes the flap valve to close; when it does so, the buoy lifts the water in the pipe relative to the water in the sea around the pipe. Whichever way the pipe is moving, the compressed air keeps a steady flow of water moving through the turbine, which constantly generates electricity.

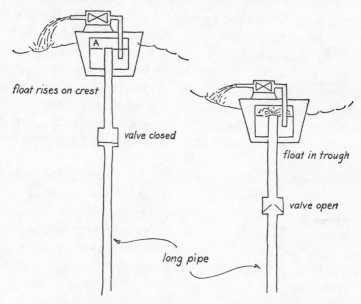

FIG. 58. Power from waves. The Isaacs wave pump is a buoy dangling a long pipe that rides up and down on passing waves. As it starts up on a crest (left) the flap valve closes and the water in the pipe is accelerated upward relative to the surrounding sea water. When the buoy descends into the trough the valve opens and the water in the pipe moves upward relative to the pipe, thus pumping water into the chamber (A) and compressing the air therein. This compressed air in the chamber keeps water steadily flowing through the turbine.

A model of this scheme was tested off Kaneohe Bay, Hawaii, in 1976. The buoy was about 6 feet across, the pipe 300 feet long and 3 inches in diameter. Motion pictures of the test show the system assembled on an airfield, picked up by a helicopter, and then vertically lowered into the ocean at the site selected. As soon as the helicopter released it and flew away, the model began pumping although the waves were not much over a foot in height. A stream of water some 20 feet high and an inch in diameter squirted straight up into the air above the buoy in an unceasing fountain.

Isaacs has calculated that a pipe 500 feet long and 3 feet in diameter in the trade-wind seas would generate about 50 kilowatts. The cost of constructing such a plant seems to be competitive with the construction costs of oil-powered, coal-powered, and nuclear plants. From then on, the wave-powered plant has the great advantage that fuel is free.

A major problem with this and other deep-water schemes is: How do you use the power or get it from where it is generated to where it is needed? For short distances ordinary submarine cables might be satisfactory. Large plants might produce some energy-intensive product in a shipboard factory, thus saving energy at some other location.

TIDAL POWER

Of the six methods for extracting energy described in this chapter, only this one is actually in use. Undoubtedly this is because it is easier to decide how to go about harnessing the tides in a specific place. The principal re-

quirement is a large bay with a narrow entrance where
the tidal range is large.

Even a fairly casual observer is impressed by the considerable amount of work done as water rushes in and out
of such a bay once or twice a day. One can see that the
currents could be used to turn a paddle wheel, or the rising water used to raise heavy floating objects, or that if
the water at high tide could be dammed for later release,
the outrush could be used to run a turbine. With a little
more thought, the first two ideas are discarded because
the energy they might produce would be very small.
Eventually the inventor concentrates on how to develop
the bay entrance with dams and turbines to get the most
out of the tidal change. It is the long-sustained rush of
large quantities of water through turbines in confined
channels that makes tidal power possible.

Because not many places in the world have the required bay and the large tides, consideration of tidal-
power schemes soon turns the talk to the existing power
plant at La Rance Bay in France or the long-discussed
but unbuilt Passamaquoddy Bay project on the border
between the United States and Canada.

The problem is to devise a plant that has the most head
for the longest period. *Head* is a hydraulic term meaning
the usable difference in elevation between the higher and
lower levels of water on opposite sides of a dam.

Tidal dams are unique in that the high-water side of
the dam alternates; this means it must hold back the pressure of water in either direction. The turbines that are
used are also very special. They have the usual multiple
blades attached to a horizontal axle that rotates, but these
blades must be adjustable so that power can be extracted
from flow in either direction. Moreover, although they are

mostly used as generators, there are times when it is helpful to use them as pumps. This requires using the generator as a motor to run the turbines.

In his fascinating book *The Tides,* Dr. Edward Clancy
describes several tidal-power installations, beginning with
Slade's Mill for grinding spices at Chelsea, Massachusetts,
built over one hundred years ago. Here four waterwheels
generated about fifty horsepower when a full head of tide
existed.

The modern tidal plant at the entrance to La Rance estuary in Brittany is much more interesting. The tidal
range there reaches a maximum of 44 feet and the area of
the bay is about 9 square miles.

Thus the construction of a dam at a point where the
bay mouth was only 2,500 feet wide could retain a huge
volume of water. This dam, which contains the power
plant and turbines, has an unusual cross section. At high
tide only the top of the dam, which is the roof of the
power plant, is above water. There are twenty-four water
conduits under the dam, each containing a turbine generator. These conduits can be opened or closed individually
by a pair of gates, and each gate contains control vanes.
This gives the operators precise control over the flow of
water at all times. The propellers that turn these
10,000-kilowatt generators (at 94 rpm) are 17.5 feet in diameter. The turbine vanes or propellers have controllable-
pitch blades so that the generator can be driven at a constant speed by flow in either direction.

The sequence for obtaining power, diagrammed in Figure 59, goes as follows: As the tide begins to come in, the
available head of water behind the dam (from the previous high tide) becomes too small for efficient generation
and the turbines are shut down, but the sluice gates remain open until the water level on both sides is the same.

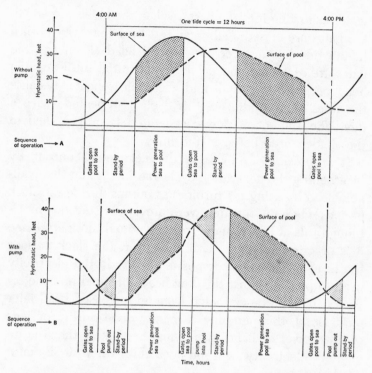

FIG. 59. Tidal power. The phases of operation at the La Rance, Brittany, plant, with crosshatched areas indicating the amount of head or quantity of energy available. The upper diagram shows the cycle without pumping; in the lower one much more energy is available in spite of the expenditure on pumping (shown as shaded triangles). (After Edward Clancy)

Then the gates are closed (1) and the water level outside begins to rise as the tide comes in. When adequate head has built up, the gates are opened (2) and water rushes in, generating power until the combination of decreasing tidal height outside and increasing water level in the basin results in too little head. (3) Again the turbines are shut down, but the sluice gates remain open as long as water is flowing into the basin. When the levels are equal, the gates are closed again (4) and kept that way until a falling tide has restored the needed head. Then (5) the gates are reopened and power is generated until (6) the head becomes too small and the cycle repeats. Because the tides are semidiurnal this cycle is repeated twice a day. The amount of power generated is proportional to the shaded area between the lines.

It is possible to increase the net power output by lengthening the generation cycle and increasing the available head by using the turbines as pumps during the slack periods when the turbines were previously shut down. Although this at first sounds like a perpetual motion scheme it is practical for two reasons. First, at the slack periods the head is low and it is possible to trade the electricity used to pump against this low head for much more electricity that can be extracted from an increased head later on. Second, this pumping is mainly done during periods of low power demand, which makes it likely that the increased electricity will be available when it is most needed.

Obviously the operation of such a plant is a complicated matter best left in the control of a computer. The maximum output is 240,000 kilowatts or 540 million kilowatt hours per year without pumping and 130 million additional kwh with pumping. *Vive la France* and *la* computer.

The Passamaquoddy Bay project is larger and more complicated but it would operate in much the same way. I leave the description of its two huge pools, its 7 miles of dams (some in 300-foot-deep water) and its possible 1,000-megawatt continuous rating to Dr. Clancy's book. He notes that in 1961 a review commission reported that "it is evident that the construction of the tidal power project by itself is economically unfeasible by a wide margin. . . ."

CURRENTS

Although the great currents of the sea encircle all the oceans, there are not many places where it may be feasible to tap these currents for power. The energy density in ocean currents is low—which means there is not much energy at any one location. A lot of power is theoretically available, however, because the volumes of water moving are so large. This suggests that large extraction plants, and many of them, will be needed to get a substantial amount of power. Because the energy available is proportional to the velocity of the water, it is important to choose a site with the fastest-moving water available.

One likely location is the Gulf Stream where it flows through the channel between Florida and the Bahamas, at a velocity of two meters (six feet) per second. This site also has the great advantage that it is near to a large population that needs power.

As with the other possible energy sources, there are various schemes for converting currents into usable power. The one chosen for description here is the combined effort of William Mouton and David Thompson; their goal is to extract 10,000 megawatts of the 116,000 available in the Florida Current.

The Mouton-Thompson plan is to use a battery of eighteen large turbines of the type shown in Figure 60. Each of these turbines would have blades 300 feet in diameter housed in a shell or nozzle with an intake diameter of 345 feet and an exit diameter of 560 feet. Each

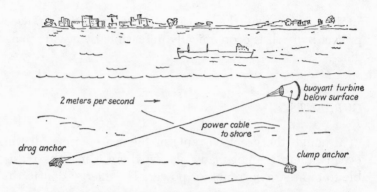

FIG. 60. Power from ocean currents. This is a proposed method of extracting energy from the Florida Current by allowing that current to drive large propeller-like turbine blades that rotate in a buoyant shell and drive a generator.

would produce about 80 megawatts. Those dimensions make such a turbine about as large a piece of hardware as has ever been built. How it would be built, transported, and installed is being studied.

In place, it would look like this: the huge turbine shell would be anchored by means of a taut wire to heavy clumps of dead weight in the sea floor directly beneath. The highest point of the turbine shell would be beneath the keels of the deepest-draft ships; buoyant chambers in the shell would cause it to tug upward while being re-strained at proper depth by cables from the clump.

A separate anchor 8,000 feet upstream, carefully de-signed to dig firmly into the bottom and resist the drag of the Florida Current, would hold the turbine vertically above the clump.

The turbine blades—and there are many of them, ra-diating from a central streamlined hub—run in a track around the interior of the shell. As they turn, they drive an electric generator system in the rim. The electricity flows through cables that lead downward to the clump anchor and thence ashore.

The inventors note that the blades turn at only one revolution per minute, so that fish will not be bothered. Initial costs are estimated at about a dollar a watt. But after that, fuel is free. There would be no significant ecological effects, but the Gulf Stream would slow down very slightly.

SALINITY GRADIENT ENERGY

It may be possible to capture a great deal of energy that is now lost when a fresh-water river flows into the ocean or into a salty lake such as the Dead Sea or Great Salt Lake. The possible availability of this energy is not generally recognized, although it may be a very promising source. When an ordinary stream discharges into the ocean, the salinity difference (30 parts per thousand) makes the energy theoretically available equal to that of a waterfall 240 meters (750 feet) high. If the same stream flowed into the Dead Sea (whose total dissolved salts are 270 parts per thousand), this would correspond to a waterfall 3,000 meters high.

Extracting this energy can most easily be demonstrated by the use of an osmotic (semipermeable) membrane. Osmosis is easiest to understand if one considers a simple tank separated into two equal chambers by means of a semipermeable membrane down the center. If we put river water on one side of the membrane and an equal amount of sea water on the other, we would soon see the membrane bulge as the fresh water passes through it to the salty side. This happens because the molecules of water on both sides are in motion, constantly striking the membrane; when they encounter a small hole in it, they can pass through. On the fresh-water side the molecules find such holes. On the salty side the large molecules of

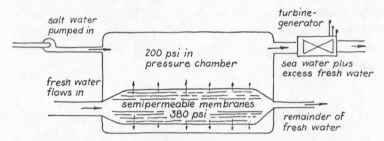

salt water
pumped in

turbine-
generator

200 psi in
pressure chamber

sea water plus
excess fresh water

fresh water
flows in

semipermeable membranes
380 psi

remainder of
fresh water

FIG. 61. Power from a salinity gradient. A chamber containing water at a pressure of about 200 pounds per square inch (psi) discharges through a turbine generator. A small amount of sea water or brine must be pumped into the chamber. Fresh water flowing through the chamber in tubes made of semipermeable membranes will pass through the membranes into the chamber because the osmotic pressure in the tubes is 380 psi. Each additional half cubic meter of water per second of fresh water passing through the turbine can produce a megawatt of electricity. (After Isaacs and Wick)

dissolved salts will not pass through these tiny holes in the membrane and prevent the water molecules from passing. Consequently much more water flows toward the salty side than away from it.

The problem is to invent a device that can use an osmotic membrane to take advantage of the salinity difference and of the flow through the membrane. One solution is shown in Figure 61. In that illustration a considerable quantity of fresh water from a river discharge flows through a series of pipe-like semipermeable membranes inside a pressurized chamber. Salty sea water is pumped into the chamber surrounding the membranes, maintaining the pressure there at about 200 pounds per square inch (psi). Because the osmotic pressure of the fresh water relative to the salt water is 380 psi, there is a differential pressure of 180 psi (six atmospheres), driving much of the fresh water out through the membrane into the chamber.

As the combined sea-water/fresh-water mixture leaves the chamber, it drives a turbine that generates electricity. The calculations of Gerald Wick and John Isaacs show that each cubic meter of fresh water per second moving through the turbine (this is in excess of the amount of sea water pumped in) theoretically can generate 2 megawatts of electricity. For a similar plant in which fresh water is mixed with Dead Sea water the power output can be 30 megawatts per cubic meter per second.

Wick and Isaacs further calculated that there is, in theory, more energy potential in the salt of most Gulf Coast salt domes than in the oil that is produced from the best of them. With a salinity gradient plant operating in the range of 5 to 25 percent efficiency these domes would remain an important source of power after the oil is exhausted.

The main problem with most applications of salinity power is that the membranes presently available are far too expensive. If adequate but less costly membranes can be devised this method will be worthy of serious consideration. However, another approach utilizes only free water surfaces, thus avoiding membranes. Small models using this method have developed relatively high power per unit area and high efficiency compared with membrane systems. This promising avenue should be explored. One important advantage of salinity power is that it is not subject to ordinary thermodynamic limitations.

BIOMASS

Another possible way to convert the sun's radiation on
the sea into a more usable form is to construct a deep-
water "marine farm" in which kelp (seaweed) can be
grown and harvested efficiently. After harvesting, the
kelp can be converted to methane or other fuels. This
scheme, called *kelp bioconversion,* was first described in
this form by Howard Wilcox of the Naval Undersea
Center.

He proposed to culture rapidly growing types of sea-
weeds in the open ocean on thousands of acres of nets or
lines supported by huge floating structures. The embryo
plants can be mass-produced in the laboratory, then
moved to polypropylene lines, and eventually installed
as juvenile plants on the farm. The lines or nets holding
the plants would be stretched horizontally 40 to 60 feet
below the surface. The water surrounding the crop would
be fertilized by pumping up cold nutrient-rich waters
from a depth of 1,500 feet or more. This is necessary because the surface waters of the deep ocean do not have
the nutrient values of coastal waters where kelp ordinarily grows.

California kelp (*Macrocystis pyrifera*) is perhaps the
fastest-growing plant known; its stalks can elongate as
much as a foot a day. Thus its ability to convert sunlight
into seaweed tissue is far better than most plants. Dr.
Wilcox suggested that the spacing between plants should
be about 10 feet for a population density of 436 plants
per acre. These plants can be harvested four times a year
without damage by the usual form of kelp harvesting
ship, which cuts off the upper 4 feet of kelp plant in
swaths, much like a harvester on land, at the rate of 300

to 400 tons per hour. A square mile of kelp is said to be capable of yielding well over a million dollars' worth of useful products per year. Such a kelp bed can also yield the equivalent of about 10,000 kilowatts per acre of "stored vegetational energy" in the form of methane. Methane is produced naturally by the anaerobic degradation of organic vegetable masses and is compatible with existing household gas systems.

Large areas of the ocean are suitable for such "farms," but those with low currents, few storms, and natural upwelling would be preferable. Many subsidiary advantages are claimed for this scheme: the kelp may be equally valuable for its drugs, chemicals, or food values, and a fishery in the kelp may develop. However, a great many technical and economic problems remain to be solved.

TEMPERATURE DIFFERENCE

The sun shining on the sea surface warms it, and wave motion mixes that warmed water downward for a short distance. This zone of warmed water is known as the *mixed layer*. The layer is thicker in the winter, when the mixing is greater, than in summer, when the waves are small. The interface between this warmed surface water and the deep cold water below is a somewhat vague boundary called the *thermocline*, whose depth below the sea surface ranges from 30 to 120 meters. Sometimes this boundary is marked by an abrupt change in temperature, but more often the change is gradual.

Because the thermocline represents a density difference, waves travel along it as described in Chapter III. For the purpose of this present discussion, however, it is enough to know that over much of the ocean there are two distinct layers of different temperatures and the temperature difference between them is 10 to 15° C.

In 1880 Jacques D'Arsonval of France invented a process that makes use of this difference to drive an engine. Nearly fifty years later his disciple Georges Claude built a plant on the coast of Cuba, to prove that the principle was sound. Claude launched a large pipe, 2 meters in diameter and over 600 meters long, by supporting the pipe on wheels and laying track down a gentle hillside into the sea whence the pipe was pulled into deep water. His plant was not a great success, but it was able to operate a small turbine that produced about 10 horsepower.

At the present time the U. S. Department of Energy is making a vigorous effort to design and build a plant that will demonstrate how a temperature-difference plant can be used to generate electricity. It calls this demonstration plant OTEC, for Ocean Thermal Energy Conversion.

The general principles of operation are illustrated in Figure 62. The present concept uses ammonia as a working fluid (the shaded pipe). Heat from the ocean must be transferred to this fluid. It is warmed by the surface water (shown entering from the left) in an evaporator that converts it to a vapor. The vapor is then used to drive a turbine, which turns an electric generator. The spent vapor then passes through a condenser (which is cooled by water brought up from several thousand feet below) and the fluid becomes liquid ammonia again. The cooled surface water and the warmed deep water are discharged at a depth below the surface where they will not influence the temperature of the inflowing waters.

Sketching an idea in this form is a long way from building a plant that will produce a substantial amount of power. Many difficult design problems remain to be solved because the method will need machinery that is huge and not ordinarily used by industry.

The deep pipe presently proposed is 60 feet in diameter and 8,000 feet long. Overcoming the many difficulties as-

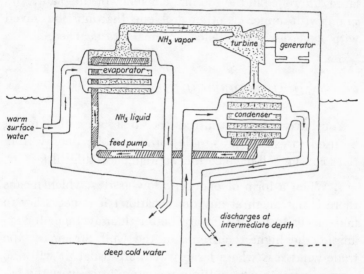

FIG. 62. Power from ocean temperature difference. This large floating structure takes in relatively warm surface water at the left to operate an evaporator and much colder water from far below for use in a condenser. Both waters, after having had their temperatures altered, are discharged at an intermediate depth. The working fluid is an ammonia compound that is volatilized at sea-surface temperatures and used to drive a turbine-generator.

sociated with building, installing, and maintaining that pipe, which will be subject to a variety of stresses plus corrosion and fouling, over the life of a plant, is a major undertaking. Then huge low-head pumps capable of moving vast amounts of water against a low pressure difference must be designed. Every warm surface that is exposed to the sea will be subject to sea growth that can slow the motion of the moving water. At the evaporators and condensers where heat flow takes place a very thin layer of thermophyllic (heat-loving) bacteria makes a large difference in the thermal efficiency of the plant. And so on, with numerous other problems that must be solved with cleverness, persistence, and many tests at sea.

FUNDAMENTAL DIFFICULTIES

You have now been introduced to six ways that might be used to extract low-grade forms of solar energy from the sea. They all have certain fundamental difficulties:

1. When a form of energy is low-grade (which means there is not much at any one location) it is necessary to find places to tap it that are better than average: for example, the highest currents of the Gulf Stream or the trade-wind seas where large waves are usual. It will also be necessary to use multiple receptors to convert the energy. Rarely will a single unit of any of the above devices be of much help; if they are to produce any substantial amount of power they must be used in clusters of 10 or 50 or 100.

2. When fluid velocities are low or the head (potential energy) is low, as they usually are with waves, tides, and currents, one must deal with large volumes of water. This means that very large structures are needed, which require large amounts of space and capital.

3. Five of the schemes described are unproven experimental ideas. Some form of each could be made to work, but their efficiency, their useful life, and other major fac-

tors are entirely unknown. Think of the problems of maintaining a group of twenty of any of the devices at sea for a period of, say, thirty years.

4. The advantage of all the schemes is that their operating fuel costs nothing. However, a great deal of fuel goes into building the parts for these plants, moving them, and installing them. On a purely energy basis it will probably take ten years or more for most of them to pay back the energy that was expended in getting them to work.

5. One value that such plants may have (those that are actually built and tested) is to demonstrate how hard we will have to work for energy once the stores of oil, gas, and coal are gone. Perhaps that will make us think a bit harder about the present huge wastage.

6. No one of these sea energy schemes will greatly help with the overall national problem, but each, used at the most effective place in its most efficient form, could contribute something. Many different techniques, each fitted to the local situation, will be needed.

It appears likely that in less than one thousand years mankind will use up most of the available fuel that has been accumulated over the last 500 million years. Those one thousand years represent less than one fifth of the well-known part of human history. What then? If we do not solve the long-term energy problem before the fossil fuels run out, mankind will slip back into the dark ages forever.

My view is that we must do more research on all sources of energy while at the same time making a much greater effort to conserve what we have now. Our great-great-grandchildren will appreciate it.

X

The Surf

WAVES HAVE MANY STAGES IN THEIR LIVES. THEY ARE BORN as ripples, grow into whitecaps, chop, wind waves, and finally into fully developed storm seas. As these seas pass out from under the winds that formed them, they diminish in height and steepness into low sine-shaped swell. As swell, waves may traverse great stretches of open ocean without much loss of energy. Eventually they reach the shoaling waters of a continental shelf. Once on the shelf the wave fronts are bent until they almost parallel the shoreline.

All this seems to be merely preparation for the final and most exciting step. The irregular waves of deep water are organized by the effect of the bottom into long regular lines of crests moving in the same direction at similar velocities. The romanticist thinks of the forces of the sea being marshaled for an exuberant death against an ancient enemy. The depth continues to decrease until finally in very shallow water it becomes impossible for the oscillating water particles to complete their orbits. When the orbits break the wave breaks. The crest tumbles forward, falling into the trough ahead as a mass of foaming white water. The momentum carries the broken water onward until the wave's last remaining energy is expended in a gentle swash that rushes up the sandy beach face and sinks from sight. The wave is gone!

This zone where waves give up their energy and where systematic water motions give way to violent turbulence is the surf. It is the most exciting part of the ocean.

BREAKING WAVES

As the swell from the deep sea moves into very shallow water, it is traveling at a speed of fifteen to twenty miles an hour, and the changes in its character over the final few dozen yards to shore come very rapidly.

In the approach to shore the drag of the bottom causes the wave velocity to decrease. The decrease causes the phenomenon of refraction, which was described earlier, and one of its effects is to shorten the wave length. As length decreases, wave steepness increases, tending to make the waves less stable. Moreover, as a wave crest moves into water whose depth is about twice the wave height, another effect is observed which further increases wave steepness. The crest "peaks up." That is, the rounded crest that is identified with swell is transformed into a higher, more pointed mass of water with steeper flanks. As the depth of water continues to decrease, the circular orbits are squeezed into a tilted ellipse and the orbital velocity at the crest increases with the increasing wave height.

This sequence of changes in wave length and steepness is the prelude to breaking. Finally, at a depth of water roughly equal to 1.3 times the wave height, the wave becomes unstable. This happens when not enough water is available in the shallow water ahead to fill in the crest and complete a symmetrical wave form. The top of the onrushing crest becomes unsupported and it collapses, falling in uncompleted orbits. The wave has broken; the result is surf.

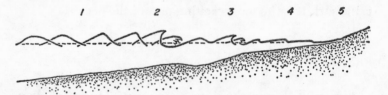

FIG. 63. The breaking of a wave: 1. Swell peaks up on entering very shallow water. 2. At depth equal to 1.3 times the wave height, it breaks. 3. Wave re-forms and breaks again. 4. Water moves beachward as wave of translation. 5. Finally rushes up the beach.

Having broken into a mass of turbulent tumbling foam, carried landward by its own momentum, the ex-wave will, if the water deepens again as it does after passing over a bar, reorganize itself into a new wave with systematic orbital motion. This reorganization is probably the result of dumping the mass of water from the wave crest into the relatively quiet water inside the breaker zone; the impulse generates a new wave. The new wave is smaller than the original one, the difference in heights representing the energy lost in breaking. The new wave, being smaller, proceeds into water equal to 1.3 times its height; then it, too, breaks.

Again a mass of water, white with bubbles of entrained air, is produced, but the water is likely to be too shallow for a new oscillatory wave to form. Now the front of the water becomes a step-shaped wave of translation—a different sort of wave in which the water actually moves forward with the wave form rather than merely oscillating as the wave form passes. Finally, at the beach face, the momentum of the water carries it into an uprush; the water slides and sprawls in a thin swash up and across the face of the beach. As it reaches its uppermost limit the wave dies; all the energy so carefully gleaned from the winds of the distant storm and hoarded for a thousand miles of ocean crossing is gone, expended in a few wild moments. Because the energy is released so rapidly, the energy density in the surf is actually much higher than in the storm which originally created the waves.

The surf changes from moment to moment, day to day, and beach to beach. The waves are influenced by the bottom and the bottom is changed by the waves. And since the waves arriving at a beach are highly variable in height, period, and direction, each wave creates a slightly different bottom configuration for the ones that come after it. The water level changes with the tide and the waves change as the storms at sea develop, shift position, and die out again. The result is that the sand bottom is forever being rearranged. Even in glass-sided wave channels where an endless number of waves, each exactly the same, can be produced, equilibrium is never reached; the sand continues to change as long as the wave machine is running.

Thus the waves change the sand at the same time the sand is changing the waves. First, consider the effect of the bottom on the waves as they break. It may make them plunge or spill.

Plunging breakers are the most impressive. Their principal characteristic is very rapid release of energy from a wave moving at high velocity. There is a sudden deficiency in water ahead of the wave which causes high-

velocity currents in the trough as the water rushes seaward to fill the cavity beneath the oncoming crest. When
there is not enough water to complete the wave form, the
water in the crest, attempting to complete its orbit, is
hurled ahead of its steep forward side and lands in the
trough. This curling mass of falling water will often en-
trap air and then, as the upper part of the wave collapses,
the air is compressed. When the compressed air finally
bursts through the watery cap, a geyser of water is hurled
into the air—sometimes over fifty feet.

If there is a strong offshore breeze, the thin crest of the
wave will be blown off as it plunges forward, leaving a
veil of rising spray behind to mark the path it has followed. This delicate tracery of spray has been likened by
poets to the "white manes of plunging horses." Anyone
who has observed such breakers, backlighted by a low
sun, will understand the comparison and agree that this
circumstance is worthy of poetic description.

To understand the reasons why breakers plunge calls
for a somewhat more scientific approach. The wave must
retain most of its energy right up to the moment of breaking. That is, there should be nothing, such as a rough bottom, a strong wind, or substantial currents, to make the
wave prematurely unstable. Any of these conditions will
degrade a wave's energy by slowing it down and warping
its orbits so that it breaks gradually rather than abruptly.
Thus, when a large clearly defined swell passes over a
steep smooth underwater slope of the proper depth on a
calm day, a perfect plunging breaker will result. If, however, the bottom is gently sloping and studded with rocky
irregularities, or if the approaching waves appear confused, a spilling breaker is more likely to be produced.

A spilling wave breaks slowly and without the violent
release of energy needed to fling the crest forward into

the trough ahead. Its crest merely tumbles down a more gently sloping forward side, sometimes over a considerable distance and lasting for several minutes. Therefore, spilling waves are much favored by novice surfers, who ride on the face of the wave, their boards doing much the same thing the tumbling white water is doing.

The famous surfboarding area at Waikiki, where surfers in outrigger canoes and on boards are frequently photographed against Diamond Head, is a fine place to observe perfect spilling breakers. There a very shallow gently-sloping coral reef extends for a mile outward from the beach. The tide range is very small so that almost all swell coming in from the Pacific is converted into low spilling breakers. The surfer can paddle out as far as he likes and be assured of a ride back at any time.

Most surf zones have larger tidal ranges and are underlain by shifting sand; instead of remaining the same as Waikiki does, their underwater topography is constantly changing. The result is that in most surf zones one can observe some combination of plunging and spilling breakers, and forms which are intermediate between the two. That is, the breaker plunges, but without sufficient momentum to hurl the water beyond the sloping forward side into the trough ahead. The falling curtain of water lands partway down the wave front and the breaker has an "intermediate section."

Some beaches have such a steeply sloping approach that a swell approaches the shore without being slowed or changed until the last possible moment. Then it will abruptly rise up and break directly on the beach face with astonishing violence. Usually these are plunging breakers.

In other areas the beach approach may shoal so gradually that the surf zone may be as much as a mile wide. On

the beaches of Oregon and Washington that have underwater slopes of about 1:100 (one foot vertical to one hundred feet horizontal) it is not unusual to have three lines
of breakers when the great winter storm waves arrive.
The outer line of breakers may be plunging, thirty feet
high, with sufficient violence to shake earthquake-measur-
ing instruments several miles inland. Having broken, they
will re-form and break twice more with decreasing violence as they cross a half mile of irregular shallows to
reach the shore.

The movement of broken waves in shallow water
creates another type of wave, the wave of translation.
This wave was first discovered and studied by J. Scott
Russell in the 1840s, when it was of much greater
scientific interest than at present. The name "solitary
wave" is now used by the mathematicians to describe this
phenomenon.

Two striking characteristics clearly differentiate the
wave of translation from the ordinary oscillatory waves
which we have been considering. First, the entire form of
this wave is above the undisturbed water level; that is, it
consists of a crest without an accompanying trough. Second, there is an actual translation of the water particles as
the wave form passes. An object floating in the water
would be carried a definite distance forward by a wave of
translation and come to rest, without exhibiting the corresponding backward motion observed in the wave of oscillation.

Russell found that the wave of translation is produced
by the sudden addition of a mass of water to a still-water
surface. When the oscillatory wave breaks, the water in
the broken crest falls onto the water surface in advance of
the oncoming wave, producing a wave of translation or a
step-shaped foamline which continues shoreward. Hence,

although this type of wave is nonexistent in the open sea, it becomes important in the shallow waters inside the breakers, where most oscillatory waves eventually are transformed into waves of translation.

These waves travel at the velocity $\sqrt{gd}$ with the unusual variation that, since the wave height is large compared to the depth of water, the two are added to give d. The velocity therefore is related to the water depth, and when there are several waves of translation moving shoreward at the same time, the later ones move faster and tend to overtake the ones ahead because they are traveling in deeper water on top of their predecessors.

SURF BEAT

One of the wave characteristics most evident to an observer standing on the shore is the variability in height of the breakers. A series of a dozen or so low waves will approach and break. Then there will be a group of several high waves—usually three or four—then another relatively quiescent period.

Sometimes this variability is caused by the arrival of two sets of swell (from two storms) of nearly the same period at the same time. When the crests of the two wave trains almost coincide, they reinforce each other and produce waves higher than those of either set. When the waves are almost completely out of phase and the crests in one train coincide with troughs in the others, the resulting waves are small. As the phase relationship changes, a pattern emerges like that shown in Figure 64. The envelope of these wave traces (shown dotted) has a wave form and a period or "beat frequency"—usually two to three minutes—but it is not a true long-period wave.

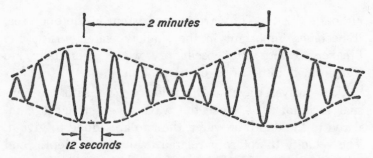

FIG. 64. Surf beat envelope. Two groups of waves, each about twelve-second period, combine to reinforce and cancel each other, causing a "beat" with a period of two minutes.

The effect of groups of breakers of alternating height is to raise and lower the average water level in the surf zone. The rise is somewhat exaggerated because the volume of water transported into the surf zone is proportional to the square of the breaker height.

Anyone wading in shallow water notices that a rapid succession of high breakers temporarily raises the water level. John Isaacs says that he has seen variations of sea level of as much as sixteen feet at Twin Rocks, Oregon, in very heavy weather caused by surf beat. The waves of translation resulting from the large breakers transport a considerable volume of water shoreward on the surface faster than it can escape seaward again along the bottom.

The consequence of this process, according to Walter Munk, whose name is conspicuously identified with surf beat, is that the shoreline tends to act as a source of new waves which return about one percent of the incoming wave energy seaward as true long-period waves. These newly-formed waves resulting from surf beat move seaward and along the coast and may be the cause of surging in harbors.

UNDERTOW AND RIP CURRENTS

One of the most ubiquitous myths of the seashore is
that of undertow. The very word frightens many would-
be surf swimmers, and some beaches have signs which
say, "Dangerous Undertow, Swim at Your Own Risk."
Even at beaches without signs, rumors of undertow often
have been passed down for several generations without
anyone's having experimented to determine the facts.

The author cannot define undertow, but timid souls
and uninformed lifeguards assert it is a mysterious current that flows seaward from the beach along the bottom
and "sucks (or tows) swimmers under."

There are currents flowing in the surf zone and there
are other water motions which may cause trouble for
swimmers, but they hardly fit the description given. Consider them one at a time. Orbital currents in the waves
perform circles equal to the height of the waves with the
period of the waves. A swimmer in waves performs these
circles as the water does; half the time these move him
down to seaward, the other half up to landward. After
each wave passes he is about where he started. If he gets
in the trough of a breaker he will indeed be sucked under
it, and as it breaks he will be upended and propelled
landward, possibly to be cast up on the sand.

The foamlines of broken water (waves of translation)
do transport water landward that must somehow return
seaward as a current. If the beach has a reasonably even
slope inside the bar, there may be a return current on the
bottom. But in order for the wave of translation to endure, the water must be quite shallow—perhaps two or
three feet. So in most circumstances a swimmer could
stand on the bottom and, even if knocked down by the

water moving landward, he certainly would not be carried out to sea along the bottom by the relatively small return current.

On very steep beaches where large waves break
directly on the beach, the uprush and backrush may be
violent surges of water as much as two feet deep. These
are quite capable of knocking a man down and rolling
him back down the beach into the path of the next
breaker, where he could be mauled and tossed about by
several waves before he could regain his footing. In such
circumstances usually the best escape is to swim seaward
and reach the calm water outside the breakers—it is only
a few feet away. Once there he can select the right wave
and ride it in, sliding far up the beach on the uprush, digging into the sand at the high point and holding there
until the backrush draws the water away, then scram-
bling to high ground before the next uprush. This maneuver can be real sport, though it is a bit dangerous. However, steep beaches with high surf are rare; certainly
there are none in the usual resort areas. But this minor
hazard does not fit the popular description of undertow.

One time on the beach at Carmel, California, a popular
swimming resort, I was discussing the question of undertow with a group of bathers who insisted that it was
"very strong" at a certain point they indicated. The sand
at Carmel is very white, the water clear; the breakers on
this occasion were about seven feet high and a hundred
feet offshore. We conducted the following experiment. A
packet of life-jacket marker-dye was tied to a cobblestone
and heaved into the water some fifty feet from shore in
the supposed zone of undertow. After the stone reached
bottom, we pulled the dye-release tab, which had been
tied to a long string. It was plain to the watchers on the
beach face that as the bright green dye spread, the water

it marked swayed with each passing wave but showed not the slightest tendency to flow as a current in any direction. This demonstration settled the point at the time, but the undertow warning signs probably are still there, as well as on many other public beaches where they have no more meaning. Such signs are well intentioned and may warn the swimmer of real danger, but they do not tell him what to do. For this I have a suggestion at the end of this section.

There is one form of current in the surf zone that can be dangerous to an inexperienced swimmer. This is the rip current, first described by Professor F. P. Shepard, of the Scripps Institution of Oceanography. The rip is also of importance in beach processes, for it is responsible for some of the strange forms that the underwater parts of a beach may take.

Rip currents are formed when waves break on a shallow underwater bar in rapid succession. The water they hurl shoreward in foamlines cannot easily return seaward along the bottom but "piles up" inside the bar. This excess water is supported there slightly above sea level by the continuous addition of water from more breakers. When the height of water is sufficient, a current starts to flow seaward across the lowest part of the bar. As it moves, it erodes a channel and from then on there is a continuous flow of water called a rip current. The channel may be narrow and the water velocity as high as four feet a second. Rips are supplied with water by feeder currents inside the bar, which collect the water from the foamlines and flow laterally along the beach, as shown in Figure 65. Out beyond the breaker zone, the channel abruptly widens and the strength of the current diminishes. Often it forms a large slow vortex.

Because the depth of water is greater in the rip channel

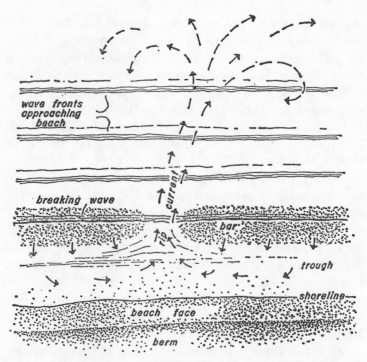

wave fronts approaching beach

breaking wave

current

rip

bar

trough

shoreline

beach face

berm

FIG. 65. Rip currents are created when waves break on a shallow bar, making waves of translation which raise the water level inside the bar. The excess water then flows seaward as a swift and narrow rip current in a channel of its own making, ending in a vortex outside the surf.

than over the bar on either side, waves rarely break in the channel. Moreover, a current flowing against the waves has the effect of increasing wave steepness. The crests become prematurely unstable and a small spilling breaker may result, or, more likely, a large number of short steep waves will develop that look something like wind chop. The result is that rip currents usually can be seen from the beach, especially if one can observe the surf zone from a vantage point.

The fact that large waves are less likely to break in the rip may actually encourage swimmers to choose the zone of high currents. Anyone who finds himself being carried outward should not try swimming shoreward against the strong current but should swim to one side or the other— usually a short distance—and get out of the current to where the effect of the breakers will be to carry him shoreward again.

The following thoughts may be helpful to would-be surf-swimmers, especially to those who do not consider themselves to be very strong swimmers. The surf can be a dangerous place, for breaking waves produce sudden violent forces and swift currents. Therefore, before you plunge in and eagerly try to swim out through the breakers, it is well to take a few minutes to look the situation over. Breakers vary considerably in size, but the high ones often come in groups about three minutes apart. So stand at a proper vantage point and just watch what's happening for, say, five minutes.

Watch the waves break—that's where the bars are. And don't forget that these bars are shallow; you may be able to stand on the bottom in water only waist-deep well out beyond places that are over your head. Generally the lighter-colored foaming water is shallower than the darker water, and it may mark a place where you can rest for a while.

If one is studying waves from the shore, or must decide whether or not to venture out into the surf in a boat, it is useful to be able in advance to judge the height of the breakers with accuracy. This is easily done, even if the line of breakers is well offshore. Simply stand on the beach face at such a level that the top of the breaker is exactly in line between your eye and the horizon. Then, as shown in Figure 66, the vertical distance between eye

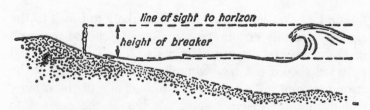

FIG. 66. When the observer's eye is aligned with the top of the breaker and the horizon, the vertical distance between the eye and the backrush is equal to the height of the breaker.

and backrush curl (which is about at the same level as the average sea surface) is equal to the height of the breaker. You may be surprised how high the larger breakers really are, but it is a lot better to be surprised on the beach than in their midst.

So check the height of the breakers, look for rip currents, and forget undertow.

SURVEYING IN THE SURF

In 1945 I had never seen the ocean, but I joined the World War II Waves Project of the University of California at Berkeley. The project had been set up to develop scientific means of determining the characteristics of beaches and of the waves that would make it difficult for landing craft to approach enemy-held beaches. Studying the surf was our business. Later, when the war was over, the project continued, its objectives becoming more broadly scientific.

M. P. O'Brien, Dean of Engineering and a member of the Beach Erosion Board, directed the work and, almost on the day I joined the project, ordered our field party north to study the waves and beaches of Northern California, Oregon, and Washington. His theory was, "If you can work there, you can work anywhere." Subsequent experience certainly proved him correct.

So we set out for the northern beaches, timing our arrival to coincide with that of the great waves from the winter storms. John Isaacs, an old hand along the coast, was party leader; I was his engineer assistant. Field-party equipment included two amphibious six-wheeled trucks called Dukws (and pronounced "ducks"), a collection of aerial cameras, walkie-talkie radios, and a Catalina PBY flying boat.

Dukws are fascinating vehicles, thirty-two feet long and eight feet wide, whose top rises ten feet above the roadway. On the highway they are formidable and even the log trucks will give them a fair share of the road, but in the surf they seem no more than a chip of wood. In the water they move by means of a screw propeller, and fortunately they turned out to be probably the world's best surf craft, or else I would not be around to write about them.

John and I each drove a Dukw up the coast—the regular drivers were to join us later—and I well remember on the bleak day we approached Eureka that John stopped his Dukw and motioned for me to join him. He pointed out across Humboldt Bay and the sandspit separating bay from ocean to a sort of white froth on the horizon a couple of miles away where an occasional geyser shot up. "Some of those breakers must be thirty feet high—plunging. Look at them explode!" Then, in a matter-of-fact way, "That's where we're going to work."

Since I had never seen a wave before, much less the Pacific Ocean, I did not quit on the spot but accepted this proposal as a normal part of university research. Thirty-foot breakers sounded like a reasonable size for an ocean as large as the Pacific. Now it seems that even this modest description should at least have generated in my mind a picture of a tumbling wall of water higher than a two-story house breaking into a foaming mass that would compare favorably with the tumult below the spillway at Grand Coulee Dam, but it did not. Having spent my previous working life in mines and tunnels, I was not quite sure what a breaker was.

We set up an observation station at Table Bluff lighthouse, a hundred feet above the beach, and began systematically photographing the waves twice a day and noting their characteristics. Square frames covered with white canvas were anchored into the beach above high tide at thousand-foot intervals. These markers would give scale to the aerial photos and establish the survey lines that we would run out through the surf. On days when the surf was high we would make simultaneous radio-fired photos of the surf zone from the flying boat overhead and from the cliff. Then, when the breakers on the outer bar were low (meaning that most of them were under fifteen feet high), we would survey the bottom along lines extending out from the air markers. The object of all this was, of course, to establish the relationship between the waves and the underwater topography and give us data for future determination, by aerial photography alone, of the nature of the approaches to enemy-held beaches.

The method of surveying the underwater part of the beach was this: We would set up pairs of range boards a hundred feet apart perpendicular to the shoreline so that the Dukw driver could keep the craft on line as it moved slowly landward along the survey line. Down the beach a thousand feet, at a point making a right angle with the range boards, a surveyor's transit was set up to measure readily the angle to the Dukw along the hypotenuse of the triangle. At frequent intervals a leadsman standing in the waist of the Dukw would call, "Mark," into the radio transmitter and heave a lead-weighted sounding line into water off the bow. As the Dukw passed the lead he would hold the line vertically and read off the depth of water beneath the trough of the wave. To this depth he would add the one third of the estimated height of the wave about to break over him and call the total into the microphone.

The transit man, following the progress of the Dukw through the telescope, would, on hearing "Mark" via the radio and seeing the lead splash, read the angle. An assistant at his side would record angle and depth. This established depths at a series of points along a line, so that we could plot a profile of the sand surface beneath the waves. Figure 71 in Chapter XI shows one of hundreds of profiles that were made in this fashion. Since the beach constantly readjusted itself, there was no end to the work.

These jobs were divided in such a manner that Isaacs always ran the transit and Bascom was the leadsman on these sorties through the surf. Somehow, in innocence and ignorance, I was persuaded that fifteen-foot breakers smashing down on a thirty-two-foot tin boat were nothing to be disturbed about. In reality, of course, we often underestimated the height and unexpectedly encountered breakers over twenty feet high. At these times our friends on the beach offered many helpful suggestions by radio.

Perhaps when the Coast Guardsmen from Humboldt Bay lifeboat station served notice that we were working at our own risk and could not count on their help if we got into trouble, I should have been more wary. They obviously were astonished that anyone would start out into what they considered to be a raging surf for any reason

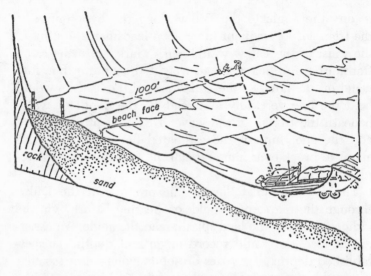

FIG. 67. Surveying in the surf. Dukw is overtaken by a breaker as it moves landward along a course marked by range poles. Man in Dukw heaves lead and calls "mark" into radio followed by measured depth. Transit man on beach reads angle; an assistant seated by the radio receiver records both depth and distance.

short of emergency life-saving. But they had the advantage of appreciating the risk, and several years had passed before it dawned on me that we were doing anything daring. We were the first, and to this day probably the only ones, foolhardy enough to take this much interest in the sand beneath the winter surf on northern Pacific beaches.

There was many a close call when a Dukw would almost get sideways to a breaker or have the canvas cover ripped off and the supporting ribs caved in. Dukws have no flotation compartments. If one went down, there was precious little chance—the outer breakers being more than half a mile from shore and the water temperature in the forties—that either the driver or the leadsman would make it back alive. Even though we always wore life jackets, our heavy clothes and the wild turbulence would quickly have exhausted us. On one occasion a breaker heaved the Dukw onto the beach face on its side, wheels pointing out to sea, throwing me clear. The next wave set it back on its wheels without damage. Somehow, no one was ever hurt. We were young and lucky, and in return for the risks we had the fun of challenging the breakers.

In order to "run a line of soundings" it usually was necessary to get out through two major lines of breakers; often we would smash head on into half a dozen big breakers and be carried backward before a series of smaller waves would arrive and let us cross the bar. At each breaker the Dukw collided with the mass of solid green water moving (relatively) at twenty miles an hour; at the moment of impact each tiny leak in the driver's cockpit was like a firehose turned on the men inside. Often the glass in the windshield would crack or the canvas rip; we nearly always lost the windshield wipers and ended up with the pumps furiously throwing out a stream of water the size of a man's leg. Though each wave washed over us, the Dukw would shudder and rise above the surface; with persistence we would get through. At such times a good strong rip current was appreciated. When these currents existed, they carved channels through the bars, and the water would be too deep for all but the largest swell to break. If the Dukw could get in a rip it had a much better chance of crossing the bar without serious pounding; besides, its speed was increased by that of the current. Amid waves breaking on all sides these passages were hard to identify. We would station a lookout on the bluff who could see the whole surf zone and, by means of the walkie-talkie radios, guide

the Dukw into the rip channels, much as aircraft pilots
are "talked" through low clouds in ground-controlled-
approach. Or sometimes, on approaching the outer line of
breakers, we would rest in the quiet zone between the
bars and watch the big ones go over for a while—occasionally deciding that the sand could just as well be
surveyed on another day. The drivers knew that any serious mistake would be their last one, and it was not unusual for them to quit "for good" when the wheels touched
safely down on shore. Then we would talk it over and decide not to sally forth into such large breakers again. Next
morning the drivers would be on the job early, ready to
go.

Surfboarding on a Dukw is great sport. I well remember bucking out through the surf just south of the
Columbia River entrance, finally getting beyond the outermost breakers and then sitting there for nearly an hour
getting up nerve enough to run the breakers. As a trough
passed, we could look down a dark watery valley that
disappeared into the fog in each direction; then we would
be lifted up on the next crest. From this temporary vantage point we could see a dozen more huge crests approaching, and looking landward see the back side of
lines of frightening breakers. They were all about the
same—nearly twenty feet high. Finally we would pick
what we thought were slightly lower waves and make a
run for it. Usually our judgment of height was wishful
thinking, but for excitement it beats a roller coaster any
day: full speed ahead at six knots until you are overtaken
by a wall of water as high as a house and moving three
times your speed. The trick is to time the run so that the
biggest wave breaks just barely ahead of you; then you
can ride in atop the breaking crest, crossing the bar just in

time to get beyond reach of the next wave. (It's a good idea, but it's hard to put into practice.)

As the wave overtakes the craft, there is a sickening moment when the stern begins to lift rapidly and the driver fights to remain square with the waves (encountering a wave sideways would mean disaster). Then as speed picks up, the craft tilts forward at thirty degrees or so and buries its bow until there is green water across the windshield. The entire craft seems about to flip end-over-end and you think, "Why did I ever get myself in a place like this? What a fool to go to sea in a truck!"

But then the wave begins to pass under, and the buoyancy of the forward end lifts the bow until it is a level platform projecting out ten to fifteen feet above the slick green water surface of the trough below. The forward wheels and axle hang down so that the rushing water of the breaker crests beats against them from behind and carries this awkward looking truck-boat forward like a surfboard. Now you are flying, perched on a wave making fifteen knots, water boiling on all sides—an exhilarating ride. Taking soundings has become second nature; you heave the lead, estimate the still-water level, call the depth.

Soon the wave sets the craft into the quiet water and continues on, leaving the Dukw to continue at its own speed, still surveying. There is another line of breakers ahead, but these are only ten feet high and now seem tame. Inside at last, the Dukw rides easily and safely on the leading edge of a foamline sometimes five or six feet high. A foamline is a boiling mass of aerated white water; as the air escapes, the mass loses height and only a foot or two of green water reaches the beach face. Once through the inner breakers, the driver engages the wheels, and as

the water shoals, the tires touch gently as weight is transferred gradually from the buoyancy of the hull to the
truck's springs. Finally, motor roaring and gears grinding,
the craft climbs out of the water and lurches to a stop at
the backrush to mark the end of the run; then up the
beach face, a truck once more. With tire pressure controlled from the cab, a Dukw can operate in the softest
sand. Happy to be safe ashore, the crew open the drain
plugs to let out the water added to our bilges by the
breakers. They check by radio with the transit party
down on the beach to see if all the data were properly received and recorded. "Okay? Now we'll run the next line
a thousand feet down the beach."

Although this method of surveying in the surf may
seem crude, we would often repeat lines to check on our-
selves; even in the rough surf there was rarely a disa-
greement of more than a foot. Since an echo sounder will
not work amid bubbles and turbulence, the old lead-line
method seems to be the only technique for obtaining such
data.

After several years of almost daily surf operations
Isaacs and I wrote a thick pamphlet which became
known as the "Dukw report." It went into considerable
detail about our experiences with these wonderful vehicles, including the fact that we lost two in the surf and
one that rolled off a mountain cliff in Oregon and plunged
two hundred feet into the sea. A result of that report
about our operations in heavy surf was that the U. S.
Coast Guard—which had previously regarded these tin-
hulled trucks with some suspicion—began using them for
surfboats at their life-saving stations.

The big breakers are so far from shore that we were
never able to get very good pictures of the Dukws in really large surf. Photographs of the surf zone at Table Bluff

taken with a long-focal-length aerial camera show the
Dukw a mere speck in a breaker over half a mile from
shore. In the summer we worked south, often in the Monterey Bay area. There, while training a new driver for the
much rougher northern work, we obtained Plate 25 of a
Dukw surfboarding on a modest twelve-foot breaker.

After five years spent largely in observing and recording waves, studying and surveying beaches, and photographing the entire U.S. Pacific Coast from ground and
air, I recorded the status of the coast as of 1950 in a three-
volume tome, *Shoreline Atlas of the Pacific Coast of the
U. S.* Many years hence, when the forces of erosion have
had time to accomplish notable changes in the coast, this
book should form a valuable basis for comparison.

SURFING

Captain James Cook seems to have been the first West-
erner to observe and record the sport of surfing. In 1777,
in Tahiti, Cook watched a native paddling a small canoe
toward "a place where the swell began to take its rise."
Then, while "watching its motion attentively," he "pad-
dled before it with great quickness until it overtook him
. . . with sufficient force to carry his canoe before it,
without passing underneath." The canoe was then "carried along at the same swift rate as the wave, till it landed
him on the beach." Most astonishing, the man then pad-
dled back out to sea "in search of another swell."

Two years later Captain Cook was in Hawaii, and one
of his lieutenants wrote that the natives indulged in this
curious amusement when the surf was at its utmost
height. Then, after a pause that writer Arthur Klein calls
the "dark days," surfing began to be revived in about

1900, primarily by George Freeth and Duke Kahana-moku. The Duke set up the first surfing club at Waikiki; Freeth restored the lost art of standing up on a surfboard, and in 1907 he brought the sport to Redondo Beach, California.

Surfing was, and still mainly is, a Pacific sport, although now there are surfers all over the world. Warm subtropical waters that have a reasonably good chance of long-period swell are most favored. Surfers have, however, been observed to wait hour after hour for a wave in weather that would make a brass monkey shiver.

Usually the objective is to ride "in the tube" or to go as far as possible on a single ride, preferably with a combination of speed and maneuvering. This requires a carefully designed board, an ideal set of waves, and a lot of know-how derived from practice and experience. The board, which must be of suitable size for the rider and the conditions, should also be smooth and have the right wetted area as well as the proper fineness (length to width ratio) to maximize the dynamic supporting force while minimizing the friction and form drag. The surfer must contribute to this process by putting his weight at the right spot on the board to adjust the shape and size of the wetted area.

The best waves for surfing are plunging breakers in which the end of the curl (breaking section) is progressing sideways along the wave front, somewhere between one and two times as fast as any point on the wave is approaching the beach. The fact that the breaker is plunging means that the surfer has a wider choice of slopes. Generally, the steeper the wave front at the point of contact with the board, the faster the ride.

Dr. Terry Hendricks, a physicist and inveterate California surfer to whom I am indebted for some of these views, has calculated that for very tubular waves the optimal slope for surfing is about 57°. This was found to agree with the positioning of top surfers measured on photographs taken at Hawaii's Bonzai Pipeline. These large plunging breakers can move at 18 feet per second or more. The surfer, however, moves faster because he is sliding sideways across the face of the wave (often just ahead of the sideways-moving curl). If that motion is half again as fast as the wave velocity, then the surfer is moving at 32 feet per second, or about 22 miles an hour.

On some large waves, rough measurements of the surfer's speed have yielded values of 25 to 30 mph. At these speeds, about one horsepower is being dissipated in drag forces.

Some features of a good surfing area are:

1. It should frequently receive swell with periods of at least 9 seconds and preferably longer.

2. The breakers should be of the plunging type so that the face of the wave is sufficiently steep to provide good board speed.

3. The lateral speed of breaking—the sideways extension of the curl along the crest—should be between one and two times the onshore speed of the wave.

4. Any wind should be light and preferably offshore.

5. The shape of the bottom should be fixed (by a rocky reef, for example, instead of sand) so that the favorable breaking condition is not changed by the waves. It should also have an even slope or a set of reefs that can maintain wave shape over a wide range of tidal heights and swell variability.

6. The beach face should absorb and dissipate the

wave that reaches it, or the shoreline should be slanted so that no significant wave reflections enter the surfing area.

7. A deep channel, with an outflowing current, is desirable for paddling out beyond the breakers.

8. The bottom should not have dangerous features such as sharp rocks or jagged coral, and the shoreline should not be so rough and rocky that lost boards are damaged or surfers endangered.

9. An "indicator" break, farther offshore, can be a helpful warning of the approach of a set of large waves.

10. Convenient sighting points onshore are helpful in relocating the best takeoff position.

11. The area should be remote, to reduce the number of surfers (according to an anonymous expert).

Few surfing spots have all of these features, but it is obvious that quite a number have enough to make riding the breakers an increasingly popular sport.

Where are the best surfing areas? Probably they have not all been found or publicized; in any case it would be hard to get agreement on the order of listing them. There would, however, be no argument that the following areas are all near the top:

The north coast of Oahu in the Hawaiian Islands, which faces into the open North Pacific, is rarely without large waves in the winter. It has several great surfing spots including the Bonzai Pipeline, Sunset Beach, Waimea, and Haleiwa. On the west coast of Oahu the surf is generally lower, but when it's "up," the place to go is Makaha and, on the south side, Ala Moana.

Off Southern California, very large swell is rare because

much of the coast faces south and all of it is protected to some extent by the offshore islands and underwater hills. In addition, it is farther from the major swell-generating areas than the Hawaiian beaches. However, there are "windows" between the islands where the North Pacific swell leaks through. At that time, Rincon and Lunada Bay near Los Angeles, and Rights-and-Lefts as well as Cojo, near Point Conception, are all popular. In the summer, occasional long-period southern swell from storms south of the equator or hurricanes off Central America and Mexico create superlative waves at Wind and Sea or Black's Beach at La Jolla or Malibu near Los Angeles. Then San Onofre at San Clemente, with its super-slow break, is a favorite with old surfers.

The famous "wedge" at Newport Beach, California, is seldom ridden with surfboards, but it gets a lot of body-surfers, belly boarders, and knee boarders.

Northern California offers a cool climate for surfing. But for ardent surfers, Steamer Lane near Santa Cruz creates great enthusiasm.

In Australia, Burleigh Heads, Dee Why, and Shark Island are very popular spots. Champion surfers hang out at K-108 off Peru; Niijima Island off Japan; or Jeffreys Bay, Durban's Bay-of-Plenty, or Nahoon Reef in South Africa.

There are many more great spots that remain unnamed —carefully guarded secrets.

It is also possible to ride the breakers a thousand miles inland in an artificial 2.5-acre lagoon called Big Surf at Tempe, Arizona. Big Surf replicates a short section of an ocean beach with perfect five-foot-high spilling breakers. From the point where the waves form in water about nine feet deep, the surfers can ride about three hundred feet to a sandy beach with palm trees.

The generator, devised by Phil Dexter, is of interest. It consists mainly of a large rectangular reservoir 47 feet high that holds 500,000 gallons of water. Pumps steadily fill the reservoir; every 50 seconds a line of gates is raised that releases some 70,000 gallons of water (270 cubic meters) in about 2 seconds from the base of the generator. As the water squirts out along the bottom of the reservoir it is deflected upward by a concrete baffle in the bottom of the lagoon to form impulsively generated waves. In about 75 feet a well-formed breaker is available to the inland surfers.

In the world of the surfer, the words used by scientists to describe waves approaching a beach are replaced by an entirely different sort of jargon, just as descriptive. Here are some examples that may help a wave researcher communicate with a surfer on a lonely beach.

Long crested waves approaching shore are *lines*. If the swell is *lined up* with the proper orientation for the *break*, this is desirable because the surfer can get a long smooth *ride*. Long fast-breaking lines are *walls*; and if the wave breaks so fast the surfer cannot keep up with the *end*, he does not *make* the wave. Surfers wait outside the usual break for a group of above-average waves to come along. When these waves are exceptionally large, they form an *outside set* and surfers in the normal *takeoff* (starting) spot may be *caught inside*. If there is no place to escape from the *white water* or *soup* from those *heavies*, that's a *closeout*.

Spilling waves with some white water and inadequate steepness of *face* are *mushy*, and irregular crests caused by cross swell are *peaky*. Plunging waves begin to break with a *pitch-out* when the *lip* of the wave starts to move faster than its main mass of water. Then the wave *curls* to form a *hollow* or *tube* that the surfer may enter. If he's trapped there he is *locked in,* and if he is caught by a wave or free-falls from the top, that's *over the falls.*

When a breaker changes from plunging to spilling, or "the curl" ceases to progress, the wave *backs off.* Local wind waves, not parallel to the breaking swell, can make the surface *bumpy,* and if the wind makes surfing unpleasant the surf is *blown out.*

As for maneuvers, a fundamental technique is to be *driving,* which means optimal trim and positioning to produce the maximum lateral speed. If the ride is good the surfer is *stoked.*

One of the effects of too late a takeoff or improper weight positioning is that the board can *pearl* or dive beneath the surface.

A *bottom turn* comes after the surfer slides straight down the face of the wave to gain maximum speed and then turns to use this speed in moving along the face of the wave. Reversing direction on the face of the wave is a *cut-back,* and if the surfer heads up toward the lip and then turns down the face of the wave to beat the lip as it starts to come over, that's *off the lip.* But if the surfer delays that top turn and follows the lip instead of preceding it and then ultimately overtakes it and gets out in front of the broken portion of the wave, that's a *re-entry.*

Finally, a surfer who loses his nerve in the face of a large breaker may *bail out* by diving to the bottom. A spill is a *wipeout* or *down the mine,* and the surfer *takes gas.* If the wave does not justify bailing out, the surfer may *straighten out* by turning toward shore and *proning out* the wave by dropping down on the board. If the wave walls up but allows time for a turn, he can *kick out* by abruptly turning up the face of the wave and shooting over the top (often parting from the board in the process).

Dr. Rick Grigg, a surfing champion in Hawaii, who in his other life is a professor of oceanography, describes the sport more as a way of life. He comments: "Surfing has become extremely popular in recent years. The number of surfers has multiplied so greatly that certain beaches are literally overrun with hordes of *gremmies* or *surf rats*. Their image is well known: blond long hair, baggy trunks, an old jalopy stacked with beat-up boards and a covey of adoring surf bunnies. For the more serious surfer, a life of surfing is an end in itself. Surfers often view the rest of the world as *up-tight* or *out of it*. They live in a world of *good vibes* and being *turned on*. Their life can be *far out*, *too much*, and *out of sight*—at least when the waves are *up*. And when they're not surfers, they lead a *mellow* existence *tuned in* to all that which is most natural. Their ticket to freedom in a world of special fun is to catch a wave."

PLATE 40. There are few more fearsome moments for a sailor than encountering breakers on the Columbia River Bar. This 1912 photo from a tug (note tow line cutting through the crest) shows the start of a breaker that was probably over twenty-five feet high. *O. Barton/Williamsons Marine Salon*

PLATE 41. Miami Beach, Florida, consists mainly of large hotels and apartment buildings built on an offshore bar. The beach front is laced with groins, and although these are not very helpful at holding sand, three million visitors come to this beach every year. *Miami Beach Tourist Development Authority*

PLATE 42. The beach at Carmel, California, with the **Pebble** Beach golf course beyond. This beach was studied intensively by Mike O'Brien and the author because it is a closed system (no sand leaves or enters Carmel Bay). *Willard Bascom*

PLATE 43. The two small berms in this pebble beach on the French Riviera were created by brief summer storms. *Willard Bascom*

PLATE 44. Chesil Beach in southwest England faces Lyme Bay on the English Channel. The crest of the berm, fourteen meters above mean sea level, was produced by the storms for which this area is famous. *National Environmental Research Council*

PLATE 45. The black sand beach at Pirae, Tahiti, is made of particles of volcanic rock transported to the sea by an adjacent stream. This beach is protected by an offshore coral reef. Elsewhere on the island there are beaches of white coral sand. *Willard Bascom*

PLATE 46. Where the Namib desert meets the South Atlantic the sand dunes rise hundreds of feet from the sea and extend over fifty miles inland. This area is known as the Skeleton Coast because it is virtually impossible for shipwrecked mariners to make their way to safety. *Willard Bascom*

PLATE 47. Large waves from a Santa Ana (easterly storm) break over buildings along the waterfront in the usually placid yacht harbor of Avalon, Catalina Island, California. *Gene's Photo Shop, Avalon*

PLATE 48. Long Beach, New Jersey, after the great storm of March 7–8, 1962. *U. S. Army Corps of Engineers*

XI

Beaches

ALONG THE BOUNDARY BETWEEN LAND AND SEA THE SOLID underlying rock is covered with a layer of rock fragments. These fragments range in size from fine sand to large cobbles, in thickness from a few inches to hundreds of feet, in color from clear white to opaque black. These are beach materials. Every coastal dweller in the world is quite sure he knows what a beach is like. Yet if you were to ask, you would find totally different opinions, and all derived from local experience.

BEACH MATERIALS

The open-sea beaches that border much of the United States from Cape Cod south along Jersey and the Carolinas to Florida, and along the California coast south of Point Conception are for the most part composed of coarse, light-colored sand, produced by the weathering of granitic rocks into their two main constituents, quartz and feldspar. Generally these beaches are steep-faced and coarse-grained. Since they contain our most popular beach resorts, many Americans tend to think that they fairly represent the world's beaches. But hundreds of miles of beach along the Oregon-Washington coast are quite different. There the sand is fine-grained and dark gray-green in color, derived from the weathering of basalt, which forms beaches that are wide, flat, and often hard as a racetrack. Much of the Florida coast is equally hard and fine-grained, but it comes from the disintegration of coral.

On the other hand, the beach at Cannes in southern France is largely composed of uncomfortable pebbles, and much of the English coast is lined with small flat stones called shingle. In fact, the word beach seems to have been the ancient word for a shingle shore.

Many beaches of Labrador and Argentina are composed of large cobbles. Those of Lower California are composed of two materials, a flat sandy portion that is exposed only at low tide, while above and behind the sand great cobble steps called ramparts rise to a height of thirty feet or more. On Tahiti, if you live on the windward side of the island, you think it is natural for a beach to be made of black volcanic sand. But if you live on the other side, where the wide coral reef furnishes the beach material, it seems reasonable for beaches to be blindingly white. In fact, beaches can be made of nearly any material that is present in quantity; rock fragments are not necessarily required. At Fort Bragg, California, a small pocket-beach consists entirely of old tin cans washed in from the city's nearby oceanic dump and arranged by the waves into the usual beach forms, as though to prove that the laws of beach physics cover all possibilities.

Thus, although beaches vary widely in appearance and composition, the principles that govern their behavior are the same, and for convenience here all beach materials will be called sand. The accompanying table shows the actual sizes of the particles and may help the reader to visualize the beaches being discussed relative to those within his own experience. Several other factors, including the shape and density of the particles, are of interest but they are of secondary importance.

A beach responds with great sensitivity to the forces that act upon it—waves, currents, winds. It is a deposit of material in transit, either alongshore or off- and onshore. The important thought in the definition is that of motion, for beaches are ever-changing, restless armies of sand particles, always on the move. Most sand movement occurs underwater, the result of waves and wave-caused currents that organize the particles into familiar forms. But the motion of a beach before the waves, even when huge quantities of sand shift in a single day, may not be noticed by a casual observer. The short-term changes are usually imperceptible.

Watch the waves break on a sandy beach; the water runs up the beach face a short way; some of it sinks in, the rest slides back down as the backwash. The moving water carries a film of sand in each direction, and the question is, what is the net effect? Is sand being added to or subtracted from the beach face?

For any small number of waves no one can give a positive answer; each wave is slightly different in height or velocity and may either add or take away a few grains of sand. But overnight, or after a week, the net effect of the waves may be easily observable. Now you notice that a rock is covered (or uncovered) by sand; you see a small vertical cliff cut into the berm or a newly added ridge of sand along the beach face; a little way offshore the waves break in a different place, indicating that the bar has shifted. The sand feels different beneath your feet—a new layer of sand, not yet compacted by the waves, is soft to walk on. These are evidence of beach motion; whenever there are waves there is constant shifting, constant readjustment.

This chapter deals only with the offshore-onshore motion of sand. Littoral transport, or the flow of a stream of tumbling particles of sand alongshore under the influence of wave-caused currents, is described in Chapter XII.

TABLE VIII

SIZES OF BEACH MATERIALS

(U. S. CORPS OF ENGINEERS STANDARD)

Millimeters

Boulders	Larger than 200		(over 8 inches)
Cobbles	76	to 200	(3 to 8 inches)
Gravel			
Coarse	79	to 76	(includes shingle
Fine	5	to 19	and pebbles)
Sand			
Coarse	2	to 5	
Medium	0.4	to 2	
Fine	0.07	to 0.4	
Silt or clay	Less than .074		(barely visible to naked eye)

SAND MOTION

The principal beach forms are shown in Figure 68, which is a generalized profile of the conditions that prevail in winter and in summer on many beaches exposed to the ocean. Remember that our definition of beaches includes all the sand in motion above and below water out to a depth of about thirty feet. Above water there is usually a nearly horizontal terrace of sand brought ashore by the waves: the berm. Below water are elongated mounds of sand that parallel the beach: called bars, or sometimes longshore bars.

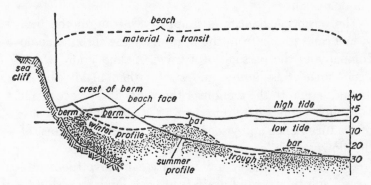

FIG. 68. Generalized profile through an intermediate slope beach showing seasonal changes in the distribution of the sand.

In summer the berm is low and wide. To the layperson it *is* the beach—the observable sand on which beach-goers sunbathe and frolic. At that time the underwater profile is likely to be smooth and barless.

In winter the berm is higher and narrower, as most of the sand moves underwater to create the bars. The reason for the shift is the change in wave action with the season. The large waves that come from winter storms cut the berm back; the small waves of summer replace it again. If the amount of sand involved is constant, as it is on a beach between two rocky headlands, the entire beach motion is merely an exchange of sand between berm and bar.

Therefore the study of beaches that are closed systems is concerned principally with the questions of why the

sand moves in each direction, which waves are responsible, and what shapes and slopes the sand takes. There is
a rather delicate balance between the forces that tend to
bring sand ashore and those that move it seaward. The
position of the main mass of sand is a measure of the
dominant forces.

The basic mechanism is simply the lifting of the individual sand grains from the bottom by the turbulence accompanying the passage of a wave. A sand grain weighs
little, since it is lighter underwater than in air (by an
amount equal to the weight of the water it displaces) and
not much energy is required to lift it. Moreover, because
of the turbulence and viscosity of the water, the grains settle slowly. While grains are in suspension, or falling
freely, currents of very low velocity can move them sidewise. Each time a sand grain is lifted it lands in a slightly
different location. Uncounted millions of sand grains are
picked up and relocated by every wave, and the beach
constantly shifts position. They need not move very far
each time, for there are some eight thousand waves a day.
Sand grains that move a tenth of an inch per wave could
migrate seventy feet in a day. Of course, all waves do not
have the same effect, and the currents may change direction. Hence, it is difficult to say whether the sand is moving to or from shore at any moment.

The key to the relation between waves and sand motion is the large change in the beach between winter and
summer. Clearly there is a difference in the kind of waves,
but what is it? In winter the waves are large and the surf
is rough; suspended sand can be seen boiling up behind a
breaking wave. Energy is being expended on the beach at
a higher rate than in summer. This rate of delivery of energy is most conveniently described in terms of wave

steepness—the ratio of wave height to wave length, commonly written H/L.

For example, a six-foot wave six hundred feet long has a steepness of 6/600 or 0.01. If the wave length is only two hundred feet, six-foot waves have a steepness of 0.03. Thus wave steepness increases either with an increase in height or a decrease in length. In wave-channel experiments J. W. Johnson of the University of California at Berkeley was able to show that when the wave steepness is greater than 0.03, bars always formed (starting with a barless beach profile). If the steepness was less than 0.025, bars never formed in the model tank. Probably on a real beach the values are different, but the essential idea is the same. There the waves are highly variable in both height and period, in contrast to those in the model tank which are all precisely the same. Moreover, it is difficult to assess the effect of sand size, which, if scaled down to conform to the rest of the model, would be too small to react properly.

The effect of wave steepness seems to be as follows. When the waves approaching the beach are small (or the wave length is long) the sand on the bottom moves shoreward with the orbital currents. These low-steepness waves pick the sand up, move it forward, and set it down. Although the orbiting water returns seaward an equal distance, the sand it carries is now more likely to be dragged along the bottom. Friction against other sand grains and the existence of a laminar, or non-turbulent, flow region at the bottom keep the sand from moving quite as far as the water does and thus from completing the orbit. Consequently the net motion of sand is landward when the steepness is small.

When relatively large waves follow close upon one another, an entirely different set of circumstances exists. Now there is general turbulence in the surf zone, which keeps the sand in suspension, particularly in shallower water. The mass transport of water by the high waves is greater, and when they break, substantial waves of translation are generated. The result of these effects is that there is a general flow of water shoreward along the surface. Since the waves are relatively close together, the berm remains saturated, and relatively little of the water traveling up and down the beach face sinks into the sand. The shoreward-moving water carries a load of suspended sand particles, and when the waves rush up the beach face, their leading edges surmount the crest of the berm and deposit their sand atop the berm, raising its height. The remainder of the water rushes back down the beach face, picking up a thin layer of sand as it goes. This sandy suspension becomes involved at the bottom with the seaward-flowing currents, which must, of course, balance the landward-moving water at the surface. These currents move the sand seaward until they reach the breaker zone, where the landward-flowing currents are generated. There they deposit their load to form a bar. (Note that this current, while strong enough to influence suspended sand, could not be detected by a swimmer.)

Thus we have an explanation of how the steep winter surf can build the berm higher while cutting it back, and how bars are formed by the erosion of the berm.

The difficulty in determining whether a berm is retreating or advancing at any moment comes from wave variability—the difference in height and length from wave to wave. Suppose that the waves arriving at a beach all have about the same period and wave length but that the height varies as it does in the examples of Figure 55

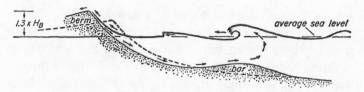

FIG. 69. Circulation of water in surf as steep waves transform
dashed profile to solid profile by moving sand from berm to bar.

(Chapter VIII). The small waves would bring sand
ashore; the large ones would take it away. And that is the
way with beaches. The sand is constantly shifting in accordance with complicated and variable water motion.
The profile of the sand itself is a rough analogue solution
to the question: Is the average wave steepness above or
below 0.03?

BERMS AND BARS

Now, equipped with a general understanding of the
mechanics of sand migration in the surf zone, we can examine more perceptively the beach forms that are produced. To do this one takes a series of profiles of a beach
over a period of time and examines the changes. Over the
same period the waves reaching the beach are observed
and recorded. The idea is to correlate the beach changes
with some specific quality of the waves. It is not easy either to obtain the information or to make sense out of it.
But eventually the persistent researcher does end up with
an accumulation of data and a "feel" for the way that
waves and beaches interact.

The Waves field party eventually surveyed beaches at
some forty Pacific Coast locations, repeating profiles at

some of them dozens of times in many kinds of weather conditions and in all seasons of the year. On each visit we surveyed three lines a thousand feet apart extending from the dunes to minus thirty feet of water to insure obtaining a representative profile. In the course of five years about five hundred profiles were made and six hundred sand samples were taken. Figures 70, 71, and 72 contain a few examples of steep, intermediate, and flat beaches that we profiled and compared with beaches elsewhere in the world. Since beaches are very irregular in slope, the

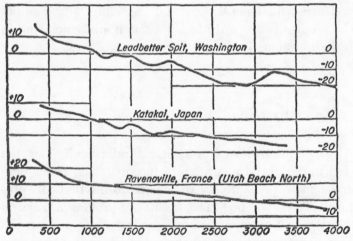

FIG. 70. Profiles of flat beaches. Note the three bars on the beach at Leadbetter Spit. (Slope exaggerated 1:5.)

words steep and flat are relative. As used here a flat beach is one on which the water is less than ten feet deep one thousand feet seaward of the zero tide level (mean lower low water), whereas a steep beach is over thirty feet deep one thousand feet out from a similar point. Note the difference in vertical exaggeration between the figures.

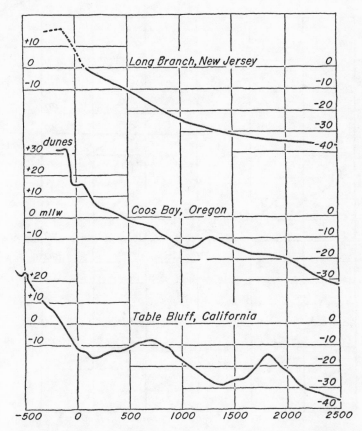

FIG. 71. Intermediate slope beaches. Contrast the barless beach profile at Long Branch with the two huge bars at Table Bluff. (Slope exaggerated 1:5.)

Each of these beach profiles was selected because it is of special interest. Utah beach, a principal landing point in the invasion of Europe, is among the flat beaches. The tidal range there is about fifteen feet. At low tide the German defenders could plant the beach tank traps and landing craft obstacles, which were such serious problems to

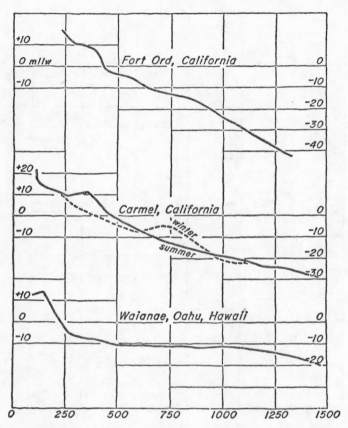

FIG. 72. Profiles of steep beaches. At Waianae only the beach
face is sand. The flat area is a coral reef over which great
breakers form and where the surfing is excellent (for an expert).
(Exaggerated 1:2.5.)

our D-Day operations. The beach at Katakai would have
been a landing site if it had been necessary to carry out
Operation Olympic, the direct invasion of Japan. Leadbetter Spit, typical of a hundred miles of beach north and
south of the Columbia River, was intensively studied be-

cause of its similarity to the Japanese beaches. After having been in and out through the surf at Leadbetter many times, we reached the conclusion that except in very low surf the attempt to land on Japan would have been an amphibious disaster.

In the intermediate slope beaches, Long Branch, New Jersey, is much like other exposed beaches of the Atlantic Coast; its barless, summer profile is shown in Figure 71.

Coos Bay, Oregon, has a pronounced bar, a clear winter berm, and a steep-fronted dune line caused by a violent storm that had cut deep into the semipermanent dunes. The huge bars at Table Bluff have an attitude of violence about them which they well deserve—or so they look to me.

The steep beaches, particularly Fort Ord, demonstrate the extreme. There it is not unusual for waves to break with great violence directly on the beach face, impelling a thick uprush or "surge" of water up and across the beach that can be dangerous to both swimmers and landing craft. A similar situation exists at Waianae, except that the breakers move shoreward across a long flat shoal before they reach the beach face. When the great Pacific swell rolls in, the surfing champions gather to compete.

But much of our data came from Carmel, where we would rest in the spring to recover from winter encounters with the northern surf. The beach is a closed system, since it is protected by headlands at each end and by a deep reef offshore. Even there, ten-foot breakers are not unusual. Throughout much of 1946 we maintained a careful watch on that beach in an attempt to keep a "budget" of the sand position—that is, to know where all the sand was all the time. Figure 73 shows the growth of the berm. In the five months between April and September it wid-

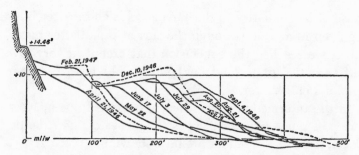

FIG. 73. The berm at Carmel, California, builds two hundred feet seaward during summer when the waves are small. Then it retreats almost to the vanishing point before the large waves of winter storms.

ened by more than two hundred feet. By December the first large storm had caused the beach face to retreat substantially, but by February it was almost back to the point of beginning. We were also able to detect berm growth by making precise surveys hour by hour and observed rates of over six feet a day. When storms start to erode the berm, particularly during neap tides, it is not unusual for a steep sandy cliff or scarp to form at the seaward edge of the berm. A vertical scarp five feet high was seen on the Oregon coast—cut overnight by a short and violent storm. On our next survey, two weeks later, small waves had replaced most of the eroded material and only the upper foot of scarp remained. The beach face, of course, is immediately seaward of this scarp, and its slope is actually flattened by the pounding waves.

Since berms are formed by wave action, it is not surprising that the height of the crest of the berm is a function of the height of the waves. Experiments by R. A. Bagnold of England in a wave channel demonstrated that the height of the berm above sea level is 1.3 times the

height of the (deep-water) waves that formed it. A similar relationship also exists in nature, but it is difficult to
confirm because sea level constantly changes with the
tides, because refraction influences the amount of deep-
water wave energy that reaches any beach, and because
every wave is different. However, it seems likely that on
ocean beaches the height of the berm is about equal to
1.3 times the significant height of the deep-water waves
multiplied by the refraction coefficient. For example, the
berm on the continuous beach rimming the gently curved
shore of Monterey Bay is sixteen feet above low water at
the exposed Fort Ord section and decreases gradually in
height toward protected Monterey harbor, where it is six
feet lower.

Even a casual beach-watcher soon notices that the
slope of the beach face and the size of the sand are somehow related. Steep beach, coarse sand; flat beach, fine
sand. But determining more precisely what the relationship is took quite a while. There are lots of places on a
beach to take sand samples and to measure slope, and on
the same beach the results vary greatly from place to
place. A good deal of sampling and measuring was done
before a "reference point" was selected. If the sand sam-
ple is taken on the beach face in the zone subjected to
wave action at mid-tide and the slope is measured at the
same place, consistent results are obtained. Figure 74
shows the relationship for *exposed* beaches. Here again
the effects of wave energy cause variations. If the berm is
retreating before the pounding of the waves, the slope is
less steep than if sand is being added.

A more important effect of exposure to wave action on
sand size and slope is illustrated in Figure 75, which
shows four beach profiles made along the continuous

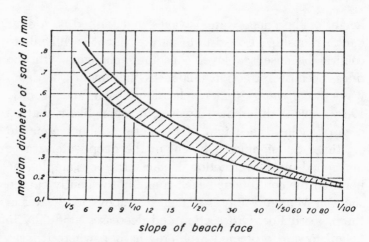

FIG. 74. Relationship between sand size and beach-face slope at the mid-tide zone on exposed beaches. Upper curve is minimum probable slope; lower is maximum.

beach at Half Moon Bay, California. There, Pillar Point completely protects the beach at profile one from the prevailing northwest swell. Profile four is exposed; between these extremes are two beaches of intermediate slope. In the protected zone behind the point, the beach is flat and the sand fine, but toward the south the beaches grow steeper and coarser. This demonstrates how beaches adjust to the wave environment.

Longshore bars, or beach bars, are underwater ridges in the beach material that parallel the shoreline. Often more than one bar is present, the number depending on the size of the waves, the bottom slope, and the tide range. We have discussed already how they are formed by currents that flow when steep storm waves arrive. Once formed, bars have a pronounced effect on the waves. Because they are abrupt shoals, they tend to act as filters causing all waves above a certain size to break at one spot (instead of breaking over a wide zone as they would on an even slope). Moreover, since bars rise abruptly and slope steeply to seaward, they tend to make the breakers plunge and release the energy suddenly.

A substantial range of tide (of five feet or more) tends to create two sets of bars. Because the tide curve is sinus-

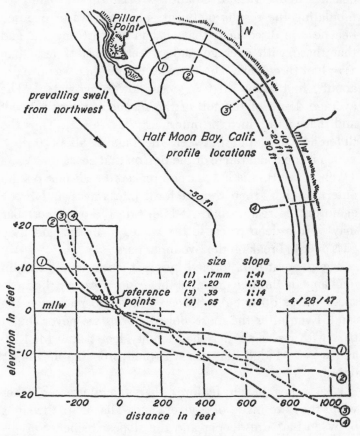

FIG. 75. The effect of a protecting headland on beach slope and sand size.

oidal, sea level lingers near high tide and low tide for extended periods but changes from one to the other with relative rapidity. Bars can develop at two levels corresponding to high and low tide, but the sand cannot shift from one to the other during the change.

Our surveys determined the depths of bars on many beaches under various conditions of storm and calm. In tabulating the results of twenty-nine surveys of exposed beaches we discovered that all had at least one bar and that those with average underwater slopes of less than 1:75 had three bars. The top of the inner bar was usually about 1 foot below MLLW (mean lower low water). The average depth of the top of the second bar was 7.5 feet and that of the third, or outermost, bar 13 feet. Thus the difference in depth between the bars is about 6 feet, which is the usual range of the tide on that coast.

When the tide is low, large breakers break first on the outermost bar; then they re-form into waves and break again on the second bar. At high tide the outermost bar may be too deep to cause the waves to break, and they pass over to break on the two inner bars.

The deepest bars formed by great storm waves remain unchanged through months of calm weather because small waves do not reach deep enough to rearrange the sand. Even after the most violent storms we never found bars with crests deeper than twenty feet below MLLW, and we concluded that this was their probable maximum depth.

Like other beach features, bars have greater relief when they are made of coarser sand. That is, the troughs between bars are deeper and the slopes steeper. Various attempts to correlate bar spacing with wave length or to find a simple relationship between depth of bars and troughs have not been successful. Since longshore currents often flow in the troughs, these may be scoured deeper or filled in, independent of wave action.

Bars have been observed on beaches ranging in size from model tanks to lakes and oceans, and subject to corresponding wave actions. As many as five have been observed on a single beach, and substantially unbroken bars twenty miles long have been observed on Leadbetter Spit, Washington. But although they have been described here as if they were continuous parallel beach features, often they are very irregular. When wave direction changes, the bars begin to shift position; if the waves quiet down before the shift is complete, the result may be an indescribably ragged arrangement of sand which will remain until the next storm produces order again.

The question of the maximum depth at which the bottom material can be moved by wave action is not settled, in spite of the arbitrary thirty feet below low tide used herein. For example, a violent storm at Madras, India, cast up on shore a quantity of pig lead that came from a vessel wrecked more than a mile offshore. Shingle and chalk ballast dumped overboard by sailing ships in water over sixty feet deep and more than seven miles from shore was brought ashore at Sunderland, England, by wave action. And captains of ships passing over Nantucket shoals, where the depth is seventy-five feet and more, report that storm waves breaking over the ship leave sand on deck. What is the mechanism of transport? No one knows exactly.

MINOR BEACH FEATURES

There are several beach features that seem to have no great geological or engineering importance, but they add interest to the study of beaches. These include swash marks, backwash marks, rills, steps, cusps, domes, pinholes, and ripple marks.

A wonderful time to observe these features is early in the morning, especially after a high tide. Often the air is still and a pleasant light fills the sky. The beach is clean and virginal, the night's waves having erased the human marks of the previous day. Then, with the sand surface free of confusion, beach-watching is most rewarding.

The flow of a thin sheet of water up the beach face that follows the final breaking of each wave on the shore is called the uprush, or sometimes the swash. At its upper edge, just before its energy is spent in the upward motion, the swash is only a film of water less than a quarter of an inch deep. Immediately ahead of the moving water is a line of sand particles, usually a little larger than most of those on the beach face, bulldozed along by the edge of the swash.

When the momentum of the moving water is spent in upward motion, the uprush stops. Part of the water sinks into the sand and part of it slides backward down the beach as the backrush. As it does so, a thin line of sand grains is left to mark its maximum upward reach. These are swash marks.

Swash marks are a sort of scorecard of the reach of a succession of waves. As the general level of surf rises and falls with surf beat, carrying on it large and small waves, you can watch the marks change position. As the level recedes and successively smaller waves create uprushes,

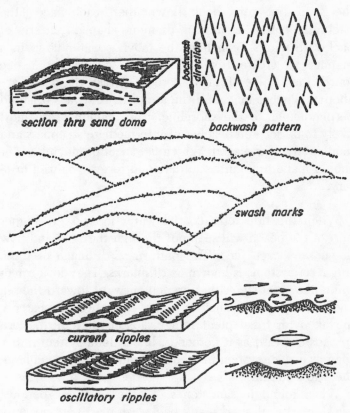

section thru sand dome

backwash direction

backwash pattern

swash marks

current ripples

oscillatory ripples

FIG. 76. Small beach features.

the swash marks make a pattern like that shown in Figure 76. But as the amplitude of the waves increases, suddenly one larger wave will erase all the previous marks, using their sand grains to make its own record mark. On a receding tide the highest marks remain until the next incoming tide, when a new series, erasing and replacing, climbs up the beach face.

The part of the swashing water that does not sink into

the sand but runs back down the beach face (the backrush) often creates a diamond-shaped pattern of backwash marks. Somehow the moving water flows in a manner to create tiny crisscrossed valleys about one fourth inch deep. Usually these backwash diamonds are about six inches long, and the long axis is always oriented perpendicular to the shoreline. The diamonds are most likely to be seen on beaches of intermediate steepness and moderately coarse sand. Why a flat sheet of moving water should make tiny gullies in diamond form remains a mystery.

When the tide retreats, the water left on the higher part of the beach will seep out through the sand and flow down the beach face. The pattern of drainage of these tiny river systems is known as rill marks. They look something like plant stems that branch outward toward the sea and, when seen in ancient rocks, have been repeatedly mistaken for fossil plant remains. Note that the pattern spreads outward as it descends, like a delta system rather than as a river system in which tributaries join to enlarge the main stream.

When found in sandstones of other geologic periods, swash marks, rill marks, and backwash marks are not only excellent evidence that the sand once was the beach of a prehistoric sea, they also point the direction of the sea and indicate the range of tide.

As the backrushing water slides down the surface of the beach its velocity increases and the surface sand grains are lifted into suspension. The momentum of this turbid sheet of water and sand carries it below the general level of the sea, and a small wave, usually less than a foot high, called the backrush breaker, curls over it. The

result is a turbulent sandy swirl whose effect is to lift the
sand grains and keep them in suspension, to be carried up
the beach face again by the next uprush. But the larger
sand grains may settle to the bottom, where they roll back
and forth as each wave passes, occasionally being lifted
and dropped again by unusually violent water motion.
The net effect of this constant shifting is segregation according to size in which the larger particles move steadily
downward. A little below the level of the lowest backrush
breaker these larger sand grains reach a depth at which
they can no longer be moved upward by most of the
waves. The result is a steplike deposit whose upper surface is the continuation of the beach face and whose
outer surface is the angle of repose of the sand. This low-
tide step, which is usually about a foot high, may be hard
to see because of the turbulence, but it is often encountered with momentary alarm by the bare feet of waders
who sink into the soft, coarse sand or step off its abrupt
edge.

Cusps are evenly-spaced crescent-shaped depressions
concave to seaward that are built by wave action on the
seaward edge of the berm. Of all the curiosities of the
shore these are surely the most puzzling, and none of the
dozens of explanations that have been given for their formation is completely satisfying. Cusps varying greatly in
shape have been observed in beaches made of fine sand
and large cobbles; they occur equally in protected bays
and on exposed beaches. Cusps have been made in the
laboratory with lengths of six to nine inches; they have
been measured by the author at San Simeon, California
(fourteen feet), at Ford Ord (ninety feet), and at Table
Bluff (average of nine measured with a Dukw milometer
—1,180 feet).

Like other beach features, cusps have more striking relief and are less regular on exposed beaches made of
coarse sand than in protected bays, where the precision of
cusps sculpted in fine sand on a flat beach is a thing to
marvel at. They seem to the author to develop at wave
steepnesses between erosion and deposition. In fact, their
shape suggests indecision or perhaps nearly balanced
forces of alternate dominance.

There is no general agreement on how cusps form or
why they should be the shapes and sizes they are, but the
rankest amateur can stand for half an hour watching
wave action in cusps and convince himself he knows how
the cusps are maintained. The two-wave cycle is often
something like this: (Figure 77). On the even wave a
straight swash, (1) bearing its usual load of suspended
sand, rushes up the beach face. It is split into segments by
the apex points and deflected along the sides of the bay
until its force is spent or it meets the water of the opposite side. (2) Once stopped, it is influenced solely by gravity and returns seaward by the steepest path, which (3)
leads it to the channel in the center of the bay. The considerable velocity of the water down this channel moves
bottom material, (4) and a small submarine delta forms.
The effect of this jet of water is to stop abruptly the water
it meets in front of the next wave, (5) making that wave
relatively ineffective at shifting sand. Even so, the part of
that wave opposite the horn is unimpeded and, as before,
it rushes up and drops its sand.

It should be noticed that the high backrush velocity
and the low slope associated with the removal of sand
from a beach exist only in the channel, whereas the
highest uprush velocities and lowest saturation are found
at the horn, which is steep and depositional. The cycle
repeats. Apparently cusp horns are built by every wave

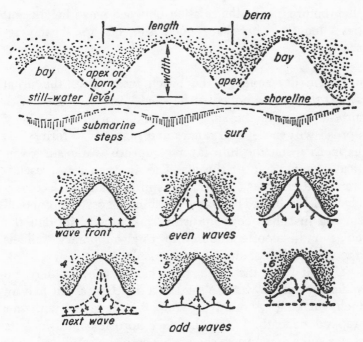

FIG. 77. Cusps are a puzzlement.

and the bays are deepened by the work of every other wave. Of course, this two-wave cycle does not repeat every time because variability in wave height and period causes the waves to get out of phase—which may be the reason that the most regular cusps are formed by the most regular waves.

Researchers generally agree that (1) conditions are best for cusp formation if the waves approach exactly parallel to the shore, and are unconfused by local currents and winds, (2) some original irregularity in the beach is necessary to start them forming, and (3) the spacing of the cusps is related to wave height. But the question why cusps should form at all is no closer to being answered than before, nor is the relation between wave height and cusp length. These are good subjects for beach researchers.

In the dry sand on the beach face above the usual swash the spaces between the sand grains are filled with air. In this area the sinking water of an unusually long uprush will cause sand domes and pinholes to form. This happens when the thin layer of uprush water sinks vertically and displaces the air. The air then migrates upward and emerges from pinholes in the sand surface as a chain of bubbles. The water swashing across the pinholed surface in subsequent uprushes sinks down through the holes and smooths them into tiny temporary funnels about an eighth of an inch in diameter.

The first of the high uprushes, however, may be sufficient only to wet the sand to a depth of about half an inch, making a relatively impervious layer with air trapped beneath. When the next uprush comes and its water sinks downward, the air beneath the saturated zone is forced together in pockets as before. But now the sand surface is sealed, and instead of the air escaping as a series of small bubbles, it becomes one large bubble. Unable to escape as the pressure rises, the bubble lifts the sand above it into a low dome perhaps a quarter of an inch in height and three inches across or sometimes twice that large. One can tap these domes with a finger and feel them collapse, or slice them carefully with a pocket knife and see the dome structure.

Sand subjected to the action of moving water frequently forms parallel ridges and troughs which are known as ripple marks. They are like small waves of sand and may be seen in sandy stream bottoms, on the face of a gently-sloping beach when the tide is out, and beneath the surf zone. Ripple marks are commonly seen in ancient strata (sometimes with dinosaur tracks), and they have been photographed on the ocean floor in water eighteen thousand feet deep. In short, whenever there is sand underwater, ripples may be formed by the motion of the water. They come in a great variety of shapes and sizes.

Ripple "wave length" may be as little as two inches and the height a fraction of an inch, or they may form sand waves several feet deep and fifty or more feet long. Ordinarily ripples are only a few inches from crest to crest and their size seems to be related to the size of the sand from which they are formed, the velocity of the current, and the amount of material in suspension.

Observation and carefully controlled experiments reveal that there are two well-defined kinds of ripples: (1) Current ripples, which are formed by water flowing in a single direction, are asymmetrical with a long gentle slope on the side from which the current comes and short steep slope on the lee side. (2) Oscillation ripples, created by the equal back-and-forth currents of flattened orbits at the bottom as oscillatory waves pass above, are symmetrical. The ripple marks seen on beaches are almost always a complicated mixture of the two, since orbit size varies from wave to wave and the direction of bottom currents usually is highly variable.

Since wave fronts generally parallel the shoreline, it might be expected that the underwater ripples would also parallel the shore, but this is true only part of the time. Even beneath the surf the asymmetrical current ripples seem to predominate. There, if the ripples are observed relative to a peg driven into the bottom, they are seen to be constantly in motion in an explicably random manner and direction. Probably they are a prime mechanism in the movement of sand by water, but unfortunately ripples do not clearly indicate the direction of the main migration.

In fact, although the sand moves in the direction of the current, the ripple form does not. If the velocity of the moving water is more than about 2.2 feet a second, the vortex motion in the lee of the crest causes the ripple form to move against the current. When the velocity exceeds 2.5 feet per second the ripples are swept away entirely as in an underwater sandstorm.

FAMOUS BEACHES OF THE WORLD

When one thinks of resort bathing, a few famous beaches immediately come to mind: Miami Beach, Waikiki, the French Riviera, the Copacabana (Rio), Brighton (England), Coney Island (New York), and Acapulco (Mexico).

What makes these beaches so desirable? Is it the kind of sand, the size of the waves, or the temperature of the water, or the climate, or the beauty of the surroundings? Or is it convenience to (or remoteness from) population centers, the likelihood that women (or men) will be present, the low (or high) costs, or the reputation and advertising? In other words, are the main attractions natural or artificial, and which are the most important? Those questions were recently asked by the government of Thailand, which felt its beaches were among the world's best and wanted to make this point with tourists and the outside world.

As I thought about that problem and tried to arrive rationally at some conclusion about what kind or color or size of sand was best, I realized that people seem to have just as much fun on the shingle beaches of England or the rocky beaches of the Riviera as they do on the bright white coral sand of Bermuda, or the black sand beaches of Tahiti. We are adaptable creatures and within fairly wide limits can have a good time in whatever way suits us at the moment. Some people are just as happy on the crowded beach at Coney Island at the end of a New York subway ride as others are on a remote island reachable only by private aircraft. The beauty and desirability of a beach are in the mind of the beholder. Under some circumstances you may like any or all of them; under other conditions (such as with a cold wind blowing or without your friends) you might not like any.

XII

The Littoral Conveyor Belt

THE MOVEMENT OF SAND ALONG A COAST BY WAVE-CAUSED currents, called littoral transport, is responsible for most shoreline problems. Either sand is being removed from some place that people wish it would stay or it is being deposited some place where it is not wanted, or both. The processes are as old as the ocean and, by man's usual standards, fairly slow; that is, years are usually required to make an appreciable change. As long as the property bordering the ocean is in the form of great ranches or public lands, no one pays much attention to a change in the position of the shoreline of fifty feet over a period of fifty years. Its exact position is usually not known and no great value is assigned to the land. When, however, a lighthouse or road is built near the water's edge so that there is a fixed object against which shoreline changes can be conveniently measured, the coastal dwellers first become dismayed by the loss of land, then alarmed.

When the ranches are subdivided into small lots on the edge of the sea cliff and sold for high prices, as has happened at many places on the California coast, the new

owners are soon in an uproar when they find their land is
disappearing at the rate of a foot a year. The process of
erosion has not changed, only the attitude toward it.
Something must be done at once!

In England in the early 1900s property owners whose
land was being eroded by wave action clamored for the
Government to take preventive action. Their island was
disappearing beneath the sea! They argued so loudly that
a Royal Commission was appointed to study the matter.
After making a careful survey, the commission reported
that over a period of thirty-five years England and Wales
lost 4,692 acres and gained 35,444 acres, giving a net gain
of nearly 900 acres a year. This finding seemed to prove
that people whose land disappeared complained more
loudly than those whose land was increasing. It must
be admitted, however, that the land lost probably was
good cliffland on the open coast which disappeared in a
spectacular way, whereas the land gained was low, sandy
and not particularly valuable. Non-geologists are usually
not aware that the very existence of a cliff is warning that
erosional processes are at work, even though the changes
seem to be very slow.

It is said that George Washington studied the erosion
of the Long Island coast and ordered that the Montauk
Point lighthouse at the eastern tip be built at least two
hundred feet back from the edge of the cliff so it would
last two hundred years. At the present rate of erosion it
will just about last that long. A recent measurement
showed about forty feet left between the base of the
lighthouse and the edge of the cliff.

Unfortunately, almost anything that either speeds up
erosion of a coast or retards the normal motion of sand
alongshore affects all the other property within the same
littoral zone. Any "remedial" action that does not con-

sider the effects on the downstream beaches only causes more problems. Thus the shoreline engineer, in addition to considering the complex immediate problem of what action to take at any one place to keep the property owners there happy, must be careful that his solution does not create worse problems somewhere else. The best he can hope for is a good solution for a few generations; eventually the long-term geological process will overwhelm anything he does.

SHORELINE EROSION

There are several mechanisms by which the sea attacks a cliff and makes sand. These are: (1) hydraulic and pneumatic action in which the pressure of water moving at high velocity against the cliff forces water into cracks in the rock and compresses the air that is trapped (this compressed air will sometimes shove large blocks of rock *away* from the cliff into the waves); (2) the impact of water laden with rock fragments, which act as cutting tools against the cliff; (3) the abrasion or rubbing together of the fragments in suspension; (4) grinding of the blocks that fall against each other as the cliff is undercut; and (5) corrosion or chemical weathering of salt water and oxygen in the zone just above sea level.

Exactly how does rock become sand?

A vivid picture of the working of the "sea mill," which grinds large boulders to fine sand, was given by J. W. Henwood in an account of the visit he made to a mine that extended out under the sea in southwest England: "When standing beneath the base of the cliff, and in that part of the mine where but nine feet of rock stood between us and the ocean, the heavy roll of the larger boulders, the ceaseless grinding of the pebbles, the fierce thundering of the billows, with the crackling and coiling as they rebounded, placed a tempest in its most appalling form too vividly before me to be ever forgotten. More than once doubting the protection of our rocky shield we retreated in affright; and it was only after repeated trials that we had confidence to pursue our investigations."

Few persons are privileged to listen to the surf from below, but similar sounds are created by large waves breaking in pocket beaches on steep rocky coasts. Where cliffs rise vertically from the sea there are often slot-like depressions carved by the waves and floored with cobble beaches. Watching from the cliff above, one sees a wave break violently in the slot with much hissing and roaring. The churning water lifts cobbles as though they were sand grains and carries them upward in a surge of green and white froth. When this happens one hears muffled "clocks" as the cobbles strike against each other. Then, at the top of the uprush, water and cobbles crash against the base of the cliff and the wave reflects. Down goes the water again, dragging its load of cobbles, causing them to clatter against one another with a loud crackling sound. The observer is readily impressed by the violence trapped in the pocket and finds no difficulty thereafter in understanding how beaches have been created from cliffs by the relentless impacting and grinding of waves.

As the rocks grind against each other and cliffs are undermined, as the moving sand abrades and then moves on, the coast retreats. Over the great lengths of geologic time it may be worn back many, many miles. Even in the short length of historic time there are many examples of substantial changes.

Old maps of the Yorkshire coast of England show the locations of many towns that have long since been swept

out of existence by the waves, their former sites now
represented by sandbanks far out in the sea. In 1829 the
famous geologist Charles Lyell reported a depth of
twenty feet in the harbor at Sheringham where only
forty-eight years before there had been a cliff fifty feet
high with houses on it. Now the harbor too is gone. Near
Cromer, also in England, the sea cliff has long been retreating at a rate of nineteen feet a year and at Covehithe
and Southwold the erosion cuts the shore back ten to
fifteen feet a year. During the great storm surge of 1953
(previously mentioned in connection with the Dutch dike
failure) a cliff forty feet high at Suffolk retreated forty
feet in a single night. A lower cliff lost ninety feet to the
sea during the same night. Such extremely rapid erosion
is the result of unusually violent waves brought to bear
against unconsolidated materials by a water level too high
for the beach to offer its usual protection. By contrast,
careful examination of the hard rocks of the Cornish coast
indicates that they probably have changed little over the
last ten thousand years.

The erosion and retreat of a shoreline is not always a
steady year-by-year wearing away of a cliff and the seasonal removal of sand. On some coasts there will be little
erosion for long periods of time and then a few years of
rapid erosion and abrupt retreat. This means that the average rate of sea-cliff erosion may not be meaningful.

Recent studies by Professor Francis Shepard and Gerald Kuhn of the coast of Southern California have shown
that it is important to appreciate such factors as bedrock
failures, block falls, and sea-cave collapses. These types of
slope failures are commonly associated with heavy rains
and major storms, which generate large waves. They note
that substantial consequences of storm-related cliff failures have been largely forgotten because few dramatic in-

stances have occurred since the 1940s. In the area studied, which includes Solana Beach and Encinitas, the
worst erosion occurs where ground waters from springs,
leaky pipes, and shrub watering have lubricated rocky
joints and fault planes. Deep roots and human activities
(grading, building, and climbing on the steep cliffs) also
accelerate coastal retreat. In the last five years the coastal
retreat in this area has ranged from negligible to about
ten feet.

A city map of Encinitas made in 1883 and updated in
1976 shows that about six city blocks have been lost to
erosion and at the maximum point the sea has cut in eight
hundred feet. Much of this retreat followed the great flood
years of 1884, 1886, 1889, and 1891. The county tax records show that as the property on the cliff edge eroded
away, it was duly decreased in value, while the assessment
of property immediately behind (with a newly improved
view of the sea) went up. Presumably this will continue.

THE LONGSHORE TRANSPORT OF SAND

Most longshore currents are generated by waves
striking the shoreline at an angle. Although wave fronts
bend as they move across shallow water and tend to become parallel to the shore, often the refraction process is
not quite complete. When the wave finally breaks at a
slight angle, either on a bar or on the beach, the water receives an impulse, part of which is in the alongshore direction. Therefore, the cumulative effect of many breaking waves is to move sand steadily alongshore.

Professor J. Munch-Petersen, who studied the Danish
coast intensively for nearly forty years, drew the follow-

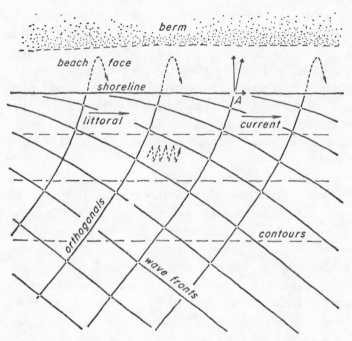

FIG. 78. Waves approaching a straight shoreline at an angle
are not completely refracted. The remaining alongshore component (marked A) is responsible for the littoral current. Paths
of sand grains moving to the right with every wave are shown
by dotted lines.

ing analogy: "One can get a good picture of the material
movement if one looks upon the wave as an excavating
machine and the wave current as a conveyor belt that
moves the material the machine has loosened. Each wave
machine lifts the sand and impels it in a more or less
oblique direction, adding it to the conveyor."

Over the years he modified the basic wave energy formula into one which he felt best described the ability of

waves to transport material along a straight sandy coast:

$$\text{Material moved} = \frac{KH^2L \cos \alpha}{8}$$

in which alpha is the angle of wave attack and K is a coefficient that depends on the size of material and the steepness of the beach.

More recently Joseph Caldwell of the Coastal Engineering Research Laboratory established a relationship between the amount of alongshore energy and the amount of sand moved which gives similar results. It suggests that the energy expended in average weather to move the conveyor belt that extends from Point Conception to Los Angeles is roughly five million foot-pounds per foot of beach per day (or for one hundred miles, about fifty thousand horsepower).

Along that part of the California coast there is a delightful assortment of puzzling problems for the shoreline engineer, all created by an almost continuous littoral current from the west. This current is a product of the shape of the coast and the constant wave direction. North of Point Conception the coast faces due west, directly into the wind and waves. But south of the point the coast turns abruptly to the east so that the same winds and waves strike the shore at an angle. The current sweeps sand along the coast, and any structure that interrupts the flow acts like a dam, halting the flow of sand and causing the beaches to its west to grow. Beaches to the east of the structure are exposed to the inexorable waves and currents, and without new sand constantly arriving they retreat rapidly.

The first major obstruction that the moving sand encounters is the Santa Barbara breakwater. As the sand moving along the beach from the west passes the tip of

that structure, it abruptly encounters the deeper, quieter
water that the breakwater was built to create. The wave-
created turbulence that has held the sand in suspension
ceases, and the particles are deposited just inside the end
of the breakwater. But the filling in of the harbor is only
half the problem. The beach to the east, deprived of its
sand supply, is quickly stripped of sand and the soft cliffs
behind are attacked. In the period 1938 to 1940 the Sand
Point bluff was cut back one hundred to two hundred feet
for over a mile. So, the solution for many years has been
to dredge the sand from inside the breakwater and pump
it into the first beach exposed to wave action, where it
would remount the conveyor belt and continue on down
the coast.

In the years 1948–50 the author made an extensive
study of the sand motion in the Santa Barbara area for
the University of California, under contract from the
U. S. Army Corps of Engineers. The principal problem
was to attempt to correlate the rate of sand motion with
wind and wave action. We began by installing recording
wind and wave meters at Santa Barbara and by making
detailed beach profiles several miles upstream and downstream from the harbor. The principal areas of interest
were, of course, the harbor itself and the first downstream
berm. We soon discovered that the sand entering the harbor enlarged the perimeter of the sandspit in such a way
that the growth was easy to measure. The new sand extended from low water down to the flat harbor bottom
along its natural angle of repose. By making weekly surveys over a period of a year and plotting them as shown
in Figure 79, we could then establish a relationship between the size of the waves and the growth of the spit.
Since all the sand reaching Santa Barbara went into the

spit, the growth was a direct measurement of sand transport along that coast.

On days when the breaker height was less than two feet on the beach outside the breakwater, the spit grew at a rate of around two hundred and fifty cubic yards of sand a day; if the breakers were over four feet high, new sand moved in at one thousand cubic yards a day; and during storm conditions the rate exceeded twenty-five hundred cubic yards a day. The average sand flow during the year and a half of our study was about six hundred cubic yards a day, but data accumulated by the U. S. Engineers over a period of years indicated long-term cyclic changes. Daily averages, obtained by dividing the amount of sand dredged out every two years by the num-

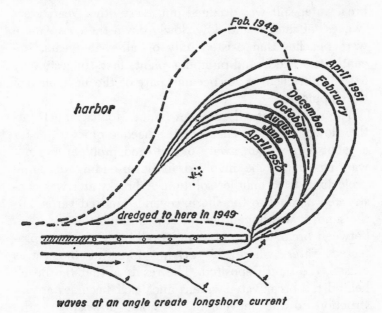

FIG. 79. Growth of the sandspit inside the end of the breakwater at Santa Barbara.

ber of intervening days, ranged from four hundred to nine hundred cubic yards. The highs and lows of these long-term variations appeared to come at about eleven-year intervals, and the author attempted without much success to correlate this rough periodicity with other natural phenomena. Doubtless it is related in some way to the position of the weather system that controls winds and waves in the Pacific. This, in turn, is probably connected with solar activity of an eleven-year period, but the mechanism that connects the two is not well understood.

Beyond Santa Barbara the moving sand encounters other obstacles, including the Ventura–Port Hueneme complex, which will be described presently. When the breakwater spit was dredged out every other year, great "waves" of sand would flow slowly down the coast; there were beaches that existed only on alternate years. Recently the fixed sand-pumping plant, first suggested by M. P. O'Brien in 1940, became part of the new plan of development.

The sand eventually reaches Santa Monica, much farther down the coast. That city also needed quiet water for a yacht harbor, but, aware of the sand problem and not wanting to become involved in never-ending dredging projects, it tried another solution. A breakwater was constructed parallel to the shore, several hundred yards out; the sand, it was hoped, would flow through the wide gap between breakwater and shore. It did not. Once in protected water, where the driving force of the waves ceased, the sand deposited. The result is that the beach behind the breakwater widens and itself becomes an obstruction to the movement of sand; downstream the beach retreats. So Santa Monica also uses a dredge to put the sand back into circulation.

The general mechanism of littoral drifting is apparent, but some of the details are obscure, so scientists are always seeking new ways of directly measuring the amount of sand suspended in the water and the depths at which it can be moved by various wave and current conditions. The use of radioactive sand for tracing the movement of beach material has been tried by scientists in Sweden, France, England, and the United States with some success. The idea is to take a sand with the proper kind of impurities (of the same size and physical properties as the sand on the beach to be studied) and expose it in a reactor until it becomes temporarily radioactive. Then the sand is placed on the beach and followed with Geiger counters. British experimenters used sand 0.18 mm in diameter activated with scandium 46, which has a half life of eighty-five days, and traced its motion for four months. They determined that only large storm waves would move sand at a depth of nineteen feet.

Similar experiments were then conducted with pebbles (shingle) on the east coast of England. The pebbles were taken from the beach to the nuclear laboratory at Harwell, where a radioactive coating was applied. The isotope used was barium 140–lanthanum 140, whose half life of twelve days made tracing of the pebbles possible for about six weeks.

Six hundred coated pebbles were dumped seven hundred yards offshore in water nineteen feet deep at low tide, and two thousand were placed in quite shallow water a dozen yards from the low tide shore. The positions of pebbles underwater were measured as often as weather conditions permitted—those offshore with Geiger counters mounted on a sled towed along the sea bottom, those on the beach face with a scintillation counter. With these instruments it was possible to locate individual radioactive pebbles among the millions on the beach, even though they were buried as deep as nine inches.

During the observation period the pebbles in deeper water did not move at all, but those in shallow water spread out as much as a mile from their original position. For the first four weeks the weather was calm and wave heights never exceeded two feet. Even so, the ninety-three pebbles that were located had moved a mean distance of sixty yards. The next week the winds blew harder and from the opposite direction and the shingle migrated rapidly the other way. In so doing, some of the pebbles crossed a river mouth, apparently without being affected by the rapid tidal currents there. The researchers concluded that the movement of the shingle was directly related to the direction and strength of the winds blowing off the North Sea.

On the extreme Southern California coast Douglas Inman, of the Scripps Institution of Oceanography, has for years been studying the motion of sand in inshore waters. Spending much time on the bottom in diving gear, he has observed sand being raised by passing waves and moved by currents, has sampled the sand in suspension with various devices, and tried to establish the laws by which sand grains of various sizes respond to waves.

On the east coast, using one of the Beach Erosion Board model tanks, Thorndike Saville, Jr., set up an experiment to determine the amount of longshore transport under various wave conditions. Waves were generated that approached the shore at an angle of 10° in deep water and broke on a beach face that had an initial slope of 1:10. The velocity of the longshore current was obtained by timing the movement of dye and was found to increase with wave steepness. The moving sand was trapped and weighed at the downstream end and an equivalent amount introduced at the upstream end. In this manner the quantity of sand in motion could be carefully measured on what was, in effect, an endless beach.

By taking samples in four traps to measure transport in different zones, Saville was able to relate wave steepness to zone of transport. When wave steepness was less than 0.03, most of the sand moved by "beach drifting" in the swash zone on the beach face. Waves of greater steepness soon created a bar on which subsequent waves broke and raised the sand into suspension. From then on, the bulk of the transport occurred in the breaker zone along the bar. Others extended the experiments to include a greater range of direction of the approach of waves. It was then determined that when the wave front made an angle of 30° with the beach, the sand transport was maximum.

In similar experiments the British Hydraulics Research Board modeled a stretch of beach at Dunwich to determine the proper spacing of groins, a form of barrier we shall discuss further. By scaling from the model, they determined that on the open beach the sand transport was equal to 455,000 yards per year. If groins 180 feet long were spaced at intervals of 350 feet, this transport was reduced to 180,000 cubic yards per year. Although the experiment was not a realistic representation of actual conditions, the results do give the shoreline engineer a rough idea of the extent to which such barriers can be effective.

LITTORAL DRIFT

The coastal engineer is constantly confronted with variations on the problem of how to keep sand moving along a shoreline and at the same time prevent the shore from eroding. If he builds any new shoreline facilities that stop the flow of sand, there will be trouble both at the place where the sand stops and the place where it would have gone. As with any problem posed by nature, the first step is to try to understand what is going on. If sand is filling a harbor, it is necessary to know where it comes from, how it is transported, and the rate at which it is arriving. If a beach is retreating, the engineer must know why before he can make plans to restore the sand. So he begins by making a study and obtaining answers to these critical questions. Then a plan of action must be developed and guided through the practical obstacle course that includes making legal, financial, and political arrangements, as well as the actual construction work.

Plans involving erosion-deposition problems inevitably rest on two solid pieces of knowledge: (1) Sand set in motion by wave-caused turbulence will settle out wherever a protective structure reduces wave action; (2) if no action is taken on erosion problems everyone shares the erosion, but as soon as one part of the shore is protected the remainder of the shore must supply the sand.

Usually the engineer's first question is: What is the net littoral drift? How much sand will we have to deal with in this problem?

The term "net littoral drift" refers to the difference between the volume of sand moving in one direction along a beach and that moving in the opposite direction (caused by shifts in the direction of attack of the waves). On a long, reasonably straight shoreline the net drift is of primary importance, and in the Santa Barbara coast it is about 300,000 cubic yards a year. But as Major General W. F. Cassidy of the Corps of Engineers points out, where the moving sand must cross an inlet, the total amount of sand in motion in both directions is important.

He cites figures for Corson Inlet, an unimproved inlet through the barrier reef on the New Jersey coast:

Southward-moving sand	600,000 cu. yd/year
Northward-moving sand	450,000 cu. yd/year
Total sand moving	1,050,000 cu. yd/year
Net sand moving south	150,000 cu. yd/year

The total sand involved at the inlet is 1,050,000 cubic yards per year, which represents the amount of sand that could be lost to the beach at that point. In fact, the inlet historically removed 300,000 cubic yards per year from the shore face although the net littoral drift is only half of that. What happens? The sand in shifting back and forth across the inlet is moved out of the littoral conveyor area by transverse tidal currents and is either carried out to sea, deposited as shoals in the channel, or is moved into the bay behind. In any case, the result is erosion of the beach, which must make up the deficiency by contributing the amount of sand withdrawn from the system. Moreover, the shift of the sand causes the inlet to migrate. If jetties were constructed to confine the flow of tidal water, at the end of a year there would be 150,000 cubic yards of sand accumulated north of the north jetty. This is the kind of situation in which it is worthwhile to think about installing a sand-transfer plant, with two objectives in mind: (1) to keep the entrance from shoaling, thus aiding navigation, and (2) to conserve 300,000 cubic yards of sand a year.

Such plants already exist in a number of places in the world, the best known at the Lake Worth Inlet, Florida, entrance to the port of Palm Beach. There a small sand-pumping plant on the updrift jetty picks up some of the sand that deposits there, pumps it through a pipeline, and discharges it on the downdrift side of the other jetty. Although this plant cannot handle all the drifting sand, it has stabilized the shoreline and, with the jetties, keeps the entrance free of shoals. It is at least the successful test of an idea. Every few years a special dredging operation moves the excess sand across the entrance and restores the balance.

There are places on the Southern California coast where such intermittent dredging has long been necessary. Clearly any new harbors or structures that interrupt the sand flow require either a fixed pumping plant or some sort of a plan for bypassing the interruption. At Port Hueneme, which is a few miles east of Santa Barbara and subject to the same littoral drifting, a harbor has been scooped in the flat coastal land and the entrance fenced with two parallel jetties, the westernmost of which stopped the sand. Periodically, as expected, it has been necessary to dredge the sand from this trap and dump it on the downdrift beaches. One difficulty is that the dredge must work under conditions that are rather hazardous for a floating pipeline dredge, exposed to the waves that move the sand. The need for enlarged harbor facilities in the area led Richard Eaton, chief technical adviser to the Beach Erosion Board, to propose a solution that seems to solve a series of problems simultaneously.

This Ventura County harbor has been carved from the dunes immediately upstream of Port Hueneme and it too has parallel jetties, much like the first ones. But now the dredging situation is different, for a breakwater has been constructed parallel to the shore just west of the jetty; as at Santa Monica, this barrier causes the sand to deposit, but it also creates a zone of quiet water where a dredge

can work without difficulty. Now, in one operation, the accumulated sand can be pumped around both harbor entrances and deposited on the beach beyond. This kind of
sand-trapping, bypassing operation will doubtless come
into more general use as the coast develops.

In another, newer version of this idea, a weir jetty is
positioned on the upstream side. Under high tide and
storm wave conditions, it permits sand to overflow into a
specially made compartment. At periodic intervals a
dredge working in the protected water can pump the
sand across to the downstream side.

A similar but perhaps even more difficult problem has
arisen sixty miles farther south, beyond the port of Los
Angeles. The problem is that the natural sand supply for
the beaches has been cut off. South and west of the Los
Angeles plain the beaches in other years had been
nourished with sand brought down from the hills by small
intermittently flowing streams. But in the last few dec-
ades the local need for water and the demand for flood
control caused these "rivers" to be dammed and their
channels lined with concrete. Now the sand is trapped in
reservoirs well back from the ocean, and the starving
beaches have steadily retreated, with erosion extending as
far as Newport Beach. The littoral current strips an estimated 200,000 cubic yards of sand a year from the
beaches and carries it south, eventually dumping it into
the Newport submarine canyon, from which it cannot be
retrieved.

When the erosion first became serious in 1947, a million
cubic yards of sand were dredged from the Anaheim Bay
channel and deposited on the beaches to widen them. By
1963 the continuing attrition had made the situation on
some of the beaches critical again—seventy-five houses

were smashed by waves in a single storm. So another three million yards will be dredged from Anaheim Bay and dumped on the upstream beaches. The littoral drift will carry it along the shore toward Newport, a wave of sand that widens the beaches as it advances. But there is a limit to how much sand is available in the nearby bays and entrances.

CURIOUS SAND FORMS

The configuration of a shoreline and the position of stream outlets are sometimes the result of wave refraction, especially along sandy coasts exposed to large waves. This happens because the height of the berm is controlled by the height of the waves and the berm acts as a dam. On straight sandy coasts, streams will often flow directly toward the sea until they reach the beach. Then they will turn right or left abruptly and flow for a considerable distance—sometimes several miles—until the dam formed by the berm is lower. At that point the stream will cut through and enter the sea. If one looks into the reason why the berm is lower, it is usually found to be some variation in the offshore topography that caused the waves building the berm to be lower at that spot. Many beaches on the west coasts of Italy and of the United States have streams that behave this way.

If there is a large rock or island a short distance offshore that protects the coast from wave attack, this has two important effects. First, it creates a zone of relatively calm water where sand or gravel will deposit. This material builds outward toward the island and finally creates a tombolo that ties the island to the mainland. A convex curve in the beach, such as forms behind offshore break-

waters or beached ships as sand builds outward, is called
the tombolo effect. A second effect of an offshore island is
to reduce the height of the berm in its lee so that streams
in the area flow into the sea behind the island. For example, James Island on the Washington coast has a tombolo with the Quillayute River flowing out one side. This
river used to adjust to wave conditions by flowing on alternate sides of the island until training jetties were built to
hold it in a permanent channel.

Sometimes the refraction caused by a submarine canyon will bend wave energy away from the beach opposite
the head of the canyon, resulting in a low berm at that
point. This happens at the Point Mugu lagoon in California. When the water in the lagoon rises, it cuts through
the low berm opposite the head of Mugu canyon. However, there is substantial sand transport to the east in this
area, caused by littoral currents, so the stream outlet then
migrates eastward as sand builds up to the west and
erodes to the east of the channel. In some years the entrance moves nearly a mile eastward before a large winter
storm throws up a new berm, the lagoon begins to fill
again, and the cycle repeats. The same phenomenon used
to happen at Newport Bay, California, before people in-
terfered with the natural process by building training jetties to hold the tidal entrance at the extreme southern end
of its excursion.

Another curious beach feature that attracted my attention long ago are the ridges along Clatsop spit, Oregon,
just south of the Columbia River entrance. Most beach
ridges (sometimes called dune ridges) are merely growth
lines attesting to a series of abrupt advances by a shoreline—possibly single large storms or periods of exceptional littoral drift that brought in and deposited huge
quantities of sand. These ridges are very common, and

Cape Canaveral in east-central Forida is made largely of the ridges that have built up over the last few thousand years. Such ridges also exist at Clatsop near the south jetty of the river.

The ones I am interested in, however, are entirely different. After driving along and across these extremely regular elongated mounds on numerous occasions and rather absent-mindedly thinking they were man-made railroad embankments it suddenly dawned on me that there was no good reason to have any railroad embankment, much less several running parallel. Not long afterward I flew over the area and took the photograph used in this book (Plate 34), which shows about two miles of the Clatsop ridges. There are two large ridges, five smaller ones, and suggestions of seven or eight more. The one at the extreme right actually has a railroad track on it.

These ridges parallel both each other and the shoreline. Obviously they were somehow built by the sea, but since they rise to forty feet above sea level it is evident that the sea used a special technique. The larger ridges are in pairs, and my examination showed elongated depressions on the seaward side of the large ones (not shown in the area photographed). I looked and dug for material that could be dated by carbon 14, without luck—but it must be there somewhere. There you have the principal evidence. What caused the ridges? My solution is given at the end of this section. In the meantime, think it over.

TIDAL ENTRANCES AND BOTTOM FEATURES

Sand transport in tidal entrances is different from that on open beaches where waves and wave-caused currents dominate. Typical tidal inlets on open coasts are in a state of dynamic equilibrium in which the motion of sand in the entrance channel is constantly being adjusted in accordance with variations in the tidal currents.

Steve Costa of the University of California at San Diego did a doctoral thesis on this subject that disclosed the relationship between the velocity of the near-bottom water, the bed forms, and the amount of sand transport. In a series of model experiments conducted at the hydraulic laboratory of the Scripps Institution of Oceanography he held the water depth constant and worked with sand of sizes ranging from 0.06 to 1.0 mm.

He, and others before, have found that as water flows over a sand bed at increasing speed, there is a threshold velocity below which no sand is moved. As the velocity increases, individual grains begin to move short distances in a jerky fashion, a process called saltation. A further increase causes asymmetrical current ripples to form, and a still greater increase brings about the formation of dunes, often with superimposed ripples. When the velocity is further increased, a transitional stage is reached; eventually the dunes are swept away and the bottom becomes flat. This produces sheet flow. At even higher velocities, long stationary sand waves and anti-dunes are formed. The anti-dune has the curious characteristic that the dune form travels upstream while its sand grains are moving downstream (as they do in all the other bed forms). Many scientists have investigated and rechecked the above matters. The problem was that only in the transitional flat-bed situation could the rate of sand transport be simply related to the hydrodynamic regime.

In the other bed forms—especially ripples and dunes, which dominate tidal inlets—the sand transport mechanism depends on the turbulent flow of the water as it interacts with the bed forms. These features cause a large increase in the near-bed turbulence, which increases the average forces acting on the sand grains and creates fluctuating forces that further enhance the transport rate.

Steve Costa found that the type of bed form present controls the way in which sand transport depends on current speed. Table IX shows that sand transport is proportional to surprisingly high powers of water velocity. Actually, the absolute value of sand transport increases continuously with velocity.

In the dune regime, characteristic of most stable inlets, the transport of sand is very sensitive to small changes in velocity. A 1 percent change in maximum tidal currents results in a 6 percent change in transport rate. This remarkable amount of leverage caused John Isaacs to suggest that if a small additional flow could be added at a time that increased the velocity of the ebbing current, certain entrances could be kept free of excess sand. Tide gates or a pump system could add to the outflow of some bays to move sand at a lesser cost than periodic dredging.

TABLE IX

POWERS OF V (BOTTOM CURRENT VELOCITY) ON WHICH SAND
TRANSPORT DEPENDS. (AFTER STEVE COSTA)

BED FORM REGIME	SAND TRANSPORT PROPORTIONAL TO:
Ripples	V^{10}
Dunes	V^6
Transition and flat bed	V^3
Standing waves	V^6
Anti-dunes	V^6

Sand waves, dunes, and ripples on the bottom of Cook Inlet, Alaska, have been intensively studied by Arnold Bouma, Monty Hampton, and others of the U. S. Geological Survey's Pacific-Arctic Marine Geology Group using side-scan sonar, a high-resolution seismic profiling system, television, and photography. The water depth in the area studied has an average of about 60 meters (180 feet) and the surrounding shores are very rocky, so this is not a beach within our definition (rock fragments subject to movement by ordinary wave action). However, the features formed are similar to those found at tidal entrances and their study is instructive.

Cook Inlet is a very rough and rugged place. The average tidal range at Anchorage is 9 meters (28 feet), and on the change of tides the flow of water in and out of the inlet reaches mean maximum velocities of 2 m/sec (3.8 knots) with 3 m/sec during tidal extremes. Winds sometimes reach 100 knots, waves can be 6 meters high, and in winter the surface is covered with floe ice. Beneath all this, the bottom currents create some remarkable bed forms: sand waves, dunes, ripples, and ribbons.

Each of these types of bed-form fields covers only a relatively small area, perhaps a kilometer wide and a few kilometers long. Their boundaries are distinct, changing abruptly from one form to another.

Sand waves are the largest feature, having a wave length ranging from 10 to 1,000 meters and a wave height of from 0.5 to more than 10 meters. In profile these waves are strongly asymmetrical, with a steep lee or down-current side and a relatively gentle slope leading up to the crest. The crests are straight, or nearly so, and the elevations of troughs and crests are about the same. In other words, they are exceedingly regular features. The wave length to wave height ratio is seldom more than 20:1. These bed forms are normally formed by moderate currents in sediments coarser than 0.1–0.2 mm. Sometimes these large waves have smaller ones on their flanks, which may be parallel to the large crests or at a large angle to them, suggesting variations in the current direction and velocity.

The observations have not been taken over a long enough period of time for the rate of transport of sand to be known. However, the waves seem to be similar to sand ridges reported from the North Sea that are not believed to have moved appreciably during the last three centuries.

B. R. Colby, also of the USGS, studied the matter and found that coarse sand is moved along the bottom when surface-current velocities are over 2 m/sec (and currents near the bottom are nearly 40 cm/sec.) This occurs only during spring tides and perhaps winter storms. He, and others, also noted a significant increase in transport power with a decrease in water temperature.

Bouma and his associates in the Cook Inlet study also found a similar but smaller sand form called a dune or mega-ripple. These are much less regular in height and plan, probably because they are formed by stronger and more turbulent currents. Dunes have a wave length of 1 to 40 meters and height up to a few meters. However, because they are steeper (their length-height ratio is less than 20:1) they show more apparent relief on the sonographs.

The smallest features seen are ordinary current ripples, which seldom exceed 5 cm in height and 30 cm in length. Their shape depends on grain size and angularity and on the bottom current, which is often deflected or modified by the larger bed forms.

Sand ribbons were also seen. These are thin, narrow bodies of sand elongated in the direction of the current, commonly resting on a floor of coarser material. Sometimes there will be several such ribbons, roughly parallel, and sometimes sand in the ribbons will be in the form of small waves. Ribbons indicate that the sand supply is scarce and that the currents are over about 1 m/sec. Parallel ribbons are common in the North Sea and the Strait of Dover to depths of 150 meters. I have observed them in the Bahamas, both on the great banks far from land in water only 8 meters deep and in even shallower water where scarce sand, rounding a point, is rapidly moved to a receiving beach across a hard coral bottom.

Television observations of the Cook Inlet bottom showed details of the distribution of grain size and permitted an estimate of sand-movement velocity on various parts of the ripples. In the Coastal Water Research Project we have used television to find out directly what current velocities are required to move bottom material. We wanted to know the minimum water velocity required to resuspend sediments in various locations. Generally we were interested in muddy sands at water depths of 20 to 80 meters. The complexities of size distribution, shape, and density of the particles, the amount of consolidation, and the extent of recent churning by marine organisms could not be reproduced very well in the laboratory. So we decided to measure the velocities in situ.

For this purpose we devised and built a "sediment stirrer"—a three-sided Plexiglas tunnel with an open bottom. It was lowered to the sea floor so that the sediments being investigated formed the bottom of the tunnel. Then a variable-speed motor (controlled from the surface) was used to drive a propeller that drew water through a convergent entrance section into the tunnel. Water velocity in the tunnel was measured by means of a small current meter at the midpoint.

A television camera and light system was attached to the steel framework that supported the tunnel so that those on the ship above could see on a TV monitor what was happening in the tunnel below. As the water velocity increased, the sand particles were soon set in motion. This happens abruptly because the stress on the sediments increases at a rate proportional to the square of the water velocity. This is the *velocity required to initiate motion.* The speed is then increased until a turbid flow is observed along the bottom; this velocity was termed the *resuspension velocity.* No significant correlation with sediment grain size was found, but where less dense organic materials were present a much lower velocity was required to initiate motion. It was possible to map the probable mobility of sediments in this fashion.

Our intention was to determine how often during the year the orbital currents caused by storm swell would be sufficient to stir the bottom. (If the bottom material is put in suspension by wave orbital currents, then very-low-speed longshore currents will transport it.) Terry Hendricks then measured water motions with a current meter and also calculated the bottom currents that would be produced by waves, using detailed wave data for the area. The result was (for 60 meters depth of water off the Palos Verdes Peninsula) that the bottom sediments would probably be reworked if the currents exceeded 6 cm/sec; that was found to occur about 39 percent of the time, or 150 days a year.

In scanning the data we found a number of occasions when the currents reached over 20 cm/sec and some when it was over 50 cm/sec. This strongly suggested that the main shifts of the bottom materials come during unusually long-period waves (over 14 seconds) or in the violent storms that occur every decade or so.

To return to the question of the high, parallel beach ridges at Clatsop spit, Oregon: my hypothesis is that the ridges were caused by ice shove. A long time ago, but within the last four thousand years during which the sea has been at its present level, a great mass of ice drifted onto this beach. Most likely it was fresh-water ice, perhaps from the breakup of glaciers far to the north or perhaps it came down the Columbia River. Fresh-water ice is likely to be in larger pieces that project higher above the water than salt-water floe ice. In any case, it was evenly distributed along at least ten miles of that sandy beach. At the same time a violent storm, with high winds and waves from the west, drove the ice hard aground on a shoreline that was well behind the present shoreline. Doubtless there were also storm tides that raised sea level slightly.

As the ice was driven shoreward it shoved sand ahead of it into the great ridges we see today. Doubtless these have been smoothed somewhat and softened by erosion. The small transverse ridges that cross all the large ones at about equal angles were probably made by winds at a later time. The depressions to the west of the ridges now filled with swamp are the final resting place of some of the blocks of ice that pushed the ridges. While they were melting, another beach developed on their seaward side, but in some places that beach reached the ridge and obliterated the ice depression.

The existence of pairs of ridges is an interesting problem. My guess is that each pair was formed by ice from the same source in the same season or at least in successive years. Perhaps after the first grounding and some

melting another great storm shoved more of the floating
ice onto the beach. Then many years passed—dozens or
hundreds—and the phenomenon repeated itself and another ridge was formed. Since we are now living in an interglacial period there may be more to come before the
Clatsop ridges are completed.

GROINS AND BEACH NOURISHMENT

For many years the accepted method of dealing with
shoreline erosion problems was to build groins. A groin is
a dam-like structure, usually a few feet high and about a
hundred feet long, constructed perpendicular to the
shoreline. Its objective is to retard the loss of a beach,
widening it by trapping the passing sand. Groins may be
made of timber, sheet-steel pilings, stone, or concrete.
Some are built solid, to be impervious to sand flow; others
—permeable groins—are constructed with openings that
permit appreciable quantities of sand to flow through. Ordinarily a system of groins is built to protect a long section of shoreline. Some parts of the New York and New
Jersey coasts have "groin fields" extending for many
miles. As material accumulates on the updrift side and
the beach there widens, the supply of sand to the down
drift side is correspondingly reduced and the beach retreats. So, the solution is to build another groin, and another, and another. The slope of the beach face on the
updrift side progressively steepens while that on the
downdrift side flattens. Often the updrift side fills and
overflows, the swashes of high tide carrying the sand over
the top and spilling it on the low side, and soon a system
of groins produces a series of short curving beaches that
give the shoreline the cuspate appearance shown in the

accompanying drawing. As each groin fills, the sand bypasses the end and proceeds down the coast.

Although properly engineered groins can capture and retain sand, their effect is usually local and temporary. Persons with beach-front property in imminent danger of being washed away are understandably eager to take fast action, and without investigation they may build a groin in the hope of restoring their beach. But there may not be any sand passing, or the groin may be built in the wrong place and actually accelerate the erosion. The motion of coastal sand is more complex than one might suppose.

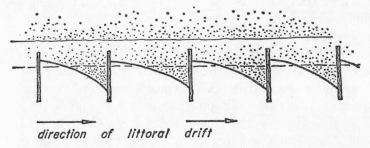

direction of littoral drift

FIG. 80. Groins are low dams intended to arrest the sand moving alongshore in the hope of maintaining or widening the original (dashed line) shoreline.

Sometimes groins are helpful. There is an instance in which a ship saved a lighthouse, instead of vice versa. In 1883 the Cape Henlopen light on the Delaware coast was in imminent danger of being undermined by the sea. The high-water mark reached around the base and various emergency protective actions were being considered. Then in a storm the *Minnie Hunter* was driven ashore, grounding about five hundred feet north of the lighthouse. The wrecked ship immediately acted as a groin which dammed the coastal flow of sand and replaced the

beach in front of the light so that the structure survived
for many more years.

When the objective is to have adequate sand on the
beach for play and the protection of shoreline structures,
an alternative to groins is beach nourishment. This simply
means that sand is added wherever people want it. The
advantage of this technique is that it is simple and direct;
the disadvantage is that the newly added sand erodes in
the same way as the sand it replaced. Usually the local
residents are happy for a while, but in a few years they
grow increasingly restive as each set of winter storms cuts
the new sand back beyond what the ocean will replace in
the summer.

There are several ways to nourish beaches. The famous
Waikiki Beach has been rebuilt several times, usually
with sand trucked down from the north end of Oahu
some miles away. Then it slowly grinds itself into fine particles that drift along offshore, so that a fine-sand dump is
formed at the seaward end of the old Ala Wai Channel.
The wide beach at Long Beach, California, is made of
sand dredged from the bottom, inside the distant breakwater; and Redondo Beach was similarly widened with
sand scooped from Santa Monica Bay. At one time my
company was involved in rebuilding Pompano Beach,
Florida. When we began our work, sections of the beach
ranged from narrow to nonexistent, and the shorefront
buildings were endangered. So we contracted to add a
strip of sand about 10 feet deep, 300 feet wide, and
15,000 feet long.

The new beach sand was pumped from about 30 feet of
water a mile offshore by a large dredge that sucked up
sand from areas where we had found deep sand pockets
by probing with a jet. At first the new sand appeared
grayish because of the tiny particles of unoxidized mate-

rial, but a few months in the sun turned it white. About 1.5 million yards was moved ashore in this fashion. The holes offshore from which sand was borrowed will refill with sand, but probably not as rapidly as material is eroded off the beach and moved downcoast by the littoral transport. Like other solutions to the problem of defending against the sea, this one is temporary.

Because groins rarely give a satisfactory long-term solution they are no longer the preferred means of maintaining a beach. In the long run they are usually more expensive and less effective than a "beach nourishment" program. So the fashion is to add more sand, supplying it to the "headwaters" of the littoral stream from inland dunes or from the bottoms of nearby lagoons.

This change of opinion about the best way to maintain beaches is illustrated by the problem now facing the state of New Jersey. The configuration of the coast is such that refracted Atlantic Ocean swell strikes heavily on the New Jersey coast's most prominent point, near Barnegat Inlet. Littoral currents move the sand away from the point in both directions, and the point is eroding rapidly. In the past fifty years nearly $50 million has been spent on shore works in an attempt to stabilize the shoreline. The present annual rate of expenditure is more than $2 million, and the results are not entirely satisfactory. Some parts of the shore have long since been stripped of sand; others are still retreating. In several places elaborate groin systems have failed.

The Beach Erosion Board studied the New Jersey problem and proposed a project to develop adequate recreational beaches and prevent further erosion. This project will nourish all the beaches along the coast by supplying new sand to the beaches in the vicinity of Barnegat Inlet. The sand will come partly by truck from inland locations and partly by pumping from Barnegat Bay; wave action and littoral currents can be relied upon to distribute it along the coast. The estimated initial investment is $28 million, but the program will require less than $1 million per year to maintain the beaches thereafter.

Many other shoreline construction projects, costing hundreds of millions of dollars, have been planned for the shores of the United States. Beach erosion is a problem of increasing importance as coastal land is developed intensively.

XIII

Man Against the Sea

THE SEA CAN BE EITHER FRIENDLY OR HOSTILE. IT IS CALM
and beautiful one day, furious and terrifying the next. On
days calm enough to make surveys and do construction
work one must not forget that before long unleashed violence will follow. The destructive power of the sea
against ships and beaches has been described. Now we
will consider what happens when waves smash against
harbor defenses and shoreline installations, and what can
be done to withstand the onslaught.

The solution to any problem begins with the attempt to
understand what is going on. What is the nature of the
forces? How do they act? What levels of energy are involved?

Previous chapters contain background information
about the various kinds of waves, the way in which they
refract as they enter shoal water and the manner in which
they are transformed into breakers. Now we must make
use of this information in the design of coastal works that
defend against the sea's attack. Experience is a good, although perhaps a hard, teacher, and it is well to begin by

recalling some instances in which violent wave action has damaged shoreline structures in the past. These serve as a warning—reminding us of the extreme forces which waves may exert once in a decade or a century. Then we will consider various means that can be used to defend our shores and harbors against the worst the sea can do.

WAVES ATTACK

Case histories of wave attack on man's coastal structures make fascinating reading, for this aspect of the lore of the sea makes its great power most apparent. Many of the following examples were collected by D. D. Gaillard and presented in *Wave Action in Relation to Engineering Structure,* published nearly sixty years ago. Lighthouses, by the very concept, are natural recipients of violent wave action since they often are built on rocky headlands or submarine ledges to keep ships at a safe distance. Some of them are called "wave-swept towers," and it is understandable that lighthouse keepers should be an endless source of stories about fabulous waves and marine disasters.

For example: During the construction of the Dhu Heartach lighthouse in 1872, fourteen stones of ten tons weight each, which had been fixed into the tower by joggles and Portland cement at the level of thirty-seven feet above high water, were torn out and carried into deep water.

A door in the Unst light, 195 feet above the sea, was once broken open by the impact of flying water, and windows in the Dunnet Head light station in north Scotland, 300 feet above the water, are sometimes broken by rocks flung up by the waves.

In 1923 the St. George Reef lighthouse near Crescent City, California, experienced a storm in which breaking waves swept over the foundation platform of the lighthouse tower, seventy feet above the water, tearing a donkey engine from its foundation.

At Trinidad Head, California, a few miles to the south, the light is set on a rocky promontory 195 feet above mean sea level, which doubtless seemed to its designers like a good safe height. This illusion was shattered in 1913 when the lightkeeper reported: "At 4:40 P.M. I observed a wave of unusual height. When it struck the bluff, the jar was heavy. The lens immediately stopped revolving. The sea shot up the face of the bluff and over it, until solid sea seemed to me to be on a level with where I stood by the lantern."

Several lighthouses are famous for having been swept away entirely by great storms and having been replaced more than once. These include the Eddystone light, Bishop's Rock light, and the original Minot's Ledge light, off the Massachusetts coast, which was destroyed several times during construction and in 1851 crumpled into the sea carrying its two lightkeepers with it. In the midst of a great storm people on the main coast heard the frantic ringing of its bell abruptly terminate. Little evidence could be found afterward that a lighthouse had ever stood there. The new stone shaft that replaced it rises ninety-seven feet directly from the sea, has now stood for over one hundred years, and the U. S. Coast Guard is proud that waves often sweep over the entire structure causing no effect except strong vibration.

Of all the stories, those about the light on Tillamook Rock, a few miles south of the Columbia River mouth, are retold most often. The rock itself, several miles at sea, has nearly vertical walls rising to a ragged surface about

90 feet above the water on which the lighthouse was built. During every severe storm the entire rock shudders and fragments torn from the base of the cliff are thrown on top of the rock. In a December storm a rock weighing 135 pounds was thrown higher than the light, which is 139 feet above the sea, and in falling back broke a hole 20 feet square in the roof of the lightkeeper's house, practically wrecking the interior of the building. On another occasion a fragment of rock weighing about half a ton was rolled across the platform at the base of the building, 91 feet above low water, smashing a wrought-iron fence. In 1902 a keeper reported that water was thrown to a height of fully 200 feet above the level of the sea, "descending in apparently solid water on the roof." Ten years later another keeper, investigating trouble with the foghorn (95 feet above the water) found it filled with small rocks. After the glass of the lantern was broken on several occasions by rocks, a heavy steel grating was installed 135 feet above the sea, just below the lens, to prevent further damage.

As a result of this process of trial and error, which now extends over two thousand years, increasingly heavy construction has been used, and the problem of maintaining lighthouses on exposed rocks seems to have been reasonably well solved—except in such special cases as the Scotch Cap light described in Chapter VI.

The only stories about wave violence that can top the lighthouse accounts are those about breakwaters. At Cherbourg, France, the breakwater was built as an immense embankment of loose stone protected in places by 700-cubic-foot concrete blocks. A wall twenty feet high surmounts the stone embankment. During a severe storm on Christmas Day many years ago stones weighing seven thousand pounds were thrown over the top of the wall and many of the concrete blocks moved as much as sixty feet.

In the Shetland Islands a block of stone weighing five and a half tons was detached from its bed situated seventy-two feet above the high tide level and moved more than twenty feet. Another block weighing eight tons was torn up and driven by the waves over several ledges with vertical faces two to seven feet high for a distance of seventy feet at an average level of twenty feet above high water.

In an especially severe gale at Buffalo, New York, in December 1899, considerable damage was inflicted by waves upon timber-crib breakwater which had been completed but a few weeks previously. This gale was of unusual violence, the wind blowing at times at the rate of 80 miles per hour from the west. The water level of the lake varied from 3 feet below mean lake level to 6.4 feet above the same datum between 4 p.m. and midnight. Tremendous seas broke over the breakwater. The waves, dashing against the vertical walls of the structure, rose to a great height above it, variously estimated at from 75 to 125 feet, enveloping the breakwater in an immense sheet of water. In falling, the water struck the top of the superstructure with such force as to crush the large timbers of which it was constructed. Because the direction of the breakwater was at right angles to the axis of the storm, the destructive power of the furious waves was accentuated. Seventy 12-by-12-inch timbers, 10 feet between supports and spaced 5 feet from center to center, were broken in the middle by the impact of the falling water. About 900 feet of superstructure in all was smashed almost to the water's edge.

The breakwater at Wick Bay in Scotland often faces into violent waves, and its failure in 1872 was described by Thomas Stevenson in *The Construction of Harbours:* "The end of the breakwater was composed of three courses of blocks weighing 80 to 100 tons each which were deposited as a foundation in a trench made in cement rubble. Above this foundation there were three courses of large stones carefully set in cement, and the whole was surmounted by a large monolith of cement rubble, measuring about 26 by 45 feet by 11 feet in thickness, weighing upward of 800 tons. As a further precaution, iron rods 3.5 inches in diameter were fixed in the uppermost of the foundation courses of cement rubble. These rods were carried through the courses of stonework by holes cut in the stone, and were finally embedded in the monolithic mass, which formed the upper portion of the pier.

"Incredible as it may seem, this huge mass succumbed to the force of the waves, and Mr. McDonald, the resident engineer, actually watched from the adjacent cliff as it was gradually slewed round by successive strokes until it was finally removed and deposited inside the pier. It was several days before an examination could be made of this singular phenomenon, but the result of the examination only gave rise to increased amazement at the feat which the waves had actually achieved. Divers found that the 800-ton monolith forming the upper portion of the pier, which the resident engineer had seen in the act of being washed away, had carried with it the whole of the lower courses, which were attached to it by the iron bolts, and that this enormous mass, weighing not less than 1,350 tons, had been removed in one piece and was resting on the rubble at the side of the pier, having sustained no damage but a slight fracture at the edges. The second course of cement blocks, on which the 1,350-ton mass rested, had been swept off after being relieved of the superincumbent weight, and some of the blocks were found entire near the head of the breakwater. The removal of this protection left the end of the breakwater exposed and the storm, which continued to rage for some days after the destruction of the cement rubble defense, carried away about 150 feet of the masonry (one-seventh of the whole)."

The structure was rebuilt and a much larger cap was added, this one weighing 2,600 tons, but five years later another storm treated it quite as roughly. There is no record of whether Mr. McDonald kept his job and made a third attempt. Captain D. D. Gaillard, U.S.A., later computed that the wave forces required to move the second cap must have been 6,340 pounds per square foot.

In November 1950 extraordinary waves from a storm on Lake Michigan moved a concrete cap on the U. S. Steel Company's breakwater at Gary, Indiana. This cap, 200 feet long and weighing 2,600 tons, moved 3 to 4 feet laterally when pounded by 7.2-second waves about 14 feet high. Knowing the mass of the concrete, to motion, the engineers computed that the wave pressure required to move the cap must have been between 1,440 and 2,500 pounds per square foot—or 1,680 tons of nearly instantaneous wave pressure.

MAN DEFENDS

The words that Captain Gaillard wrote more than sixty years ago to describe the effects of waves on structures are as valid as ever: "If wave motion is arrested by any interposing barrier, a part at least of the energy of the wave will be exerted against the barrier itself, and unless the latter is strong enough to resist the successive attacks of the waves, its destruction will ensue.

"No other force of equal intensity so severely tries every part of the structure against which it is exerted, and so unerringly detects each weak place or faulty detail of construction.

"The reason for this is found in the diversity of ways in which the wave force may be exerted and transmitted; for example: (1) The force may be a static pressure due to the head of a column of water; or (2) it may result from the kinetic effect of rapidly moving particles of the fluid; or (3) from the impact of a body floating upon the surface of the water and hurled by the wave against the structure; or (4) the rapid subsidence of the mass of water thrown against a structure may produce a partial vacuum, causing sudden pressures to be exerted from within.

"These effects may be transmitted through joints or cracks in the structure itself; (a) by hydraulic pressure, or (b) pneumatic pressure, or by a combination of the two; or (c) the shock produced by the impact of the waves may be transmitted as vibrations through the materials of which the structure is composed."

In order to design any kind of structure that will stand against wave action, one must have numbers that describe the amounts of energy involved and the magnitude of the forces imposed.

The energy in a wave is equally divided between potential energy and kinetic energy. The potential energy, resulting from the elevation or depression of the water surface, advances with the wave form; the kinetic energy is a summation of the motion of the particles in the wave train and advances with the group velocity (in shallow water this is equal to the wave velocity).

The amount of energy in a wave is the product of the wave length and the *square* of the wave height, as follows:

$$E = \frac{wLH^2}{8}$$

where w is the weight of a cubic foot of water (64 pounds).

Thus we can compare the energy in three waves of ten-second period, one 4 feet high, one 8 feet high, and one 12 feet high. The 4-foot wave contains 65,600 foot-pounds of energy (per foot of wave crust) or 33 foot-tons; the 8-foot wave has 131 foot-tons, and the 12-foot wave 295 foot-tons. A big difference! For practical purposes the deep-water formula applies to shallow-water waves.

The question of exactly how much pressure large waves exert against structures was investigated by Thomas Stevenson, beginning in 1842. He invented a simple, rugged dynamometer and made the first measurements of wave force. The instrument consisted merely of a plate six inches in diameter facing into the waves, mounted on a stiff horizontal spring. Behind the spring was a rod held by a friction grip in such a fashion that it would move as the plate moved but remain at the maximum distance to which the plate pushed it. As each increasingly large wave impacted against the plate, the rod would be pushed to a new position. The distance moved times the spring constant gave the maximum wave force exerted on the plate during the storm.

He reported that at Skerryvore Rocks in the Atlantic the maximum force of waves in a storm which had an average height of 10 feet was 3,041 pounds per square foot (psf), for 20-foot swell 4,502 psf, and for strong gales with waves in excess of 20 feet, 6,083 psf.

The disadvantage of this type of instrument is that it registers only the dynamic pressure of moving water and ignores the hydrostatic pressure; moreover, there is only a single maximum reading per storm. Years later Captain Gaillard decided to build a diaphragm type of dynamometer that would measure total force and use it to probe the pressure of wave impact in more detail. After using the new instrument for a while he worked out a formula for the maximum pressure exerted by a breaking wave:

$$\text{Pressure} = 1.31(C + V)^2 \frac{\rho}{2g}$$

in which C is the wave velocity, V is the maximum orbital velocity at the crest of the wave, and ρ is the mass density of water. For a wave 10 feet high with a period of 5 seconds, a typical Great Lakes storm wave, the pressure calculated from Gaillard's formula is 1,240 pounds per square foot, which agrees well with the 1,210 psf registered by his instrument. By installing a series of dynamometers at various heights above and below the average water level he found that for breaking waves the pressure increases with the height above the trough, reaching a maximum of about half the breaker's height (roughly the still-water level at that moment).

More recently R. R. Minikin, a British engineer, has established a different series of relationships between wave pressures, thrust against structures and overturning moments, but these give approximately equivalent answers. Now, armed with modern crystal pressure transducers, electronic amplifiers and continuously recording apparatus, the store of data is rapidly increasing, and the results can be examined statistically. The highest wave-pressure measurement on record was taken at Dieppe, France, in

PLATE 49. A 100:1 scale model of Oceanside, California, being subjected to large waves at an angle with the shoreline to determine the effectiveness of groins and offshore breakwaters for controlling the movement of sand. *U. S. Army Corps of Engineers*

PLATE 50. The two principal tanks at the David Taylor Naval Ship Research and Development Center. Models as much as 30 feet long weighing several tons are towed at speeds up to 60 knots down the main tank, which is 3,078 feet long and 51 feet wide. At the left is the 21-foot-wide "high-speed" tank. *U. S. Navy Photo*

PLATE 51. Small ships are designed to be theoretically capable of supporting the weight of their bow and stern if the midsection is balanced on top of a steep wave. Rarely is a ship so tested as was the *Princess May* by a very low tide in the Inland Passage. *Williamsons Marine Salon*

PLATE 52. The Ocean Test Structure, sponsored primarily by Exxon, is probably the largest wave-measuring device ever built. Since December 1976 this $3.5 million, 120-foot-high, quarter-size version of a drilling-production platform has been collecting data on the forces produced by real waves so that these can be compared with theoretical computations. *Robert Haring, Exxon*

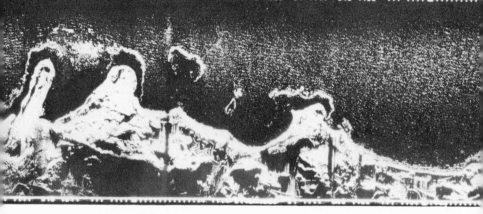

PLATE 53. Side-looking Airborne Radar produces a photo-like image of the sea surface that can be used to obtain approximate wind speed and wave length. This example is of the coast of Puerto Rico. The high contrast between land and sea means that much less of the radar energy is backscattered by the sea. *Duncan Ross, NOAA*

PLATE 54. Entrance to Fire Island inlet, June 1958. Sand moving westward along the south coast of Long Island built the beach out to the end of the jetty, which it is now bypassing to form spits in the channel. *Fairchild Aerial Surveys*

PLATE 55. From 1903 to 1935 Daytona Beach, Florida, was used for auto racing and speed record attempts by many drivers (including Sir Malcolm Campbell, who set a world mark there of 276.82 mph). Then stock car racing took over until 1959, when a speedway was built. This is the parade lap of one of the last races. *Daytona Beach Resort Area*

PLATE 56. In a most remarkable coastal construction job, Consolidated Diamond Mines of Southwest Africa extended their minable area over 300 meters seaward by means of a colossal dike that in some places was built in water previously 20 meters deep. The area in the foreground now being mined was previously beneath very rough surf. *DeBeers Consolidated Mines Ltd.*

PLATE 57. Dolos armor units weighing forty-two tons each being placed on the south jetty at Humboldt Bay, California, in 1971. Large swell spends its energy in turbulence amid these complex shapes. *U. S. Army Corps of Engineers*

1938, where A. de Rouvelle reported instantaneous pressures of 12,700 psf (the pressure above 6,000 psf lasted only for 1/100 of a second).

THE DESIGN OF SHORELINE STRUCTURES

There are four major kinds of shoreline structures: jetties, breakwaters, seawalls, and dikes. All are made usually of some combination of rock and concrete. Jetties, usually in pairs, extend into the ocean at river entrances or bay mouths to confine the flow of water to a narrow zone. If concentrated between a pair of jetties, the ebb and flow of tidal water keeps the sand in motion and prevents shoaling in the channel. A breakwater is a structure that protects a shore area, harbor, or anchorage from wave action. Often it is built well out from shore to provide a substantial area of quiet water. A seawall is built at the shoreline separating land from water. It is the man-made equivalent of a rocky cliff, designed to protect softer material from erosion. A dike is a special form of impermeable breakwater that acts as a dam. When the zone it protects is pumped dry, it becomes a special kind of seawall.

What can the engineer do to ensure that such structures survive against wave attack? He has several choices which he tries to combine into the most efficient solution. He can carefully locate the structure so that its position and shape and orientation give it the most favorable chance for survival; he can build in such a fashion that wave energy is reflected or absorbed; he can build with large and dense materials, simply resisting the wave forces with weight. Always, he considers all factors that enter into the various possibilities and tries to optimize his solution. The final plan is not necessarily the best possible structure to resist waves but the best thing that can be done considering cost, time, use of existing facilities, kind of rock that is available, probable increase in the use of the installation, and, of course, political influences of many kinds. The engineer must fight as hard as he can for the best solution, but he is overruled often and ends up building a structure of which he may not wholeheartedly approve.

Here we will review only the technical areas within which the designer can maneuver to obtain the best engineering solution. No matter what other factors may ultimately influence the decision on what is to be constructed, this is always the first step.

The location of the structure comes first. For breakwaters the underwater topography and the refraction conditions usually influence the design most. In Chapter IV the process of making statistical studies of waves and drawing refraction diagrams was described. Briefly, the idea is to obtain as much information as possible about the waves arriving at the proposed harbor by hindcasting from old weather charts. The charts will give the dominant wave direction and period as well as the probable height of the largest or most damaging waves. Then refraction diagrams are prepared; these are basic design data for the breakwater builder. Now taking into consideration the underwater topography, the general configuration of the coast, and the proposed locations of piers and wharves, the engineer can lay out various breakwater locations. Probably he will not want the structure to be exactly parallel to the wave fronts from the most probable direction. If it were, a wave could impact along the whole length of the structure at the same instant. Usually he will spread the stress out by presenting an angular front to the worst seas. Perhaps he will make model tests, first in a ripple tank, then in a larger wave tank.

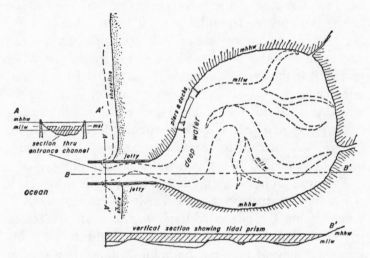

FIG. 81. Bay harbor showing tidal prism (the volume of water between mean higher high water and mean lower low water).

In locating jetty pairs, which often are parallel rocky structures extending directly into the ocean, a major problem is to space them properly so that the velocity of the moving tidal water will be sufficiently high to scour the sand from the entrance channel and keep it deep enough for ship traffic. If the distance between them is too great, the water will flow at lower velocity, and its energy will be diffused so that the channels will be shallow and sandbars will obstruct the entrance. On the other hand, if the jetties are too close together the currents are likely to scour the sand from beneath the stones and undermine them. One can get an idea of the proper spacing by studying the natural channels. In the late 1930s M. P. O'Brien examined a number of bays along the U.S. Pacific Coast and determined that a constant ratio exists between the area of the entrance section and the volume of the tidal prism. The tidal prism is the volume of water inside a bay or harbor that is enclosed by planes of mean higher high water and mean lower low water. In other words, it is the average volume of water that flows in and out during a 12.4-hour tidal cycle. Shoreline engineers who disregard this fundamental design law and arbitrarily space jetties at a greater distance than indicated by Figure 82 can look forward to years of dredging to keep open a channel that could be maintained by natural forces.

The next problem of the design engineer is to devise a shape for the structure that will reflect, absorb, or otherwise cushion the effects of large waves. It is possible to get rid of some of the wave energy by reflecting it; this approach may or may not be helpful, depending on the circumstances. If the structure in question rises almost vertically from water too deep for the waves to break, the wave can be reflected back to sea with little loss of energy. But few breakwaters are designed to reflect more than a small part of the energy. More often they absorb the wave with rough faces of rock. Seawalls, on the other hand, usually are designed to reflect a substantial part of the wave energy that reaches them. Often they have a series of steps, each about two feet high, from which the water reflects without loading the whole structure simultaneously. Others have an overhanging recurved surface which has the effect of throwing the landward-rushing water seaward, back upon itself. But if the face of the seawall curves so as to guide the water straight upward, as

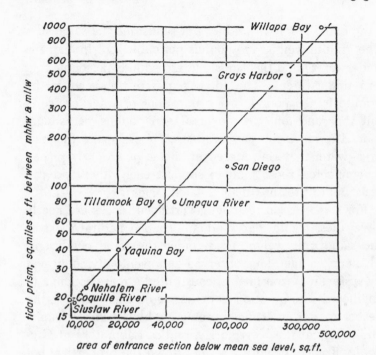

FIG. 82. Relationship between tidal prism and entrance section. (After O'Brien)

some old designs did, the water will fall back on the wall with great force, possibly damaging it and eroding the land it is intended to protect. A properly-designed wave reflector has the effect of starting a new wave moving seaward which tends to cancel the next oncoming wave it encounters, or at least reduce its force.

The resistance of rocks in a shoreline structure such as a breakwater or jetty to overturning or sliding is obviously of great interest to the shore-protection engineer. Dense rock is far more useful, as the following example shows. Compare a block of granite 5 feet on each side

(125 cubic feet) with a block of sandstone the same size. The granite weighs 170 pounds per cubic foot in air (106 underwater) and the sandstone 140 pounds per cubic foot (76 underwater). The force required to overturn the granite is 540 pounds per square foot of wave pressure, but the sandstone goes over at 390 pounds per square foot. Therefore the largest, densest rocks make the best breakwater material. Moreover, a line of properly placed or connected rocks tend to support each other and can resist more pressure than isolated blocks.

For some reason rectangular artificial blocks are nearly always less stable than randomly shaped natural rocks of the same unit weight used under the same conditions. This curious fact, long observed and eventually confirmed by systematic experiments, constituted a real challenge to engineers. The question to be answered was: What is the best shape for an artificial protecting block? Pierre Daniel and others at the Neyrpic Hydraulics Laboratory at Grenoble, France, began by setting down the properties that the new blocks—of whatever shape—should have. They decided these should be permeable so that the water could freely flow through. This solution would avoid creating any internal or back pressure (which at the Mers-el-Kebir naval base had bodily lifted a revetment composed of 400-ton blocks); it would reduce overtopping and reflection. The block should be shaped so as to have few plane surfaces; in fact, it should be as rough as possible to dissipate wave energy in turbulence; it should have maximum resistance. Combinations of blocks should interlock so that they could mutually support each other.

After many preliminary tests a sort of sea monster with four tentacles was patented under the name of "tetrapod." The most suitable proportions between legs and body were worked out with due consideration for the problem of manufacture, and not long afterward tetrapods began to appear in shoreline structures. They are most useful when placed in a double outer layer facing the worst wave action over a core of natural stone and rubble.

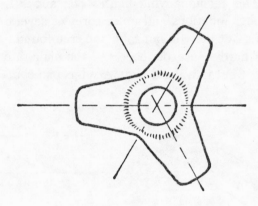

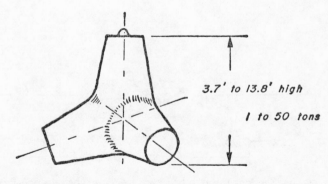

3.7' to 13.8' high

1 to 50 tons

FIG. 83. Tetrapods: four-legged sea monsters of concrete used for breakwater facing.

By bringing to bear all the factors mentioned here, successful shoreline structures can be designed. From the outside, to the uninitiated, the seawall may look like a rather ordinary piece of concrete with steps built for the convenience of bathers. Or the breakwater may look like a carelessly-dumped pile of rock instead of carefully built-up layers. The accompanying figures (84 and 85) show the physical foundations and inner cores of several kinds of structures, but they do not show the true foundation—the years of hard-won experience and the elaborate computations that went into the design. A subject so com-

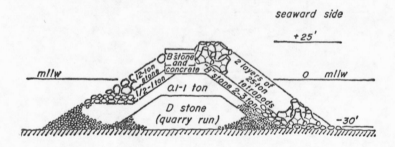

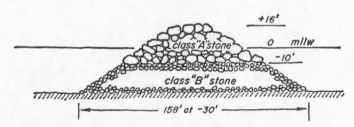

FIG. 84. Sections through breakwaters. *Top:* The tetrapod-faced breakwater at Crescent City, California. *Bottom:* The rubble-mound breakwater at Morro Bay, California.

plicated has many variations depending on local conditions and requirements, and this chapter obviously can do no more than give a hasty survey. If any reader has been stimulated to look further, I can recommend the *Proceedings of the Conferences on Coastal Engineering*, edited by J. W. Johnson and Robert Wiegel, of the Council on Wave Research, University of California at Berkeley.

Another form of coastal defense is the sand dune. Like

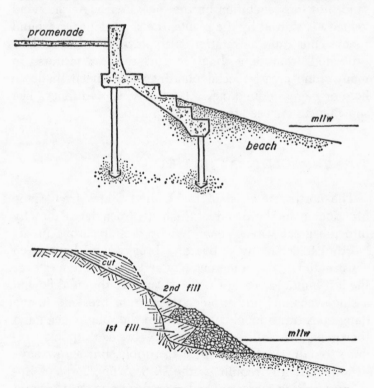

FIG. 85. Two kinds of seawalls. *Top:* A concrete-step seawall with a re-entrant curved section, resting on sheet piling driven deep into the beach. *Bottom:* A soft cliff is graded to a new slope and protected by a rubble-mound wall.

the beach itself, dunes can be nourished and encouraged by human acts. A zone of dunes behind a beach can act as a dike to prevent flooding of inhabited areas by unusually high tides or waves and, of course, the sand will resupply the beach if wave erosion becomes intense. When not acting in these emergency capacities, dunes make fine recreational areas.

Dunes usually develop when the wind blows dry beach sand into the vegetation on the back beach. As the wind velocity is slowed by the plants, the sand deposits around them. Thus dune vegetation is important and should be protected from dune buggies and careless visitors. In many dune areas, special plantings have been made to hold or increase the dunes. Alternately, slatted fences like snow fences are used for the same purpose.

THE HUMBOLDT BAY JETTIES

The northwest coast of the United States from Cape Mendocino to the Strait of Juan de Fuca faces directly into the great waves generated by winter storms in the North Pacific. Many jetties and breakwaters have been constructed at the numerous bay and river entrances over the last hundred years. These concentrate the tidal flow in a single channel and protect ships from breakers in the dangerous transitional zone between the rough ocean and the quiet inland water. Rampaging breakers quickly reduce some of these structures to rubble, but a few have been persistently rebuilt by the U. S. Army Corps of Engineers, whose increasingly larger design wave is now a breaker forty feet high.

The history of the jetties at the entrance to Humboldt Bay at Eureka, California, 225 miles north of San Francisco, is instructive. It has been recorded by Orville Magoon, an engineer for the corps, as an example of the difficulty of maintaining structures where the sea prefers not to have them.

The beginning was not auspicious. In 1878 the Board of Engineers for the Pacific Coast arrived off the entrance aboard a survey ship to make the first official inspection of the proposed jetty site. Even though it was summer and the weather appeared to be moderate, the pilot refused to take the ship across the bar into the bay. He may have been influenced by an earlier report that said, in part, "It has been reported by masters of vessels that no such heavy seas have been encountered elsewhere in the world unless perhaps at Cape Horn. Waves have been seen to break in 8 to 10 fathoms of water." (This meant forty- to fifty-foot breakers.)

The engineers decided to proceed anyway; the initial contract for the construction of a south jetty was signed in 1888, and within two years a north jetty was started. Both were to extend out to the 18-foot contour, with their tops at the plane of high water. By 1891 the south jetty was 4,000 feet long, and the north jetty was 1,500 feet. The latter used 28,000 cubic yards of brush and 100,000 tons of stone. Why brush?

The brush was used to make "mattresses." According to an eyewitness report: "Upon a grillage of poles, bound at each intersection, layers of bundles of brush are placed. The brush is about 12 feet long, the bundles in each layer being at right angles with those of the next. When the brush is 6 feet thick another grillage is added; the mass is compressed with screws and secured with wire. Then the mattress is ready. Small railroad cars filled with rock are brought up on the trestle above. Six men are stationed on surrounding timbers standing with uplifted axes to cut the mattress lashings. Other men stand ready to open the car dumps and release their rock. The signal is given, and in an instant the mattress strikes the water, followed in a second by a rattling volley of rock which drives it out of sight to the bottom."

Such was the way of jetty construction ninety years ago. The result was a fixed channel 700 feet wide and 25 feet deep. Sixteen years later the channel had shoaled and the outer ends of the jetties were buried in the sand.

Between 1911 and 1915 the south jetty was rebuilt. Piling could not be driven through the old stonework below, so the engineers shifted to the "cap" method. A concrete cap twenty-two feet wide and eighteen inches thick covered the jetties and the south jetty ended in a one-thousand-ton monolith. These were reinforced with railroad rails and secured with cables. When the job was finished, the jetty reached into thirty-one feet of water and the upper surface was twelve feet above high water. The north jetty was armored with six- to twenty-ton stones sloping 1:2 (one vertical unit for two horizontal ones). More railroad rails were added, and a monolith of concrete seven feet thick and thirty feet square was poured.

When the work was finally completed in 1927, the engineers must have stepped back proudly surveying their work and thinking, "There, that will do it!" But by 1932 repairs were needed; for these, eleven-foot cubes of concrete, each weighing one hundred tons, were cast and slid into place. By the 1940s twelve-ton tetrahedrons were used for further repairs.

During the winter of 1957–58 severe storms deteriorated both jetties, and repair became a major construction project. This time twelve-ton stones were used to raise the jetties to about fifteen feet above high-tide level. They were covered with a layer of one-hundred-ton blocks, but most of these were washed away during the winter storms of 1964–65. By 1970 another major rehabilitation job was required. This time extensive model studies were used and the adopted design consisted of placing 246 forty-two-ton Dolos armor units on a slope of 1:5 against the heads of the jetties. Two layers of Dolos units were used, with those in the upper layer carefully positioned to provide the greatest interlocking stability.

As of 1978 there has been some breakage and settling, but the structural integrity of the jetties is not yet impaired. Can the engineer in charge finally survey his work and say, "We've finally licked the sea for all time"? No; the storm waves will return again and again. Some day another engineer will once more repair the Humboldt Bay jetties.

The ocean is huge, powerful, and eternal. Puny humans can scarcely expect to win by overwhelming it, and anyone who counters its attack with brute-force solutions is doomed to expensive disappointment. Rather, the engineer must try to understand how the sea acts and learn to take advantage of the geographic and oceanographic conditions so that everything possible is in his favor. Then, on a battleground of his choosing for the short span of human interest, he may be able to hold his own. The first and most valuable lesson one can learn about the sea is to respect it.

XIV

Storms and Waves in Literature

IT IS VERY DIFFICULT TO CAPTURE THE ESSENCE OF WAVES IN words. The very large waves that inhabit the great storms inspire a subjective response that defies description in ordinary prose. But once in thousands of tries, some great storyteller will choose just the right words to describe to readers the unstable summits of fast-moving water that make the most experienced sailor quiver in his sea boots. But usually, this deficiency in description is not for want of trying. Here are five examples that span three thousand years.

Homer's poetic account of Odysseus' attempt to return home from the Trojan War against the wishes of Poseidon, the sea god, was a great beginning. In this excerpt from the *Odyssey*, Odysseus has just escaped from the land of the Cicones (after participating in considerable killing, sacking, and raping).

Zeus, who marshals the clouds, now sent my fleet a terrible gale from the north. He covered land and sea alike with a canopy of cloud; and darkness swept down on us

from the sky. Our ships were driven sidelong by the
wind, and the force of the gusts tore their sails to rags
and tatters. With the fear of death upon us, we lowered
these onto the decks, and rowed the bare ships landward
with all our might. Thus we lay for two days and two
nights on end, with exhaustion and anxiety gnawing at
our hearts. But on the third morning, which a beautiful
dawn had ushered in, we stepped the masts, hauled up
the white sails, and sat down, leaving the wind and the
helmsmen between them to keep our vessels straight. In
fact I should have reached my own land safe and sound,
had not the swell, the current, and the North Wind combined, as I was doubling Malea, to drive me off my
course and send me drifting past Cythera.

For nine days I was chased by those accursed winds
across the fish-infested seas. But on the tenth we made
the country of the Lotus-eaters.

Later Odysseus builds a boat with the help of the goddess Calypso (with whom he has been living for seven
years) and heads for home. His old enemy Poseidon is in-
censed by this attempt.

Whereupon Poseidon marshalled the clouds and seizing
his trident in his hands stirred up the sea. He roused the
stormy blasts of every wind that blows, and covered land
and water alike with a canopy of cloud. Darkness
swooped down from the sky. East Wind and South and
the tempestuous West fell to on one another, and from
the North came a white squall, rolling a great wave in its
van. Odysseus' knees shook and his spirit quailed. In an-
guish he communed with that great heart of his: "Poor
wretch, what will your end be now? I fear the goddess
prophesied all too well when she told me I should have
my full measure of agony on the sea before I reached my
native land. Every word she said is coming true, as I can

tell by the sky, with its vast coronet of clouds from Zeus, and by the sea that he has raised with angry squalls from every quarter."

As he spoke, a mountainous wave, advancing with majestic sweep, crashed down upon him from above and whirled his vessel round. The steering-oar was torn from his hands, and he himself was tossed off the boat, while at the same moment the warring winds joined forces in one tremendous gust, which snapped the mast in two and flung the sail and yard far out into the sea. For a long time Odysseus was kept under water. Weighed down by the clothes which the goddess Calypso had given him, he found it no easy matter to fight his way up against the downrush of that mighty wave. But at last he reached the air and spat out the bitter brine that kept streaming down his face. Exhausted though he was, he did not forget his boat, but raced after her through the surf, scrambled up, and squatting amidships felt safe from immediate death. The heavy seas thrust him with the current this way and that. As the North Wind at harvest-time tosses about the fields a ball of thistles that have stuck together, so did the gusts drive his craft hither and thither over the sea.

Sailing Alone Around the World, by Captain Joshua Slocum, first published in 1899, is one of the world's great adventure stories. Captain Slocum was that wonderful combination of seafarer and storyteller who could sail a small boat around the world just for fun and then write an account that makes the adventure real:

The first day of the storm gave the *Spray* her actual test in the worst sea that Cape Horn or its wild regions could afford, and in no part of the world could a rougher sea be found than at this particular point, namely, off Cape Pillar, the grim sentinel of the Horn.

Farther offshore, while the sea was majestic, there was

less apprehension of danger. There the *Spray* rode, now like a bird on the crest of a wave, and now like a waif deep down in the hollow between seas; and so she drove on. Whole days passed, counted as other days, but always a thrill—yes, of delight.

On the fourth day of the gale, rapidly nearing the pitch of Cape Horn, I inspected my chart and pricked off the course and distance to Port Stanley, in the Falkland Islands, where I might find my way and refit, when I saw through a rift in the clouds a high mountain, about seven leagues away on the port beam. The fierce edge of the gale by this time had blown off, and I had already bent a squaresail on the boom in place of the mainsail, which was torn to rags. I hauled in the trailing ropes, hoisted this awkward sail reefed, the forestaysail being already set, and under this sail brought her at once on the wind heading for the land, which appeared as an island in the sea. So it turned out to be, though not the one I had supposed.

I was exultant over the prospect of once more entering the Strait of Magellan and beating through again into the Pacific, for it was more than rough on the outside coast of Tierra del Fuego. It was indeed a mountainous sea. When the sloop was in the fiercest squalls, with only the reefed forestaysail set, even that small sail shook her from keelson to truck when it shivered by the leech. Had I harbored the shadow of a doubt for her safety, it would have been that she might spring a leak in the garboard at the heel of the mast; but she never called me once to the pump. Under pressure of the smallest sail I could set she made for the land like a racehorse, and steering her over the crests of the waves so that she might not trip was nice work. I stood at the helm now and made the most of it.

Night closed in before the sloop reached the land, leaving her feeling the way in pitchy darkness. I saw breakers ahead before long. At this I wore ship and stood offshore,

but was immediately startled by the tremendous roaring
of breakers again ahead and on the lee bow. This puzzled
me, for there should have been no broken water where I
supposed myself to be. I kept off a good bit, then wore
round, but finding broken water also there, threw her
head again offshore. In this way, among dangers, I spent
the rest of the night. Hail and sleet in the fierce squalls
cut my flesh till the blood trickled over my face; but what
of that? It was daylight, and the sloop was in the midst of
the Milky Way of the sea, which is northwest of Cape
Horn, and it was the white breakers of a huge sea over
sunken rocks which had threatened to engulf her through
the night. It was Fury Island I had sighted and steered
for, and what a panorama was before me now, and all
around! It was not the time to complain of a broken skin.
What could I do but fill away among the breakers and
find a channel between them, now that it was day? Since
she had escaped the rocks through the night, surely she
would find her way by daylight. This was the greatest sea
adventure of my life. God knows how my vessel escaped.

The sloop at last reached inside of small islands that
sheltered her in smooth water. Then I climbed the mast
to survey the wild scene astern. The great naturalist Darwin looked over this seascape from the deck of the *Beagle*, and wrote in his journal, "Any landsman seeing the
Milky Way would have nightmares for a week." He
might have added, "or seaman" as well.

Charles Darwin, later famous for his theory of evolu-
tion, was twenty-two years old when he began his voyage
around the world on Her Majesty's Ship *Beagle*. The mis-
sion of the ship was to survey the poorly known southern
coast of South America. Darwin's presence as the naturalist aboard made the trip a very important scientific expe-
dition. The ship's departure from England was twice
delayed by heavy southwestern gales, and rough weather

was encountered on many other occasions. However, Darwin's account in the *Voyage of the Beagle* about the unsuccessful attempt to round Cape Horn is the one that impressed Captain Slocum:

After having detained six days in Wigwam Cove by very bad weather, we put to sea on the 30th of December. When at sea we had a constant succession of gales, and the current was against us: we drifted to 57° 23′ south. On the 11th of January, 1833, by carrying a press of sail, we fetched within a few miles of the great rugged mountain of York Minster (so called by Captain Cook) when a violent squall compelled us to shorten sail and stand out to sea. The surf was breaking fearfully on the coast, and the spray was carried over a cliff estimated at 200 feet in height. On the 12th the gale was very heavy, and we did not know exactly where we were: it was a most unpleasant sound to hear constantly repeated, "keep a good lookout to leeward." On the 13th the storm raged with its full fury: our horizon was narrowly limited by the sheets of spray borne by the wind. The sea looked ominous, like a dreary waving plain with patches of drifted snow: whilst the ship laboured heavily, the albatross glided with its expanded wings right up the wind. At noon a great sea broke over us, and filled one of the whale-boats, which was obliged to be instantly cut away. The poor *Beagle* trembled at the shock, and for a few minutes would not obey her helm; but soon, like a good ship that she was, she righted and came up to the wind again. Had another sea followed the first, our fate would have been decided soon, and for ever. We had now been twenty-four days trying in vain to get westward; the men were worn out with fatigue, and they had not for many nights or days a dry thing to put on. Captain Fitz Roy gave up the attempt to get westward by the outside coast. In the evening we ran in behind False Cape Horn, and dropped our

anchor in forty-seven fathoms, fire flashing from the wind-
lass as the chain rushed round it. How delightful was
that still night, after having been so long involved in the
din of the warring elements!

A typhoon is the ultimate storm, and the best description of one ever written is by Joseph Conrad. *Typhoon*
matches the stolid personality of Captain McWhirr of the
steamer *Nan-Shan* against the violent winds and waves of
a typhoon in the South China Sea. It is a tale that could
have been told only by a man with sea experience like
Conrad, who had personally weathered twenty years of
storms as a ship's officer before becoming a literary figure.
He has put more honest-to-God information about the development and feel of a great storm into this story than
exist in dozens of scientific volumes.

Jukes was as ready a man as any half-dozen young mates
that may be caught by casting a net upon the waters; and
though he had been somewhat taken aback by the startling viciousness of the first squall, he had pulled himself
together on the instant, had called out the hands and had
rushed them along to secure such openings about the
deck as had not been already battened down earlier in
the evening.

But at the same time he was growing aware that this
was rather more than he had expected. From the first stir
of the air felt on his cheek the gale seemed to take upon
itself the accumulated impetus of an avalanche. Heavy
sprays enveloped the *Nan-Shan* from stem to stern, and
instantly in the midst of her regular rolling she began to
jerk and plunge as though she had gone mad with fright.
A faint burst of lightning quivered all round, as if flashed
into a cavern—into a black and secret chamber of the sea,
with a floor of foaming crests.

It unveiled for a sinister, fluttering moment a ragged

mass of clouds hanging low, the lurch of the long outlines of the ship, the black figures of men caught on the bridge, heads forward, as if petrified in the act of butting. The darkness palpitated down upon all this, and then the real thing came at last.

It was something formidable and swift, like the sudden smashing of a vial of wrath. It seemed to explode all round the ship with an overpowering concussion and a rush of great waters, as if an immense dam had been blown up to windward. In an instant the men lost touch of each other. This is the disintegrating power of a great wind: it isolates one from one's kind. An earthquake, a landslip, an avalanche, overtake a man incidentally, as it were—without passion. A furious gale attacks him like a personal enemy, tries to grasp his limbs, fastens upon his mind, seeks to rout his very spirit out of him. . . .

He saw the head of the wave topple over, adding the might of its crash to the tremendous uproar raging around him, and almost at the same instant the stanchion was wrenched away from his embracing arms. After a crushing thump on his back he found himself suddenly afloat and borne upwards. His first irresistible notion was that the whole China Sea had climbed on the bridge. Then, more sanely, he concluded himself gone overboard. All the time he was being tossed, flung, and rolled in great volumes of water, he kept on repeating mentally, with the utmost precipitation, the words: "My God! My God! My God! My God!"

Nobody—not even Captain MacWhirr, who alone on deck had caught sight of a white line of foam coming on at such a height that he couldn't believe his eyes—nobody was to know the steepness of that sea and the awful depth of the hollow the hurricane had scooped out behind the running wall of water.

It raced to meet the ship, and, with a pause, as of girding the loins, the *Nan-Shan* lifted her bows and

leaped. . . . With a tearing crash and a swirling, raving
tumult, tons of water fell upon the deck, as though the
ship had darted under the foot of a cataract. . . .

She dipped into the hollow straight down, as if going
over the edge of the world. . . .

At last she rose slowly, staggering, as if she had to lift a
mountain with her bows. When the wash of water rolling
on the deck died away for a moment, it seemed to Jukes,
yet quivering from his exertion, that in his mad struggle
. . . he had overcome the wind somehow: that a silence
had fallen upon the ship, a silence in which the sea struck
thunderously at her sides.

Arthur Clarke is considered by many to be the greatest
science fiction writer of our time. In *Rendezvous with
Rama* he not only invents a space object complete with its
own sea but sets a tsunami in motion on that sea that
challenges his heroine's knowledge of wave mechanics. It
all happens in the year 2130:

On a billion television screens, there appeared a tiny, fea-
tureless cylinder, growing rapidly second by second. By
the time it had doubled its size, no one could pretend any
longer that Rama was a natural object.

Its body was a cylinder so geometrically perfect that it
might have been turned on a lathe—one with centers fifty
kilometers apart. The two ends were quite flat, apart
from some small structures at the center of one face, and
were twenty kilometers across; from a distance, when
there was no sense of scale, Rama looked almost comi-
cally like an ordinary domestic boiler. . . .

It was far too light to be a solid body. To nobody's
great surprise, it was clear that Rama must be hollow.

The long-hoped-for, long-feared encounter had come at
last. Mankind was about to receive the first visitor from
the stars.

Commander Norton is dispatched in the spaceship *En-deavour* to check it out. The ship lands at the axis of the cylinder (which rotates once every four minutes so that the force of gravity at its interior is the same as that on earth) and sends a party inside to explore:

"The fifty-kilometer-long cylindrical section between the two bowls we've called the Central Plain. It may seem crazy to use the word 'plain' to describe something so obviously curved, but we feel it's justified. It will appear flat to us when we get down there—just as the interior of a bottle must seem flat to an ant crawling around inside it.

"The most striking feature of the Central Plain is the ten-kilometer-wide dark band running completely around it at the halfway mark. . . . We've christened it the Cylindrical Sea!"

Sergeant Ruby Barnes of Norton's crew had one thought in her mind.

Ever since she had set eyes upon the sea, she had been determined to make this voyage. In all the thousands of years that man had had dealings with the waters of his own world, no sailor had ever faced anything remotely like this. In the last few days a silly little jingle had been running through her mind, and she could not get rid of it: "To sail the Cylindrical Sea. . . ." The twenty-kilowatt motor started to whirr, the chain drives of the reduction gear blurred, and *Resolution* surged away. [As it] hummed steadily forward, it seemed again and again that they were caught in the trough of a gigantic wave, a wave that curved up on either side until it became vertical, then overhung until the two flanks met in a liquid arch sixteen kilometers above their heads. Despite everything that reason and logic told them, none of the voyagers could for long throw off the impression that at any

minute those millions of tons of water would come crash-
ing down from the sky.

All goes well for a while. Then the land party feels a
shock and radios a message.

"*Resolution!* Are you OK? Did you feel that?"
  "Feel *what?*"
  "We think it was an earthquake. . . ."
  There was a sudden shout from the helm. "Skipper—
look—up there in the sky!"
  Norton lifted his eyes and swiftly scanned the circuit of
the sea. He saw nothing until his gaze had almost
reached the zenith and he was staring at the other side of
the world. . . .
  A tidal wave was racing toward them down the eternal
curve of the Cylindrical Sea. The wave was about ten kilometers away, and stretched the full width of the sea
from northern to southern shore. Near the land it was a
foaming wall of white, but in deeper water it was a
barely visible blue line, moving much faster than the
breakers on either flank. The drag of the shoreward shallows was already bending it into a bow, with the central
portion getting farther and farther ahead. . . . [*Resolution* swung around] until it was just under way, heading
directly toward the approaching wave. Norton judged
that the swiftly moving central portion would reach them
in less than five minutes, but he could also see that it
presented no serious danger. It was only a racing ripple a
fraction of a meter high, and would scarcely rock the
boat. The walls of foam lagging far behind it were the
real menace.
  Suddenly, in the very center of the sea, a line of
breakers appeared. The wave had clearly hit a submerged wall, several kilometers in length, not far below

the surface. At the same time, the breakers on the two flanks collapsed as they ran into deeper water.

Antislosh plates, Norton told himself—exactly the same as in *Endeavour's* own propellant tanks, but on a thousandfold greater scale. There must be a complex pattern of them all around the sea, to damp out any waves as quickly as possible. The only thing that matters now is: are we right on top of one?

Sergeant Barnes was one jump ahead of him. She brought *Resolution* to a full stop and threw out the anchor. It hit bottom at only five meters.

"Haul it up!" she called to her crewmates. "We've got to get away from here!"

Norton agreed heartily. But in which direction? The Sergeant was headed full speed *toward* the wave, which was now only five kilometers away. For the first time, he could hear the sound of its approach—a distant, unmistakable roar, which he had never expected to hear inside Rama. Then it changed in intensity. The central portion was collapsing again, and the flanks again were building up.

He tried to estimate the distance between the submerged baffles, assuming that they were spaced at equal intervals. If he was right, there should be one more to come; if they could station the raft in the deep water between them, they would be perfectly safe.

Sergeant Barnes cut the motor and threw out the anchor again. It went down thirty meters without hitting bottom.

"We're OK," she said, with a sigh of relief. "But I'll keep the motor running." . . .

Then, only two kilometers ahead of them, the sea started to foam once more. It humped up in white-maned fury, and now its roaring seemed to fill the world. Upon the sixteen-kilometer-high wave of the Cylindrical Sea, a smaller ripple was superimposed, like an avalanche thundering down a mountain slope. And that ripple was quite large enough to kill them. . . .

The wave continued to rise, curving upward and over. The slope above them probably exaggerated its height, but it looked enormous, an irresistible force of nature that would overwhelm everything in its path.

Then, within seconds, it collapsed, as if its foundations had been pulled out from underneath it. It was over the submerged barrier, in deep water again. When it reached them a minute later, *Resolution* merely bounced up and down a few times. . . .

Epilogue

MANY OF THE PLEASANTEST HOURS OF THE AUTHOR'S LIFE
have been spent in watching waves and examining
beaches, trying to understand them. Walking and medi-
tating, photographing, digging and surveying—the curious quest, already in progress for over thirty-three years,
has been great fun in spite of uncounted salt-water
drenchings and numerous scientific disappointments. It
has covered thousands of miles of shoreline in twenty
countries without losing any of its fascination, and without producing any hope of complete understanding. The
subject is too complex. But somehow there is satisfaction
in being aware enough of the ways of waves and
beaches to detect the special softness of a new layer of
sand underfoot that means the berm is building or to observe a slight change in the appearance of the breakers
and think, "There must be a new storm in the Gulf of
Alaska."

The inner peace that comes with the quiet contem-
plation of a beach on a still calm morning, or the feeling
of exhilaration that comes from riding a great wave in a

small boat, is more reward than most men ever know. Fortunately the beaches of the world are cleaned every night by the tide. A fresh look always awaits the student, and every wave is a masterpiece of originality.

It will ever be so. Go and see.

Additional Reading

For those who wish to go a little deeper into the subject of waves and hear a different point of view, see:

E. P. Clancy. *The Tides: Pulse of the Earth*. Garden City, N.Y.: Doubleday & Company, 1968.

Adlard K. Coles. *Heavy Weather Sailing*. Tuckahoe, N.Y.: John de Graff, 1975.

H. A. and M. C. Klein. *Surf's Up! An Anthology of Surfing*. New York: Bobbs-Merrill Co., 1966.

W. G. Van Dorn. *Oceanography and Seamanship*. New York: Dodd, Mead & Co., 1974.

You can go very much deeper into waves with either of two mathematical treatments:

Blair Kinsman. *Wind Waves: Their Generation and Propagation on the Ocean Surface*. Englewood Cliffs, N.J.: Prentice-Hall, 1965.

O. M. Phillips. *The Dynamics of the Upper Ocean*. Cambridge, England: Cambridge University Press, 1966.

On Beaches and Shorelines:

F. P. Shepard. *Submarine Geology*. New York: Harper and Row, 1973.

C. A. M. King. *Beaches and Coasts*. New York: St. Martin's Press, 1960.

On shoreline engineering and naval architecture:

U. S. Army Corps of Engineers, Coastal Engineering Research Center. *Shore Protection Manual*. 1977.

Harold Saunders. *Hydrodynamics in Ship Design*. New York: Society of Naval Architects & Marine Engineers, 1965.

Edward V. Lewis. *Ships*. New York: Time-Life Books, 1965.

Waves in literature:

Homer. *The Odyssey*. E. V. Rieu, transl. New York: Penguin Books, 1946.

Joshua Slocum. *Sailing Alone Around the World*. New York: Sheridan House, 1954.

Charles Darwin. *The Voyage of the Beagle*. New York: Bantam Books, 1972.

Joseph Conrad. *Typhoon*. New York: Bantam Books, 1971.

Arthur C. Clarke. *Rendezvous with Rama*. New York: Ballantine Books, 1974.

Index